Computer-Assisted Mechanical Design

Computer-Assisted Mechanical Design

J. Ed Akin

Rice University

Prentice Hall, Englewood Cliffs, New Jersey 07632

Library of Congress Cataloging-in-Publication Data

Akin, J. E.
  Computer-assisted mechanical design / J. Ed Akin.
    p.   cm.
  Bibliography: p.
  Includes index.
ISBN 0–13–165895–6
  1. Engineering design—Data processing.   2. Computer-aided design.
I. Title.
TA174.A419 1990
620'.00425'02851—dc20   89–31583
                                                             CIP

Editorial/production supervision and
  interior design: Marjorie Shustak/Mary Anne Shahidi
Cover design: Wanda Lubelska
Manufacturing buyer: Mary Noonan/Denise Duggan
Cover photo: Solid model and stress results for an impeller.
          Courtesy of Aries Technology, Inc.

  © 1990 by Prentice-Hall, Inc.
A Division of Simon & Schuster
Englewood Cliffs, New Jersey 07632

Printed in the United States of America
10 9 8 7 6 5 4 3 2 1

ISBN 0-13-165895-6

Prentice-Hall International (UK) Limited, *London*
Prentice-Hall of Australia Pty. Limited, *Sydney*
Prentice-Hall Canada Inc., *Toronto*
Prentice-Hall Hispanoamericana, S.A., *Mexico*
Prentice-Hall of India Private Limited, *New Delhi*
Prentice-Hall of Japan, Inc., *Tokyo*
Simon & Schuster Asia Pte. Ltd., *Singapore*
Editora Prentice-Hall do Brasil, Ltda., *Rio de Janeiro*

To my wife, Pryntha.

CONTENTS

Contents

PREFACE

This book is based on courses and workshops taught at the University of Tennessee and Rice University during the last ten years. It also reflects practical considerations developed through several years of consulting in this subject area. It is primarily intended for engineering students and practicing engineers who wish to employ and understand the common techniques used in computer-assisted mechanical design.

There is a large amount of commercial and public domain software available to assist engineers with the processes of design and analysis. It is dangerous to utilize such tools without understanding the concepts on which they are based and the limitations of such procedures. Thus, some elementary theory is included in the presentation of various design aids. This book will cover the eight subjects that I think are currently most important to today's design procedures. These topics should allow the engineer to ask more of the "what if" questions that are so important to design.

Chapter 1 discusses optimization and introduces the simplex search algorithms as a simple but robust tool. Chapter 2 deals with matrix operations that are common to both rigid body kinematics and computer graphics. It combines the matrix kinematics with the optimization procedure to illustrate the design of mechanisms.

Chapter 3 deals with parametric geometry. That subject is important in computer graphics, surface modeling, numerically controlled machining, solid modeling, finite element analysis, the theory of shells, and so on. Matrix notation is employed to be consistent with most computer graphics and finite element texts. Chapter 4 gives a short presentation on solid modeling. Emphasis is placed on cellular or hierarchical methods combined with Boolean operations. The discussion of boundary representations methods provides other uses of the parametric surfaces in Chapter 3.

Chapter 5 introduces the important topic of finite element analysis. It is becoming increasingly linked to the material in Chapters 3 and 4. Because there are numerous texts on finite element theory, much of the emphasis here is placed on how one should effectively utilize this tool. Particular detail is paid to efficient modeling skills that can speed the design process. Combining FEA with optimization procedures is also discussed.

The next most useful design aid following finite element and optimization procedures is probably the use of simulation techniques. This subject is covered by example in Chapter 6 to show how the computer frees the designer from burdensome computations and allows several "what if" questions to be answered quickly.

Chapter 7 gives an elementary introduction to the increasingly important topics of case selectors and rule-based systems. One of the oldest topics, computer-assisted drafting, is surveyed in Chapter 8. Its use continues to increase, but the main concern here is how it best integrates with the above topics. The appendixes provide additional terminology, suggested reading, and sample software for educational and practical use.

There are important topics not included here. Surveys show that engineers may spend 20 percent of their time designing, and up to 80 percent of their time in preparing reports, communications, cost estimates, and so on. Thus, another important activity for engineers is to learn to use effectively spreadsheets, database management software, and word processing tools. Then they can increase productivity and enjoyment by spending a larger percentage of their time on the design process.

NOTE: The software in this book is available on diskette and magnetic tape for several computers. It is available, at an extra cost, from the publisher.

ACKNOWLEDGMENTS

I would like to thank my students, colleagues, and friends for their constructive criticisms and comments on this work. It has been a pleasure to see them employ these tools to improve other courses and design projects.

Ms. Linda Anderson again did an excellent job of preparing most of the manuscript. Ms. Sally Cone completed the final revisions. Their patience and dedication is greatly appreciated. Mr. Massood Mofid and my son, Jeff, prepared most of the figures.

Ed Akin
Rice University
Houston, TX

Computer-Assisted Mechanical Design

1

OPTIMIZATION

1.1 INTRODUCTION

The process of mechanical design, or synthesis, may often be viewed as an optimization task. Computer assisted engineering typically gives the analyst the ability to investigate several "what if" questions during the synthesis process. Such questions can involve many variables and are often subject to various constraints or design rules. The total group of variables needed for the design are called the analysis variables.

The quantities for which values are to be chosen to produce the design are a subset of the analysis variables typically called the **design variables, design parameters**, or the **trial vector**. We denote this list or vector of n quantities as

$$\mathbf{x} = (x_1, x_2, \ldots, x_n)^T.$$

For example, if we were optimizing a helical spring we might consider its modulus of elasticity, E, the diameter of the wire, d, the number of coils, N, the mean diameter of the spring, D, its free length, L, and its cost, \$. Then the trial vector would be

$$\mathbf{x}^T = (E, d, N, D, L, \$)$$
$$= (x_1, x_2, x_3, x_4, x_5, x_6).$$

Some of the analysis variables that affect a design will be known and are not subject to change. We will denote these quantities as **data** or **prescribed variables**. Fixed data items will not be included in the trial vector.

Of course, almost any engineering design is going to require some analysis. A design is analyzed by evaluating a mathematical model of the system by calculating various functions that we call **analysis functions,** or **state variables**. The designer selects other items, conditions, or functions to be utilized in evaluating the objective or merit function. These will be called the **design functions**. Here we use the word function in a mathematical sense and do not directly refer to the performance of the system being designed. The selection of the design variables and functions from the analysis space is often referred to as mapping between the analysis and design space.

1.2 ANALYSIS AND DESIGN SPACES

The mathematical optimization of a design assumes that a single **measure of merit, objective function**, or **merit function** exists and can be expressed formally in terms of the design parameters. We denote this scalar merit function by $F(\mathbf{x})$. Thus, the optimization problem can be simply stated as:

$$\text{Minimize } F(\mathbf{x}).$$

It is assumed that there exist one or more trial vectors, $\mathbf{x}^*$, at which the function F has a local minimum. This also allows us to treat design problems where a quantity is to be maximized. This is true since the minimum of $F(\mathbf{x})$ occurs where the maximum of $-F(\mathbf{x})$ occurs, as shown in Figure 1.2.1.

Of course, the optimization process is not quite as simple as the preceding statement suggests. We have already mentioned that certain **constraints** or design restrictions must be satisfied while selecting the trial vector, $\mathbf{x}$. A design that meets all requirements is called a **feasible design**, or an **acceptable design**. Otherwise, it is an infeasible or unacceptable design. A constraint that restricts the upper and lower limits on the design parameters will be called a **regional constraint**, or **side constraint**. A constraint that is derived from performance or functional requirements that are explicitly considered is called a **behavior constraint**, or **functional constraint**.

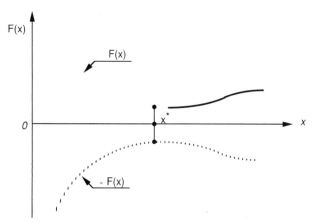

Figure 1.2.1   Minimizing a function is the same as maximizing its negative.

Thus, we will rephrase the previous statement and say that we search for a feasible design given by the design vector, $\mathbf{x}^*$ ε R such that

$$F(\mathbf{x}^*) = \min F(\mathbf{x})$$

subject to the regional constraints that

$$G_i(\mathbf{x}^*) < 0 \quad \text{for } i = 1, 2, \ldots, p$$

and to the functional constraints

$$H_j(\mathbf{x}^*) = 0 \quad \text{for } j = 1, 2, \ldots, q.$$

Here R denotes the **design space** made up by varying each of the n design parameters. Each local minimum corresponds to an optimal set of design variables. The best design must be selected from the feasible local minima. The global minimum is the lowest value of any of the local minima. In the synthesis of mechanical systems, there is no assurance that the global minimum corresponds to the optimal feasible design. Each local feasible design must be considered on its own merits. In other words, a solution may not exist, and if one exists, it may not be unique.

There are many approaches to the solution of an optimization. Basically, there are search methods that use the function values, F, alone; gradient methods that use the function values and its first partial derivatives, $\partial F/\partial x_i$; and finally, methods that also require the second partial derivatives, $\partial^2 F/\partial x_i\, \partial x_j$. The most common solution techniques are

1. Search methods
2. Gradient (first derivative) methods
3. Second derivative methods
4. Linear programming
5. Nonlinear programming

Search methods include: exhaustive search, bisection search, grid search, random search, golden search, simplex search. Popular gradient methods are steepest descent, conjugate gradients, Newton's method. The more popular methods include the method of steepest descent, conjugate directions, Powell's direct search, method of least squares, the simplex search method, etc. The search, or "hill climbing" methods are easier to understand and are computationally cheaper, since they do not require computing derivatives. Obviously, there are problems where utilizing derivative information will greatly speed the convergence to a local minimum. We will use the simplex search method.

It is important to distinguish between design and analysis. Generally a **design** will utilize **analysis variables** in one or more **analysis functions**. Design is a process of selecting the values or limits of the analysis variables. The design variables are a subset of the analysis variables that the designer selects for manipulation in order to attempt to improve the design merit function. During the design process the designer may find it necessary to make changes such as the following:

- Change the allowable range of design variables.
- Select a new set of design variables.
- Change the design constraints.
- Save for later recall the design variables set that result in a feasible design.
- Select the optimal design from many feasible designs.
- Interchange analysis variables with an independent analysis program.

In practice it is becoming increasingly necessary to employ software and graphics hardware to reduce the burden of evaluating the analysis functions and to speed up the search for the optimum design. Relatively small programs, such as **SIMPLX** (see Appendix III) can give the designer the freedom to ask the important "what if" questions that can lead to major improvements in a design.

More advanced software aids include interactive graphics and interactive input to improve the use interface. They frequently offer

- Contour plots or color surfaces of the design space or its subsets
- A history plot of design variables versus iteration number
- Interactive adjustments of the design variables
- Interactive selection of design variables from the list of analysis variables
- Sensitivity studies of design variables
- Option to save and recall design data
- "Black box" interfaces to major analysis or graphics software.

The **OPTDES.BYU** program is an example of an inexpensive public-domain software product that offers such features.

Examples of typical problem statements that can be viewed as optimizations are the following:

1. Find the values of $\mathbf{x} = (x_1, \ x_2)$ that minimize the merit function

$$M(\mathbf{x}) = (x_1 - 1)^2 + (x_2 - 2)^2 \tag{1.2.1}$$

2. Repeat (1) except for the constraint that $x_2 \leq 1.3$

3. Build a nonlinear empirical model to fit tabulated data for inputs $Z_1(I)$, $Z_2(I)$, and $Z_3(I)$ and the outputs Y(I). Let the model be

$$y = a_1 Z_1 Z_2/(1 + a_2 Z_3 + a_3 Z_1)^2 \tag{1.2.2}$$

where the best (optimum) coefficients a_j are desired. Here let $\mathbf{x} = (a_1, a_2, a_3)$ and

$$M(x) = \sum_{I=1}^{N} \left[Y(I) - \frac{a_1 Z_1(I) \, Z_2(I)}{(1 + a_2 Z_3(I) + a_3 Z_1(I))^2} \right]^2$$

be the merit function to be minimized.

1.3 ENGINEERING SYNTHESIS PROBLEM FORMULATION

As an example, consider the design of a hollow circular column of length L, which is to carry a compressive load of P. Its material has an elastic modulus of E and a weight density of γ. We will consider the weight only for cost purposes and for simplicity will omit the additional loads it induces. The hollow circular cross section has a mean diameter of D and a wall thickness of T. The geometric properties of this section, from Figure 1.3.1, are its area

$$A = \pi TD$$

and the second moment of inertia

$$I = \frac{\pi}{8} TD\,(D^2 + T^2).$$

The weight of the column is

$$W = \gamma\,AL.$$

Its cost includes the material, W, construction costs, and shipping costs (proportional to D). Thus, we assume the cost is

$$\$ = c_1 W \; + \; c_2 D$$

where the c_i are known constants. This will be chosen as the merit function to be minimized, $F = \$$.

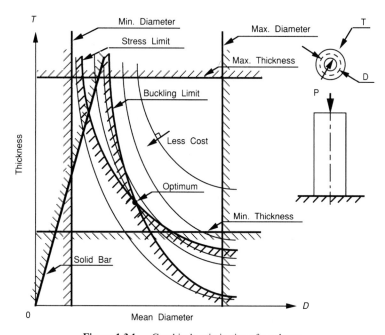

Figure 1.3.1   Graphical optimization of a column.

Of course, we must be concerned with other quantities such as the axial stress, S:

$$S = \frac{P}{A}$$

and how it compares with the known material yield stress, S_y, and the stress at which the column would fail by buckling, S_b. The buckling stress depends on the critical buckling load, P_b:

$$S_b = \frac{P_b}{A.}$$

The simplest buckling load is the Euler approximation

$$P_b = \frac{KEI}{L^2}$$

where K is a constant that depends on how the two column ends are supported. If the bottom is clamped and the top is free then

$$K = \frac{\pi^2}{4.}$$

Other buckling estimates are much more complicated. Finally, we will assume that both the length and thickness have known upper and lower limits. At this point we should consider the analysis and design spaces shown in Table 1.3.1.

Table 1.3.1 illustrates that we choose to use the diameter and thickness to minimize the cost. Of course, this design is subject to constraints on the stress and the design variables. We could have also considered the deflection of the column and

TABLE 1.3.1 ANALYSIS AND DESIGN SPACES

Analysis Variables	Design Variables
Length, L	
Diameter, D	Diameter, D
Thickness, T	Thickness, T
Weight Density, γ	
Cost Constants, c_i	
Load, P	
Supports, K	
Modulus, E	
Yield Stress, S_y	

Analysis Functions	Design Functions
Cost, $\$$	Minimize, $F = \$$
Stress, S	$S < S_y$
Buckling Stress, S_b	$S < S_b$
	$T_n < T < T_x$
	$D_n < D < D_x$

placed a limit on its maximum value. We might also decide that the length is important enough to be a design variable. Here we will select our trial vector to be

$$\mathbf{x} = \begin{Bmatrix} D \\ T \end{Bmatrix} = \begin{Bmatrix} x_1 \\ x_2 \end{Bmatrix}.$$

The merit function to be minimized is

$$F(\mathbf{x}) = c_1 W + c_2 D = c_1 \pi \gamma TDL + c_2 D.$$

This implies that zero or negative diameters would minimize F, but that is clearly not going to be physically acceptable. Thus, a minimum value for D must be selected. The limit on maximum stress gives $S \leq S_y$, or

$$\frac{P}{\pi\, TD} \leq S_y$$

and the edge of that region is

$$TD = \frac{P}{\pi\, S_y}.$$

The buckling limit is $S \leq S_b$ and the limit of that region is $S = S_b$, or $P = P_b$, so that

$$P \leq (D^2 + T^2) TDKE\, \pi/8L^2 .$$

We will employ the subscripts n and x to denote the **min** and **max** ranges, respectively. A sketch of the feasible search area for the two variables begins with a rectangular region set by the limits of the design variables (D_n, D_x, T_n, T_x). The yield line excludes the region from the axes to TD = constant. The Euler buckling line excludes the region between the axes and $TD\,(T^2 + D^2)$ = constant. There is also a physical limit that for a solid cylinder the mean diameter equals the thickness, $D = T$, so in general $T \leq D$. Usually the thickness is small compared to the diameter. A typical set of curves for such an arrangement is shown in the figure. Here the optimum value of F happens to occur on the boundary of the feasible region. This is often true. For the sketch shown in Figure 1.3.1 it occurs at the intersection of the yield curve and buckling curve.

1.4 THE SIMPLEX SEARCH ALGORITHM

The **simplex search algorithm** is a heuristic method that utilizes the idea of a simplex. If we have K design variables, then our feasible design space is a K-dimensional space. We can visualize this easily when $K = 1$ or 2 and sometimes when $K = 3$. A simplex is defined as a region in K-space defined by $(K + 1)$ vertices. Thus, our most common simplex regions are the line $(K = 1)$, the triangle $(K = 2)$, and the tetrahedron $(K = 3)$. These are shown in Figure 1.4.1. The trial space (simplex) has one vertex defined by the trial vector $(x_1, x_2, \ldots, x_K)$, whereas information about the current step sizes $(\Delta x_1, \Delta x_2, \ldots, \Delta x_K)$ is used to define the other K vertices. Thus, we have a total of $(K + 1)$ vertices and their corresponding merit function values, say M_k, $k = 1, \ldots, K + 1$.

To clarify the concepts we define the heuristic rules and illustrate them for the two-dimensional case (triangular simplex). These sequences are illustrated in Figure 1.4.2. The rules are as follows:

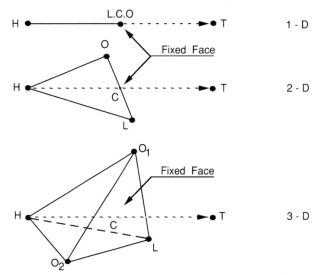

Figure 1.4.1   The first simplex shapes.

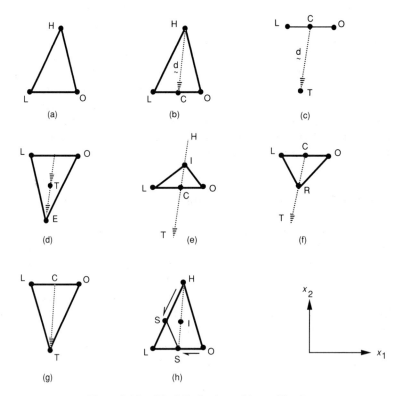

Figure 1.4.2   The 2-D simplex and its modifications.

1. Evaluate all the merit function values. Identify the location of the highest value (**H**), the lowest value (**L**), and the face containing **L** and the other values (**O**).

2. Evaluate the centroid point, **C**, of all vertices, excluding the high point:

$$\mathbf{C} = \bar{X} = \frac{1}{K} \sum_{i=1}^{K+1} X_i \quad i \neq H$$

The line through **HC** describes the possible new locations where we hope to replace **H** with a lower value. The displacement vector, say **d**, from **H** to **C** is to be used as a step size indicator.

3. Define a new test vertex **T** ≡ **C** + **d** = **H** + 2**d** and evaluate the merit function. This is called a reflection of H through C.

4. Four situations are considered before replacing the highest value vertex, **H**, with another point:

   a. If the test value, T, is less than the lowest value, L, then we are moving in the proper direction. Thus, we make an additional extension to **E** = **T** + **d** and define the new simplex to be **L O E**.

   b. If the test T is greater than H then we have gone in the wrong direction. Thus, we contract from T back to an interior point I at **d** /2 from **H**. Then the new simplex is **L O I**.

   c. If the test T is greater than the lowest L and the other points O but less than or equal to the high value H, then we retreat halfway from **T** to **C** and form a new vertex **R** and keep the simplex **L O R**.

   d. If the test T is greater than or equal to the lowest, L, and less than or equal to the other value, O, then accept **T** as the new vertex for the simplex **L O T**.

Since these rules are heuristic, there are other variations that can be tried. For example, if step 4b gives a value at interior point I that is greater than or equal to the highest value, then all other vertices can be contracted, or shrunk, halfway toward the best value, L. This type of rule has the disadvantage that instead of moving one vertex, you move all but the low-valued vertex. Then all of the simplex vertices must be reordered to re-establish the high and low vertices. These various options are combined in Figure 1.4.3. The first four rules are shown graphically in Figure 1.4.4.

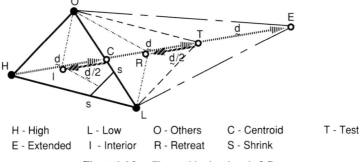

H - High	L - Low	O - Others	C - Centroid	T - Test
E - Extended	I - Interior	R - Retreat	S - Shrink	

Figure 1.4.3   The combined options in 2-D.

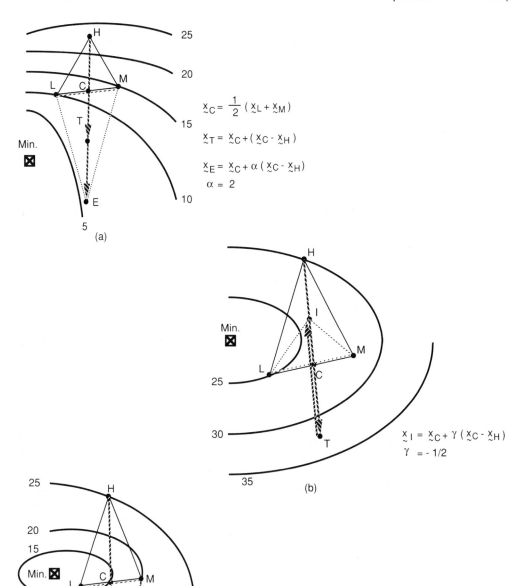

$$\underset{\sim}{x}_C = \frac{1}{2}\left(\underset{\sim}{x}_L + \underset{\sim}{x}_M\right)$$

$$\underset{\sim}{x}_T = \underset{\sim}{x}_C + \left(\underset{\sim}{x}_C - \underset{\sim}{x}_H\right)$$

$$\underset{\sim}{x}_E = \underset{\sim}{x}_C + \alpha\left(\underset{\sim}{x}_C - \underset{\sim}{x}_H\right)$$
$$\alpha = 2$$

(a)

$$\underset{\sim}{x}_I = \underset{\sim}{x}_C + \gamma\left(\underset{\sim}{x}_C - \underset{\sim}{x}_H\right)$$
$$\gamma = -1/2$$

(b)

$$\underset{\sim}{x}_R = \underset{\sim}{x}_C + \beta\left(\underset{\sim}{x}_C - \underset{\sim}{x}_H\right)$$
$$\beta = 1/2$$

(c)

Figure 1.4.4   Graphical rule illustration.

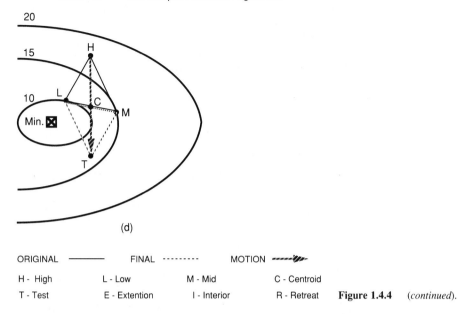

(d)

ORIGINAL ———   FINAL ·········   MOTION ◄◄◄◄

H - High	L - Low	M - Mid	C - Centroid
T - Test	E - Extention	I - Interior	R - Retreat

Figure 1.4.4   (*continued*).

The simplex search procedure can be visualized as fixing one face of the simplex, moving the worst vertex through (or toward) that face, reordering to find the new "fixed" face and repeating the procedure. Usually the simplex either keeps the same volume or changes by a factor of two. In the two-dimensional case we can visualize the simplex triangle moving about the merit function surface. The triangle moves by flipping about one edge. During each flip the triangle either remains the same size, doubles in size, reduces to half its size, or shrinks to one-fourth the original size. All but the last procedure is sketched in Figure 1.4.5. A typical simplex search flow chart is shown in Figure 1.4.6. The size of the original simplex is often important. The initial step sizes define that size and the location of initial vertices. These step sizes should be a significant percentage of the allowable range of the design variables. In other words,

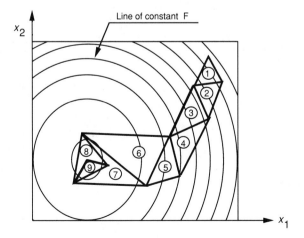

Figure 1.4.5   The 2-D simplex flipping about the edge.

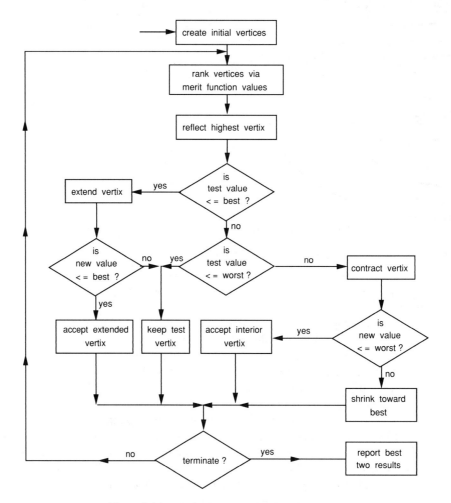

Figure 1.4.6   A simplex search algorithm flowchart.

we do not want the initial simplex to appear with the relative size of a point in the search space. One should clearly "see" it as a simplex when viewing the whole allowable search space.

Typical algorithms for such a search have been published in FORTRAN by Nedler and Mead [4], Olsson [6], and Kuester and Mize [3]. A Pascal version is given by Caceci and Cacheris [1]. The source version, **SIMPLX**, given here in Appendix III is a modification of the work by Olsson. It is designed to be easily modified and to run interactively. This program requires the user to supply a function, FN, that is evaluated by using the trial vector, **x**. It is called every iteration and should be as efficient as possible. Upon termination, a final call is made to another user supplied subroutine, SUMARY, to give the analyst the option to complete auxiliary calculations using the final trial vector, **x**.

1.5 CONSTRAINTS VIA PENALTY FUNCTIONS

Recall that we can have equality constraints of the form

$$H_j(\mathbf{x}^*) = 0.$$

For an arbitrary trial vector, $\mathbf{x}$, the equation will not be satisfied. Thus, instead we have a residual error, E;

$$H_j(\mathbf{x}) = E_j$$

whenever $\mathbf{x}$ lies in a nonfeasible region. We can raise the error to a positive power, n, multiply by a large, positive weighting constant, and add this quantity to the merit function to form an effective merit function. This additional term is called a **penalty function**. Figure 1.5.1 shows such a penalty, P($\mathbf{x}$), the original merit function, f($\mathbf{x}$), and the combined or enhanced merit function, F($\mathbf{x}$):

$$F(\mathbf{x}) = f(\mathbf{x}) + \sum_j W_j \, E_j^{2n}.$$

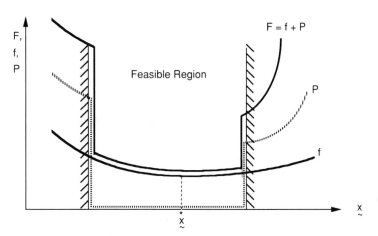

Figure 1.5.1   Adding a concave penalty function to enforce constraints.

With the inequality constraint we have

$$G_i(\mathbf{x}^*) \le 0$$

so in an infeasible domain we have

$$G_i(\mathbf{x}) = e_i$$

where e_i is a positive error term. This term can also be raised to a positive power, m, weighted, and added as another penalty. Then the combined merit becomes

$$F(\mathbf{x}) = f(\mathbf{x}) + \sum_j W_j \, E_j^{2n} + \sum_i w_i \, e_i^{2m}$$

so that at the optimum, $\mathbf{x}^*$,

$$e_i(\mathbf{x}^*) = 0 = E_j(\mathbf{x}^*)$$

and

$$F(\mathbf{x}^*) = f(\mathbf{X}^*).$$

This type of concave penalty constraints has the advantage that it clearly indicates the downhill direction back to the feasible search region. The penalty shown in Figure 1.5.1 is called an **exterior penalty**, since it goes into effect only when the trial vector, $\mathbf{x}$, moves exterior to the feasible space. We could apply another approach and employ an **interior penalty** based on the value of $-1/G_i(\mathbf{x})$, since it approaches infinity as G_i approaches zero. In that case we use a very small value of the weight W_i on the interior region. We mainly utilize the exterior penalty approach.

1.6 TYPICAL APPLICATIONS

The simplex search algorithm (SSA) can be applied to many problems. These include the solution of linear equations, nonlinear equation sets, curve fitting, and minimization problems.

Generally sets of linear equations would be more efficiently solved by other techniques. However, nonlinear algebraic equations are well suited to solution by the SSA. There are several popular methods for solving nonlinear equations. The most common method is probably **Newton's method** and its generalization for systems of nonlinear equations (the Newton-Raphson procedure). It is well suited to finding the roots, x^*, of

$$F(x^*) = 0.$$

It is an iterative procedure where the current estimate of the root, x_j, is used to obtain an improved estimate:

$$x_{j+1} = x_j - \frac{F(x_j)}{\dfrac{dF(x_j)}{dx}}.$$

Clearly this procedure stops when the exact root is found as the correction term will vanish, since F is zero at the root. It can be shown that Newton's method has a quadratic rate of convergence. However, it can also diverge. Its success is typically sensitive to the choice of starting point. Typical convergent and divergent solutions by Newton's method are shown in Figure 1.6.1. The rate of convergence can be increased by adding terms involving the second derivative (curvature) of the function. However, this is rarely done. Most modern equation writers and nonlinear solvers such as **TK Solver** employ the Newton-Raphson procedure. The SSA has the desirable feature that it does not diverge. It may converge slowly and require more calculations, but it is robust and will yield a solution.

1.6.1 Function Minimization

To illustrate some typical application dependent software for the SSA we will begin with the two-dimensional merit function given in Equation (1.2.1). That expression would form a continuous quadratic surface similar to the one shown in Figure 1.4.5, and the simplex is a triangle. Almost any starting simplex should find the minimum quickly. However, very small initial step sizes could lead to slow convergence. In that case the initial simplex is almost a point in the design space. This suggests that we should consider scaling the design variables into some nondimensional range, such as -1 to +1. We will not do that here, but commercial codes usually do. Here our merit function program is shown in Figure 1.6.2 for the unscaled components of the trial vector, $\mathbf{x}$.

For completeness, we have included a postprocessing calculation of another quantity, the average of x_1 and x_2, to illustrate how the designer could pass data through a COMMON. Usually in FN we would calculate only items needed to evaluate the merit function and pass their last value out for postprocessing in SUMARY. This is done because FN may be called thousands of times but SUMARY is called only after the final trial vector has been selected. Figure 1.6.3 shows the typical history file output for this simple function.

From Figure 1.4.5 we see that a regional constraint such that $x_2 \le 1.3$ would essentially reduce this to a one-dimensional problem for finding the value of x_1 that

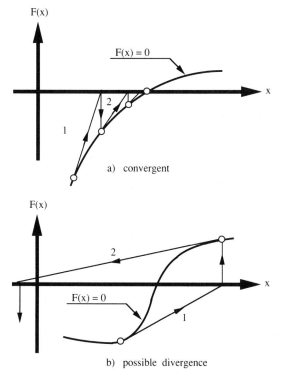

Figure 1.6.1   Newtons' method for roots of $F(x) = 0$.

```
      FUNCTION  FN ( N, X )
C     ------------------------------------------------------------
C        *** APPLICATION DEPENDENT MERIT FUNCTION ***
C     ------------------------------------------------------------
      IMPLICIT REAL*8 (A-H,O-Z)
      DIMENSION  X(N)
C     USE  COMMON /OUT/ TO SEND LAST DATA TO SUMMARY
      COMMON /OUT/  AVE
      AVE = ( X(1) + X(2) )/2.D0
      FN = ( X(1) - 1.D0 )**2 + ( X(2) - 2.D0 )**2
      RETURN
      END
      SUBROUTINE  SUMMARY ( N, X )
C     ------------------------------------------------------------
C     *** APPLICATION DEPENDENT FINAL OUTPUT ***
C     ------------------------------------------------------------
      IMPLICIT REAL*8 (A-H,O-Z)
      DIMENSION  X(N)
C     USE  COMMON /OUT/ TO GET LAST DATA FROM FN
      COMMON /OUT/  AVE
C       CALL WITH XMIN TO GET BEST VALUE
      WRITE (6,*) ' AVERAGE VALUE IS ', AVE
      WRITE (8,*) ' AVERAGE VALUE IS ', AVE
      RETURN
      END
```

Figure 1.6.2 A simple merit function.

minimizes M when $x_2 = 1.3$. In realistic problems we could not always visualize the effect of such a constraint and we would have to retain x_2 in our trial vector.

1.6.2 Curve and Surface Fitting

Fitting functions to experimental or tabulated data is a common task in engineering and optimization problems. The SSA is well suited to evaluating the required coefficients in an empirical curve or surface function. Usually a nonlinear least squares procedure is utilized. As an example, consider a curve to be approximated by the **rational polynomial**

$$z = \frac{a_1 + a_2 y + \cdots + a_n y^{(n-1)}}{b_1 + b_2 y + \cdots + b_n y^{(n-1)}}. \tag{1.6.2}$$

where known pairs of y and z are available and the coefficients to be determined are the a_j and b_j. They are the quantities in our trial vector, $\mathbf{x}$. Assuming a set of values for the coefficients, $\mathbf{x}$, one can substitute a tabulated y_j value and compute the estimate, z_j. This should agree with the corresponding tabulated value, say Z_j. Typically, these quantities will not agree. Then we can define a least squares merit function such as

```
INPUT A LINE OF DESCRIPTIVE TEXT
Name.with.no.blanks

ALL NUMERIC DATA REQUESTED ARE TO BE INPUT IN
FREE FORMAT, PIECES OF DATA MUST BE SEPARATED
BY A COMMA OR A SINGLE SPACE

INPUT ON ONE LINE THE FOLLOWING DATA:
1. ICOUNT = MAXIMUM NUMBER OF ITERATIONS
2. N = NUMBER OF VARIABLES
3. REQMIN = CONVERGENCE CRITERION
   111      2 1.00000d-12

INPUT THE STARTING VALUES OF THE  2 VARIABLES
 1.4000d+00   3.3000d+00

INPUT INITIAL STEP SIZES OF THE  2 VARIABLES
 1.0000d-01   2.0000d-01

INPUT NAME OF DESIGN VARIABLE    1: x
INPUT NAME OF DESIGN VARIABLE    2: y
INPUT NAME OF MERIT FUNCTION     : f.of.xy


Name.with.no.blanks
  111    TRIALS USED, RESULTS ARE:
   DESIGN VARIABLE      NEXT TO BEST         BEST
 x                   1.000000d+00     1.000000d+00
 y                   2.000000d+00     2.000000d+00
  MERIT FUNCTION      NEXT TO BEST         BEST
 f.of.xy             2.252621d-16     0.000000d+00
   AVERAGE VALUE IS     1.49999999246909
```

Figure 1.6.3 A typical session history file.

$$F(\mathbf{x}) = \sum_k w_k [Z_k - z_k(\mathbf{x})]^2$$

where w_k denotes a weight constant associated with each data pair. Here we will assume that all the w_k are unity.

Some curves or surfaces have forms based on theoretical considerations. For example, the Michaelis-Menten equation [3] should give reaction rates, z, that depend on concentration levels, y, in the form

$$z = \frac{a_2 y}{b_1 + y}$$

(so that $a_1 = 0$ and $b_2 = 1$). Thus, our trial vector contains the coefficients $\mathbf{x} =$

$[a_2 \ b_1]^T$. If the tabulated data are

k	y_k	z_k
1	1.68	0.172
2	3.33	0.250
3	5.00	0.286
4	6.67	0.303
5	10.0	0.334
6	20.0	0.384

then the computed trial vector is $\mathbf{x}^T = [0.4238 \ \ 2.4519]$, so that

$$z = \frac{0.4238y}{2.4519 + y}.$$

The availability of a tool like the SSA allows one to select more general forms. For example, in this case we could expand the trial vector to include the exponents of the dependent variable as an unknown. Thus, we could have selected

$$z = \frac{a_2 y}{b_1 + b_2 y^m}$$

with a trial vector $\mathbf{x}^T = [a_2 \ b_1 \ b_2 \ m]$.

Useful surfaces can also be defined in a similar manner. The commonly used thermodynamic steam tables of Keenan and Keyes [2] employ empirical equations of the form

$$\log_{10} \frac{p_c}{p} = \frac{x}{T} \left[\frac{a + bs + cx^3 + ex^4}{1 + dx} \right]$$

where p is the vapor pressure, p_c is the critical pressure, T is the temperature, x is $(T_c - T)$ where T_c is the critical temperature and a, b, c, d, and e are fitted constants given in [2]. Utilizing these curves can avoid storing large tables, searching them, and interpolating between given values.

1.6.3 Maximizing of Profit

To illustrate a problem involving maximization we will consider a typical production problem. A certain company produces four products. The requirements in raw materials, storage space, production rates, and profits are shown in Table 1.6.1. There is a limited amount of available raw material per day for manufacturing all four products. The total storage space available is also limited. We would like to utilize the full seven hours available for production.

Let x_i be the number of pieces of the i-th product produced each day. There are several terms of interest computed from Table 1.6.1.

Material used: $RM_i * x_i = (kg/part)*(part/d) = kg/d$

Space required: $SS_i * x_i = (m^2/part)*(part/d) = m^2/d$

Table 1.6.1 PRODUCTION DATA

Product number	1	2	3	4
Raw material (kg per piece) RM:	5	4	3	4
Storage space (sq. meter per piece) SS:	4	5	4	3
Production rate (pieces per hour) PR:	35	65	25	30
Profit (dollars per piece) $P:	10	12	13	11

Labor time: $x_i / PR_i = (\text{part/d})/(\text{part/hr}) = \text{hr/d}$

Piece profit: $\$P_i * x_i = (\$/\text{part})*(\text{part/d}) = \$/\text{d}$

If we sum over all the parts, $i = 1, \ldots, n$, we would obtain the results for the entire day's production. Assume that the material is limited to 380 kg/d and that the storage is limited to 460 m^2/d. Then using the material used per product, we can write the desired relation that

$$5x_1 + 4x_2 + 3x_3 + 4x_4 \leq 380 \text{ kg/d}$$

The storage necessary for each kind of product is also given in the table. Therefore, a statement representing total space is written:

$$4x_1 + 5x_2 + 4x_3 + 3x_4 \leq 460 \text{ m}^2/\text{d}.$$

Best use of the seven hours of the working day is similarly expressed. The table gives the production rate, which is inverted to give the number of hours per piece:

$$\frac{x_i}{35} + \frac{x_2}{65} + \frac{x_3}{25} + \frac{x_4}{30} = 7\text{hr/d}.$$

These are the functional constraints on the problem. The merit function to be maximized is a statement of the total profit, which is

$$10x_1 + 12x_2 + 13x_3 + 11x_4 = P \text{ dollars/d}.$$

This formulation can be utilized to determine the number of pieces of each product per day required for the maximum profit. An initial SSA formulation of this problem is shown in Figure 1.6.4. Four sample output results are shown in Figure 1.6.5.

Note that we are not able to reach a seven hour production day because we run out of raw materials or storage space. Another difficulty is that some solutions suggest a negative number for one of the parts. Clearly, such a product should be discontinued, and we should modify the solution to prevent negative values for the x_i. Reformulation of the model for more efficient resource allocation and increased profit is possible by adding more design variables or by relaxing the initial constraints imposed on the solution. These could include increasing the amount of raw material and/or the amount of

```
      FUNCTION  FN ( N, X)
C     ----------------------------------------------------
C     MAXIMIZE PROFIT FROM PRODUCTION
      IMPLICIT REAL*8 (A-H, O-Z)
      DOUBLE PRECISION  MATER
      DIMENSION X(4), RM(4), SS(4), PR(4), PP(4)
      COMMON /OUT/ MATER, STORE, TIME, PROFIT, PARTS
      DATA BIG / 1.D8 /
C        INITIAL DATA
      DATA RM / 5.D0, 4.D0, 3.D0, 4.D0 /
      DATA SS / 4.D0, 5.D0, 4.D0, 3.D0 /
      DATA PR / 35.D0, 65.D0, 25.D0, 30.D0 /
      DATA PP / 10.D0, 12.D0, 13.D0, 11.D0 /
C        INITIALIZE
      P = 0.D0
      STORE  = 0.D0
      TIME   = 0.D0
      PRTMAX = 380.D0 / 3.D0
      MATER  = 0.D0
      PROFIT = 0.D0
      PARTS  = 0.D0
C         EVALUATE AND PENALIZE
      DO 10  I = 1,4
       PARTS = PARTS + X(I)
       MATER = MATER + X(I)*RM(I)
       STORE = STORE + X(I)*SS(I)
       TIME  = TIME  + X(I)/PR(I)
       PROFIT = PROFIT + X(I)*PP(I)
       IF ( X(I) .LT. 0.D0 )   P = P + (X(I)-2.D0)**4
   10  IF ( X(I) .GT. PRTMAX ) P = P + (X(I)-1.D0)**2
      IF ( PARTS .GT. PRTMAX ) P = P + (PARTS-1.D0)**2
      IF ( MATER .GT. 380.D0 ) P = P + (MATER-190.D0)**2
      IF ( STORE .GT. 460.D0 ) P = P + (STORE-230.D0)**2
      IF ( TIME  .NE. 7.D0 )   P = P + (TIME-7.D0)**2
      IF ( PROFIT .LE. 0.D0 )  P = P + PROFIT**2
      FN = BIG*P - PROFIT**2
      RETURN
      END
```

Figure 1.6.4a Profit-maximizing merit function.

storage space. If we allow these to exceed the current limits, then we need to determine what we should pay for these additional resources.

The results in Figure 1.6.5 imply producing only the third and fourth product. But the current constraints are not practical. If we find that we can obtain additional material, above 380 kg, at 50 cents per kg and rent extra space, above 460 m^2, at 5 cents per square meter, then we obtain a completely different conclusion. Under that

```
      SUBROUTINE  SUMMARY ( N, X)
C     --------------------------------------------------
C     PRODUCTION SUMMARY
      IMPLICIT REAL*8 (A-H,O-Z)
      DOUBLE PRECISION  MATER
      DIMENSION  X(N)
      COMMON /OUT/ MATER, STORE, TIME, PROFIT, PARTS
      WRITE (6,*) ' FINAL RESULTS'
      WRITE (8,*) ' FINAL RESULTS'
      WRITE (6,20) MATER, STORE, TIME, PROFIT, PARTS
      WRITE (8,20) MATER, STORE, TIME, PROFIT, PARTS
 20   FORMAT (' MATERIAL USED........ ', 1PD14.5, /,
     1         ' STORAGE SPACE........ ', 1PD14.5, /,
     2         ' PRODUCTION TIME...... ', 1PD14.5, /,
     3         ' PROFIT TOTAL......... ', 1PD14.5, /,
     4         ' NUMBER OF PARTS ..... ', 1PD14.5)
      RETURN
      END
```

Figure 1.6.4b   Profit-maximizing merit function.

condition we want to produce only the second product. We get a full production time
and the profit per day increases by more than a factor of 3.

1.6.4 Gear Train Inertia Minimization

Consider a gear train as shown in Figure 1.6.6. We wish to minimize the effective
inertia of the system. What is the best way to do this? Do we want a single, double, or
triple reduction? What are the best gear ratios?

To build our model we begin by reviewing a typical pinion and gear pair. First
we consider the kinematic relations. Let r_P and r_G denote the radii of the pinion and
gear, respectively. Their angular velocities are ω_P and ω_G and they have a common
velocity, V, at their point of contact. Assuming fixed center points we have the
kinematic relation

$$V = r_P\, \omega_P = r_G\, \omega_G \qquad (1.6.3)$$

so the angular velocities are related by

$$\omega_G = \left(\frac{r_P}{r_G} \right)\omega_P = \frac{1}{x}\, \omega_P \qquad (1.6.4)$$

where x represents a gear reduction ratio. Next we assume that the gears are cylinders
of equal thickness. Recall that the polar inertia of a cylinder is

$$I = \tfrac{1}{2}mr^2$$

```
Production.Study
  DESIGN VARIABLE      NEXT TO BEST            BEST
jig                    2.368859d-05        4.543872d-06
widget                 8.562920d-05        2.053055d-04
wheel                  6.189131d+01        6.189127d+01
thing                  4.858102d+01        4.858104d+01
  FINAL RESULTS
MATERIAL USED........    3.79998d+02
STORAGE SPACE........    3.93308d+02
PRODUCTION TIME......    4.09501d+00
PROFIT TOTAL.........    1.33898d+03
NUMBER OF PARTS .....    1.10472d+02


  DESIGN VARIABLE      NEXT TO BEST            BEST
jig                    1.699137d+01        1.699134d+01
widget                 4.201999d+00        4.202025d+00
wheel                  9.274462d+01        9.274463d+01
thing                  3.507385d-07        1.367165d-07
  FINAL RESULTS
MATERIAL USED........    3.79999d+02
STORAGE SPACE........    4.59954d+02
PRODUCTION TIME......    4.25990d+00
PROFIT TOTAL.........    1.42602d+03
NUMBER OF PARTS .....    1.13938d+02


  DESIGN VARIABLE      NEXT TO BEST            BEST
jig                    7.002792d-07        2.309977d-07
widget                 2.547955d-01        2.547956d-01
wheel                  1.029091d+02        1.029091d+02
thing                  1.569650d+01        1.569650d+01
  FINAL RESULTS
MATERIAL USED........    3.72533d+02
STORAGE SPACE........    4.60000d+02
PRODUCTION TIME......    4.64350d+00
PROFIT TOTAL.........    1.51354d+03
NUMBER OF PARTS .....    1.18860d+02


  DESIGN VARIABLE      NEXT TO BEST            BEST
jig                    4.515458d-02        4.515453d-02
widget                 5.705529d-08        3.483161d-08
wheel                  9.996825d+01        9.996825d+01
thing                  1.996737d+01        1.996737d+01
  FINAL RESULTS
MATERIAL USED........    3.80000d+02
STORAGE SPACE........    4.59956d+02
PRODUCTION TIME......    4.66560d+00
PROFIT TOTAL.........    1.51968d+03
NUMBER OF PARTS .....    1.19981d+02
```

Figure 1.6.5 First profit solution sets.

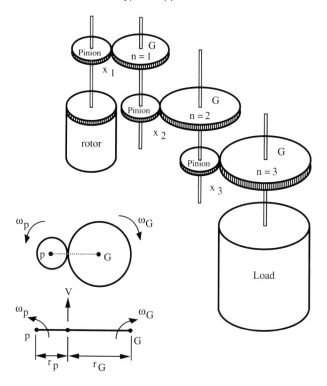

Figure 1.6.6   A gear train system.

where the mass is

$$m = \rho A = \rho \pi r^2$$

when ρ denotes the mass per unit area. Thus, the inertias of the pinion and gear are

$$I_P = \tfrac{1}{2}\rho \pi r_P^4$$

and

$$I_G = \tfrac{1}{2}\rho \pi r_G^4.$$

But for this gear ratio, $r_G = r_P x$, so

$$I_G = \tfrac{1}{2}\rho \pi (r_P\ x)^4$$

or

$$I_G = I_P\ x^4. \tag{1.6.5}$$

The kinetic energy of the part rotating about a fixed point is

$$T = \tfrac{1}{2}\ I \omega^2.$$

Adding the kinetic energy of the motor, each gear-pinion pair, and the end load gives

$$T = \tfrac{1}{2}(I_M + I_P)\omega_1^2 + \tfrac{1}{2}(I_{G1} + I_P)\omega_2^2$$
$$+ \tfrac{1}{2}(I_{G2} + I_P)\omega_3^2 + \tfrac{1}{2}(I_{G3} + I_L)\omega_4^2.$$

If we denote the gear ratios of the first three reductions by x_1, x_2, and x_3, respectively, then

$$\omega_2 = \frac{\omega_1}{x_1}$$

$$\omega_3 = \frac{\omega_2}{x_2} = \frac{\omega_1}{x_1 x_2}$$

$$\omega_4 = \frac{\omega_3}{x_3} = \frac{\omega_1}{x_1 x_2 x_3} = \frac{\omega_1}{R} \qquad (1.6.6)$$

where $R = x_1 x_2 x_3$ denotes the total gear reduction ratio. Let $\omega_1 = \omega$ and simplify the kinetic energy expression:

$$T = \tfrac{1}{2}(I_m + I_P)\omega^2 + \tfrac{1}{2}(I_{G1} + I_P)\left[\frac{\omega}{x_1}\right]^2$$
$$+ \tfrac{1}{2}(I_{G2} + I_P)\left[\frac{\omega}{x_1 x_2}\right]^2 + \tfrac{1}{2}(I_{G3} + I_L)\left[\frac{\omega}{x_1 x_2 x_3}\right]^2.$$

Substituting I_G in terms of I_P from Equation (1.6.5) and using the reduction ratio gives:

$$T = \tfrac{1}{2}(I_m + I_P)\omega^2 + \tfrac{1}{2}[x_1^4 I_P + I_P]\left[\frac{\omega}{x_1}\right]^2$$
$$+ \tfrac{1}{2}[x_2^4 I_P + I_P]\left[\frac{\omega}{x_1 x_2}\right]^2 + \tfrac{1}{2}[x_3^4 I_P + I_L]\left[\frac{\omega}{x_1 x_2 x_3}\right]^2.$$

or

$$T = \tfrac{1}{2} I_m \omega^2 + \tfrac{1}{2} I_P \left[1 + x_1^2 + \frac{1}{x_1^2} + \frac{x_2^2}{x_1^2} + \frac{1}{x_1^2 x_2^2} + \frac{x_3^2}{x_1^2 x_2^2}\right]\omega^2$$
$$+ \tfrac{1}{2} I_L \frac{\omega^2}{x_1^2 x_2^2 x_3^2}.$$

This energy measure depends only on the motor speed and the gear reductions. Thus, we define an effective inertia, I_E, as

$$T \equiv \tfrac{1}{2} I_E \omega^2.$$

Thus, the problem is to pick the design variables x_1, x_2, and x_3 in order to minimize the inertia

$$I_E(x_1, x_2 \, x_3) = I_M + I_P \left[1 + x_1^2 + \frac{1}{x_1^2} + \frac{x_2^2}{x_1^2} + \frac{1}{x_1^2 x_2^2} + \frac{x_3^2}{x_2^2 x_1^2} \right]$$

$$+ \frac{I_L}{x_1^2 x_2^2 x_3^2} \, . \tag{1.6.7}$$

Since $R = x_1 x_2 x_3$ is a known constant, only two of the gear ratios are independent design variables. This also means that only the second term enters the minimization process. If the shafts had identical inertias, say I_s, that were significant, then we would have to include their kinetic energy

$$T_s = \tfrac{1}{2} I_s (\omega_1^2 + \omega_2^2 + \omega_3^2 + \omega_4^2)$$

$$= \tfrac{1}{2} I_s \left[1 + \frac{1}{x_1^2} + \frac{1}{x_1^2 x_2^2} + \frac{1}{x_1^2 x_2^2 x_3^2} \right] \omega^2 \tag{1.6.8}$$

and also include a similar contribution to the effective inertia. A given reduction ratio, R, suggests the inequality constants

$$0 < x_1 \le R$$

$$0 < x_2 \le R$$

$$0 < x_3 \le R.$$

If $I_s \approx 0$, then the effective inertia depends only on two of the gear reduction ratios, say x_1 and x_2. If we do not consider the inequality constraints, then we can apply the methods of calculus and require

$$\frac{\partial I_E}{\partial x_1} = 0$$

and

$$\frac{\partial I_E}{\partial x_2} = 0.$$

This yields

$$x_1^6 x_2^4 - x_1^2 x_2^4 - x_1^2 x_2^6 - x_1^2 x_2^2 - 2R^2 = 0$$

and

$$x_1^2 x_2^6 - x_1^2 x_2^2 - 2R^2 = 0.$$

These two nonlinear equations must be solved simultaneously. Combining, this simplifies to

$$x_1^6 x_2^4 - x_1^2 x_2^4 - 2x_1^2 x_2^6 = 0$$

or

$$x_1^4 - 1 - 2x_2^2 = 0.$$

By trial and error we find that one such solution is approximately

$$x_1 = 1.7434$$

$$x_2 = 2.0298.$$

This may or may not satisfy our constraints. Note that this approach did not depend on R. The third gear reduction would always be $x_3 = R/x_1 x_2 = 0.283R$. A better approach would be to keep all three reductions and impose the equality and inequality constraints. Also, for more gears in the reduction train, it becomes much more difficult to find a solution from calculus. However, the simplex search method provides a good way to solve these nonlinear relations. To illustrate the generalization of this problem, assume that there are N gear reductions: x_i, $i = 1, \ldots, N$. The total reduction ratio is

$$R = \prod_{i=1}^{N} x_i \tag{1.6.9}$$

and the effective inertia is

$$I_E = I_M + \frac{I_L}{R^2} + I_P \left[1 + \sum_{j=1}^{N-1} \frac{1}{\prod_{k=1}^{j} x_k^2} + \sum_{j=1}^{N-1} \frac{x_j^4}{\prod_{k=1}^{j} x_k^2} + \frac{x_N^4}{R^2} \right]$$

$$+ I_s \left[1 + \sum_{y=1}^{N-1} \frac{1}{\prod_{k=1}^{j} x_k^2} \right]$$

where

$$0 < x_i \le R \qquad i = 1, \ldots, N. \tag{1.6.10}$$

The problem is to determine the trial vector containing the N x_i that satisfies the constraints and minimizes the effective inertia.

1.7 COMBINING OPTIMIZATION AND ANALYSIS SYSTEMS

Most designs are going to require the engineer to utilize one or more analysis systems. A practical optimization system should provide some option for exchanging information with an analysis system. The **OPTDES** system is an example of optimization software that provides such a feature.

Many mechanical engineering design problems will require interaction with a finite element analysis system for thermal, stress, and/or frequency analysis. Commercial finite element analysis (FEA) systems are usually quite large and are computationally intensive. Thus, approximate optimization procedures may be used with such analysis systems. Such procedures are discussed in the chapter on finite element analysis.

1.8 REFERENCES

1. Caceci, M. S., and Cacheris, W. P. "Fitting Curves to Data." *Byte* 9, no. 5 (1984): 340–62.

2. Keenan, J. H., and Keyes, F. G. *Thermodynamic Properties of Steam.* New York: John Wiley, 1961.

3. Kuester, J. L., and Mize, J. H. *Optimization Techniques with FORTRAN.* New York: McGraw-Hill, 1973.

4. Nedler, J. A., and Mead, R. "A Simplex Method for Function Minimization." *Computer J.* 7 (1965): 308–13.

5. Oden, J. T. *Finite Elements of Nonlinear Continua.* New York: McGraw-Hill, 1972.

6. Olsson, D. M. "A Sequential Simplex Program for Solving Minimization Problems." *J. Quality Technology* 6, no. 1 (1974): 53–57.

7. Parkinson, A. R., et al. "Exploring Design Space: Optimization as a Synthesizer of Design and Analysis." *Computers in Mechanical Engineering* (March, 1985): 28–36.

8. Parkinson, A., Balling, R., Free, J. *OPTDES.BYU User's Manual.* Design Optimization Lab., Brigham Young University, 1986.

9. Siddall, J. N. *Optimal Engineering Design,* New York: Dekker, 1982.

10. Suh, C. H., and Radcliffe, C. W. *Kinematics and Mechanism Design.* Melbourne, Fla.: R. E. Krieger Pub. Co., 1983.

11. Townsend, M. A., and Zarak, C. E. "Accelerating Flexible Polyhedron Searches for Nonlinear Minimization." ASME 82-WA/DE-31, 1982.

12. Vanderplaats, G. N. *Numerical Optimization Techniques for Engineering Design.* New York: McGraw-Hill, 1984.

1.9 EXERCISES

1. Find the minimum of $F(x_1, x_2) = (x_1 - 1)^2 + (x_2 - 2)^2$ by using typical calculus procedures. Discuss a technique that you could use without utilizing derivatives.

2. Minimize $F(x) = x^4 - 8.5x^3 - 31x^2 - 7.5x + 45$, and report the minimum value and where it occurred. (*Ans:* $x^* = 8.278$)

3. Minimize $F(x) = x^5 - 5x^3 - 20x + 5$ and report x optimum and the value of F. (*Ans:* $F = -43$)

4. Minimize $F(x) = (x + 4)(x + 5)(x + 8)(x - 16)(x + 2)^2$. (*Ans:* $x^* = 12.68$)

5. Minimize $F(\mathbf{x}) = [1.5 - x_1(1 - x_2)]^2 + [2.25 - x_1(1 - x_2^2)]^2 + [2.625 - x_1(1 - x_2^3)]^2$. (*Ans:* $\mathbf{x}^* = [3, 0.5]^T, F(\mathbf{x}^*) = 0$)

6. Minimize F$(\mathbf{x}) = [e^{x_1} - x_3]^4 + 100(x_2 - x_3)^6 + Tan^4(x_3 - x_4) + x_1^8 + (x_4 - 1)^2$. (*Ans:* $F(\mathbf{x}^*) = 0$)

7. Consider a one-dimensional minimization problem, F(x). The simplex is shown in Figure 1.4.1. Sketch a series of curves that would cause new simplex shapes analogous to those in Figure 1.4.2d through h.

8. Write a merit function subroutine to evaluate Equation (1.2.1b).

9. Evaluate the model constants in Equation (1.2.2) using the data.

y	z_1	z_2	z_3
0.344	0.0239	0.968	0.0085
0.707	0.0791	0.904	0.0171
0.344	0.0596	0.881	0.0597
0.053	0.0322	0.866	0.1020
0.308	0.0893	0.804	0.1070

(*Ans:* $a_1 \approx 14.3$, $a_2 \approx 8.4$)

10. The yield, Y, and concentration, C, of a process are dependent on the non-dimensional temperature, T, and pressure, P. Maximize the yield subject to the constraint that $C \geq 90$. The fitted empirical equations are

$$C = 85.7 + 21.9T + 8.6P - 6.3TP - 9.2T^2 - 5.2P^2$$

$$Y = 55.8 + 7.3T + 26.7P + 2.7TP - 3.0T^2 - 7.0P^2.$$

(*Ans:* $T \approx 1.07$, $P \approx 1.48$)

11. A disk of constant thickness is to be used to store kinetic energy. It has inner and outer radii of b and a, respectively, and a thickness of h. The material is homogeneous with elastic modulus, E, Poisson ratio, ν, yield stress, σ_y, and mass density, ρ. The kinetic energy is

$$T = \tfrac{1}{2} I \, \omega^2$$

where ω is the angular velocity and the mass moment of inertia is

$$I = \tfrac{\pi}{2} \rho h (a^4 - b^4) = \tfrac{1}{2} m (a^2 + b^2)$$

for a mass of

$$m = \pi \rho \, h (a^2 - b^2).$$

The maximum hoop stress, at $r = b$,

$$\sigma = \frac{3 + \nu}{4} \rho \, \omega^2 (a^2 + \frac{1 - \nu}{3 + \nu} b^2)$$

is always larger than the radial stress. For a given material, find the four design variables (a, b, h and ω) that maximize the kinetic energy stored. The constraints on the design are

$$\sigma \leq \sigma_y \qquad\qquad m \leq m_x$$
$$0 < b_n \leq b \qquad\qquad a \leq a_x$$
$$h \leq h_x \qquad\qquad b < a\,.$$

The spatial limits are

$$b_n = 0.05m \qquad a_x = 1m \qquad h_x = 0.2m$$

and the mass limit is $m_x = 2000$ kg. Use titanium so that $E = 11 \times 10^{10}$ N/m^2, $\nu = 0.3$, $\rho = 4533$ kg/m^3, and $\sigma_y = 960 \times 10^6$ N/m^2.

12. Maximize the profit in Section 1.6 if additional material costs \$0.50 per kg and additional space costs \$0.05 per square meter per day.

13. Repeat the inertia minimization problem in Section 1.6.4 for a train with (a) four gears, (b) five gears.

2

MATRIX
TRANSFORMATIONS

2.1 INTRODUCTION

A lot of engineering analysis is presented through the use of vector analysis. However, matrix formulations have become increasingly popular for high-speed computer operations. This is especially true in the areas of computer graphics, robotics, and kinematic analysis. Their speed advantage comes from the fact that microprocessors are available to execute these matrix operations in hardware rather than software. Several engineering workstations now have these chips installed and allow the user to access them through subroutine calls.

The notation to be employed here follows the usual engineering practice of representing vector quantities as column matrices. This differs from the common practice in computer graphics of representing vectors as row matrices. There are numerous computer graphics texts, such as Foley and Van Dam [1], that would be useful references in this section. However, we must convert the notation of one system to the other. This is easily done, since a valid relation in one form is simply the transpose of the valid expression in the other. For example, we will often write product expressions of the form

$$\mathbf{V}' = \mathbf{D}\,\mathbf{V} \tag{2.1.1}$$

where $\mathbf{V}$ and $\mathbf{V}'$ are vectors and $\mathbf{D}$ is a rectangular (usually square) matrix. If this is a valid relation, then it is still valid after we transpose both sides. From matrix algebra

$$\mathbf{V}'^{T} = (\mathbf{D}\ \mathbf{V})^{T}$$
$$= \mathbf{V}^{T}\ \mathbf{D}^{T}\ . \tag{2.1.2}$$

But the transpose of a column matrix is a row matrix. Let such a row be defined as

$$\mathbf{V}^T \equiv \mathbf{r}$$

so the valid expression becomes

$$\mathbf{r}' = \mathbf{r} \ \mathbf{D}^T \equiv \mathbf{r} \ \mathbf{M}. \tag{2.1.3}$$

Thus, we see that the operating matrix in one form is simply the transpose of the matrix in the alternate form:

$$\mathbf{M} = \mathbf{D}^T, \qquad \mathbf{D} = \mathbf{M}^T$$

In one case it premultiplies the vector, whereas in the other it postmultiplies the row. A series of operations converts in a similar fashion. For example, if a computer graphics text shows four operations, resulting in

$$\mathbf{r}' = \mathbf{r} \ \mathbf{A} \ \mathbf{B} \ \mathbf{C} \ \mathbf{D}$$

then the corresponding identity in our notation is

$$\mathbf{V}' = \mathbf{D}^T \ \mathbf{C}^T \ \mathbf{B}^T \ \mathbf{A}^T \ \mathbf{V}.$$

2.2 FINITE SPATIAL ROTATIONS ABOUT AN AXIS

Consider a vector $\mathbf{V}$ with components of $\mathbf{V}^T = (v_x, v_y, v_z)$ in the three Cartesian coordinate directions. The new components, $\mathbf{V}'$, resulting from a rotation about one of the Cartesian axes can be defined by a matrix transformation. For example, a right-hand rule rotation of $\theta_z = \theta$ about the z-axis is shown in Figure 2.1.1. For rotation about the z-axis the z component will not change. Thus, there is an identity that $V'_z = V_z$, and only the x and y components will change. The rotation of $\mathbf{V}$ to form $\mathbf{V}'$ can also be viewed as the simultaneous rotation of the original components, v_x and v_y. When rotated they both contribute to the new components of $\mathbf{V}'$. For example, the figure shows the new x-component to be

$$v'_x = v_x \cos \theta - v_y \sin \theta.$$

Likewise,

$$v'_y = v_x \sin \theta + v_y \cos \theta.$$

Writing these relations in matrix form:

$$\left\{ \begin{array}{c} v_x \\ v_y \\ v_z \end{array} \right\}' = \left[\begin{array}{ccc} \cos \theta & -\sin \theta & 0 \\ \sin \theta & \cos \theta & 0 \\ 0 & 0 & 1 \end{array} \right] \left\{ \begin{array}{c} v_x \\ v_y \\ v_z \end{array} \right\} \tag{2.2.1}$$

or, symbolically,

$$\{V'\} = [RZ]\{V\}$$

or

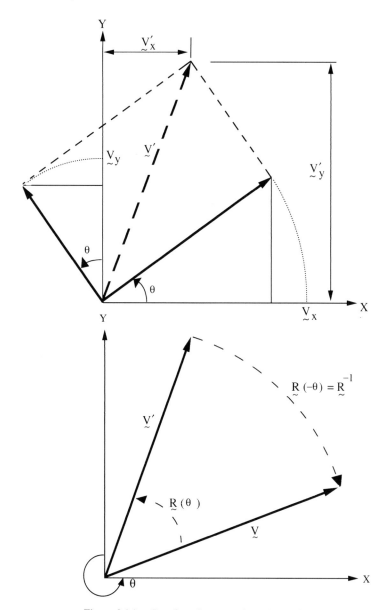

Figure 2.1.1   Rotation of a vector about the z-axis.

$$\mathbf{V}' = \mathbf{RZ}\ \mathbf{V}. \tag{2.2.2}$$

In a similar manner a rotation about the y-axis with $\theta_y = \theta$, by the right-hand rule, gives

$$\begin{Bmatrix} v_x \\ v_y \\ v_z \end{Bmatrix}' = \begin{bmatrix} \cos\theta & 0 & \sin\theta \\ 0 & 1 & 0 \\ -\sin\theta & 0 & \cos\theta \end{bmatrix} \begin{Bmatrix} v_x \\ v_y \\ v_z \end{Bmatrix} \tag{2.2.3}$$

or

$$\mathbf{V'} = \mathbf{RY}\ \mathbf{V}.$$

Likewise, a rotation about the x-axis gives

$$\mathbf{V'} = \mathbf{RX}\ \mathbf{V}$$

with

$$\mathbf{RX} = \begin{bmatrix} 1 & 0 & 0 \\ 0 & \cos\theta & -\sin\theta \\ 0 & \sin\theta & \cos\theta \end{bmatrix}. \qquad (2.2.4)$$

We have seen previously, in introductory dynamics, that finite rigid body rotations do not add vectorally (are not communicative). That is, the order of the rotations is important, as shown in Figure 2.2.2. Thus, if we want to rotate about the z-axis, then the y-axis, and finally the x-axis, the result is

$$\mathbf{V'} = (\mathbf{RX}\ (\mathbf{RY}\ (\mathbf{RZ}\ \mathbf{V})))$$

$$\mathbf{V'} = \mathbf{RX}\ \mathbf{RY}\ \mathbf{RZ}\ \mathbf{V}\ . \qquad (2.2.5)$$

This is read "$\mathbf{V}$ premultiplied by $\mathbf{RZ}$, premultiplied by $\mathbf{RY}$, premultiplied by $\mathbf{RX}$". To increase the efficiency of these operations we can compute the resultant rotation transformation as

$$\mathbf{RZYX} \equiv \mathbf{RX}\ \mathbf{RY}\ \mathbf{RZ} = \begin{bmatrix} (C_z C_y) & (-S_z C_y) & (S_y) \\ (S_z C_x + C_z S_y S_x) & (C_z C_x + S_z S_y S_x) & (-C_y S_x) \\ (S_z S_x - C_z S_y C_x) & (C_z S_x + S_z S_y C_x) & (C_y C_x) \end{bmatrix} \qquad (2.2.6)$$

where C_x and S_x denote $\cos\theta_x$ and $\sin\theta_x$, respectively. This result is not the same as that where the order of rotation is reversed. That result is

$$\mathbf{V'} = (\mathbf{RZ}\ (\mathbf{RY}\ (\mathbf{RX}\ \mathbf{V})))$$

$$= \mathbf{RZ}\ \mathbf{RY}\ \mathbf{RX}\ \mathbf{V} \equiv \mathbf{RXYZ}\ \mathbf{V}$$

but, since matrix multiplication (like rigid body rotation) is generally not commutative, $\mathbf{RZ}\ \mathbf{RY}\ \mathbf{RX} \neq \mathbf{RX}\ \mathbf{RY}\ \mathbf{RZ}$. That is, $\mathbf{RXYZ} \neq \mathbf{RZYX}$.

As a result of the importance of the order of rotation one must use care in defining the desired result. A very commonly used set of rotations are the Euler angles ψ, θ, ϕ, shown in Figure 2.2.3. They are often used in kinematics and kinetics. The resulting position can be defined by various sequences of relative motions. One sequence is to have the **spin** angle $\theta_z = \phi$, about the z-axis be followed by **mutation** angle, $\theta_x = \theta$, about the original x-axis and then followed by a **precession** angle, $\theta_z = \psi$, about the original z-axis. The result is

$$\mathbf{V'} = (\mathbf{RZ}\,(\psi)\ (\mathbf{RX}\,(\theta)\ (\mathbf{RZ}\,(\phi)\ \mathbf{V})))$$

$$= \mathbf{RZ}\ \mathbf{RX}\ \mathbf{RZ}\ \mathbf{V} \equiv \mathbf{E}\ \mathbf{V}$$

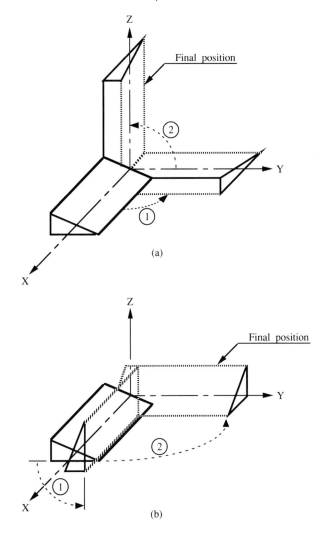

(a)

(b)

Figure 2.2.2   Finite rotations are not communicative.

where the resulting Euler rotation matrix, **E**, is

$$\mathbf{E} = \begin{bmatrix} (C\,\psi C\,\phi - S\,\psi C\,\theta S\,\phi) & (-C\,\psi S\,\phi - S\,\psi C\,\theta C\,\phi) & (S\,\psi S\,\theta) \\ (S\,\psi C\,\phi + C\,\psi C\,\theta S\,\phi) & (-S\,\psi S\,\phi + C\,\psi C\,\theta C\,\phi) & (-C\,\psi S\,\theta) \\ (S\,\theta S\,\phi) & (S\,\theta C\,\phi) & (C\,\theta) \end{bmatrix}. \quad (2.2.9)$$

Another type of important rotation is that about an arbitrary axis in space, which is considered later.

Often it is necessary to compute the inverse (or opposite) of an operation such as a rotation. For example, if we rotate by θ_z about the z-axis and then by $-\theta_z$ about the z-axis, we should recover the original vector, as shown in Figure 2.2.1:

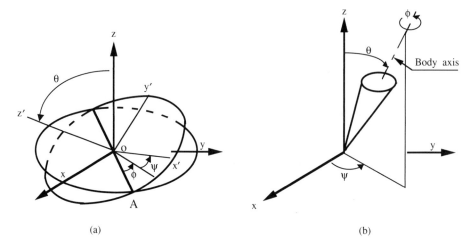

Figure 2.2.3   A set of Euler angles.

$$\mathbf{V}' = \mathbf{RZ}\ \mathbf{V}$$

so we define

$$\mathbf{V} = \mathbf{RZ}^{-1}\ \mathbf{V}' \tag{2.2.10}$$

as the inverse operation and call $\mathbf{RZ}^{-1}$ the inverse of $\mathbf{RZ}$. Here then

$$\mathbf{V} = \mathbf{RZ}^{-1}(\mathbf{RZ}\ \mathbf{V})$$

$$= \mathbf{RZ}^{-1}\ \mathbf{RZ}\ \mathbf{V} \equiv \mathbf{I}\ \mathbf{V}$$

where $\mathbf{I}$ is the (diagonal) identity matrix. That is,

$$\mathbf{RZ}^{-1}\ \mathbf{RZ} = \mathbf{I}.$$

Here we can find $\mathbf{RZ}^{-1}$ by inspection, since we know that $\cos(-\theta_z) = \cos\theta_z$ and $\sin(-\theta_z) = -\sin\theta_z$. Thus, since $\mathbf{RZ}^{-1}$ must be the same as $\mathbf{RZ}$ taken in a negative rotation

$$\mathbf{RZ}^{-1}(\theta) = \mathbf{RZ}(-\theta) \tag{2.2.11}$$

or

$$\mathbf{RZ}^{-1} = \begin{bmatrix} \cos\theta & \sin\theta & 0 \\ -\sin\theta & \cos\theta & 0 \\ 0 & 0 & 1 \end{bmatrix} = \mathbf{RZ}^{T}. \tag{2.2.12}$$

Therefore, we note that the inverse of the rotation matrix is its transpose, $\mathbf{RZ}^{-1} = \mathbf{RZ}^{T}$. This is generally true, since rotation transformations are defined by orthogonal matrices. Likewise, we also have

$$\mathbf{RY}^{-1} = \mathbf{RY}^{T}$$

$$\mathbf{RX}^{-1} = \mathbf{RX}^{T}$$

$$\mathbf{RZYX}^{-1} = (\mathbf{RX\ RY\ RZ})^{-1} = (\mathbf{RZ}^{-1}\ \mathbf{RY}^{-1}\ \mathbf{RX}^{-1})$$

$$= (\mathbf{RZ}^{T}\ \mathbf{RY}^{T}\ \mathbf{RX}^{T}) = (\mathbf{RX\ RY\ RZ})^{T}$$

$$= \mathbf{RZYX}^{T}.$$

2.3 ROTATION ABOUT A LINE

It is much more common to need to rotate an object about a line in space rather than one of the coordinate axes. The general rotation about a line can be described in various ways. The intermediate steps differ, but the final result is the same in each procedure. We describe a procedure of five steps that employ the axis rotations just defined. Assume the line lies in the positive octant of space. The operations shown in Figure 2.3.1 are

1. Rotate the line of interest about the x-axis by an angle γ (based on the right-hand rule) so that it lies in the x-z plane.
2. Rotate about the y-axis by an angle of $-\beta$ so the line now lies on the z-axis.
3. Rotate about the line, now on the z-axis, by the desired amount, ϕ.
4. Reverse the process by rotating about the y-axis by the angle β.
5. Rotate about the x-axis by $-\gamma$ to return the line to its original position.

The important information in this process is what was the original direction of the line and what is the desired amount of rotation, ϕ. The direction of the line would usually be given by a unit vector, $\mathbf{U}$, or the direction cosines, (u_x, u_y, u_z), that are its components. We should expect that the final result depends only on these four things and that the intermediate steps are not important. Indeed, the combined transformation

$$\mathbf{v}' = [\mathbf{RX}(-\gamma)\ [\mathbf{RY}(\beta)\ [\mathbf{RZ}(\phi)\ [\mathbf{RY}(-\beta)\ [\mathbf{RX}(+\gamma)\ \mathbf{v}\ ]]]]] \qquad (2.3.1)$$

where $\tan \gamma = u_y/u_z$, $\tan \beta = u_x/\sqrt{u_y^2 + u_z^2}$ reduces to

$$\mathbf{v}' = \mathbf{RU}(\phi)\ \mathbf{v}$$

$$\mathbf{RU} = \begin{bmatrix} (u_x\ u_x\ V + C) & (u_x\ u_y\ V - u_z\ S) & (u_x\ u_z\ V + u_y\ S) \\ (u_x\ u_y\ V + u_z\ S) & (u_y\ u_y\ V + C) & (u_y\ u_z\ V - u_x\ S) \\ (u_x\ u_z\ V - u_y\ S) & (u_y\ u_z\ V + u_x\ S) & (u_z\ u_z\ V + C) \end{bmatrix} \qquad (2.3.2)$$

with $C = \cos \phi$, $S = \sin \phi$, $V = 1 - C = vers(\phi)$. This result can be checked by letting the unit vector lie along each of the coordinate axes. For example if $u_y \equiv 1$, $u_x = u_y = 0$ then

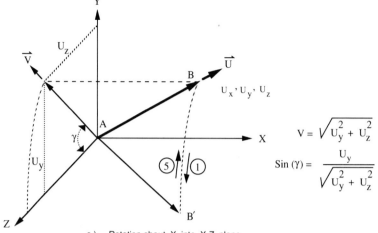

a)   Rotation about X into X-Z plane

$$V = \sqrt{U_y^2 + U_z^2}$$

$$Sin\,(\gamma) = \frac{U_y}{\sqrt{U_y^2 + U_z^2}}$$

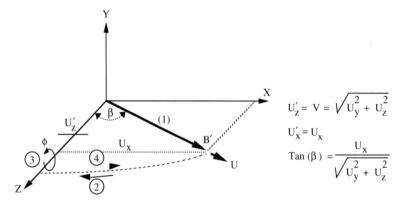

b)   Rotation about Y onto Z-axis

$$U_z' = V = \sqrt{U_y^2 + U_z^2}$$

$$U_x' = U_x$$

$$Tan\,(\beta) = \frac{U_x}{\sqrt{U_y^2 + U_z^2}}$$

Figure 2.3.1   Transforming line AB onto Z-axis.

$$\mathbf{RU} = \begin{bmatrix} (0+C) & (0) & S \\ 0 & (V+C) & 0 \\ (0-S) & (0) & C \end{bmatrix}$$

$$= \begin{bmatrix} C & 0 & S \\ 0 & 1 & 0 \\ -S & 0 & C \end{bmatrix} = \mathbf{RY}.$$

Likewise, if $u_x = 1$, $u_y = u_z = 0$ then $\mathbf{RU} = \mathbf{RX}$, as expected. If there is no rotation then $\mathbf{R} = \mathbf{I}$, the identity matrix.

The above procedures show how to find the new values of the three rotated components of a vector. Sometimes we want to simply translate a vector from one point to another. For example, if we translate a point, P_1, on a rigid body so that it occupies a new point, P_2, then all points on the rigid body have the same change in position. The position of any point (x, y, z) then changes to (x', y', z'), where

$$x' = x + t_1 \qquad\qquad t_1 = x_1 - x_2 = \Delta x$$

$$y' = y + t_2 \qquad\qquad t_2 = \Delta y \qquad\qquad\qquad (2.3.3)$$

$$z' = z + t_3 \qquad\qquad t_3 = \Delta z.$$

In matrix form we could write

$$\mathbf{V}' = \mathbf{V} + \mathbf{t} \qquad\qquad\qquad (2.3.4)$$

where $\mathbf{t}$ is the above translation vector, $\mathbf{V}$ is the original position of a point, and $\mathbf{V}'$ is the new position of that point. Comparing the above two equations with Equations (2.2.1 and 2.2.2) we see that two different operations are involved. Rotations require a matrix multiplication and translations require a matrix addition. It is desirable to find an alternate approach that requires only one operation.

2.4 FINITE DISPLACEMENTS

A general finite displacement (or affine transformation) can be written as the linear equations

$$x' = a_{11} x + a_{12} y + a_{13} z + a_{14}$$

$$y' = a_{21} x + a_{22} y + a_{23} z + a_{24}$$

$$z' = a_{31} x + a_{32} y + a_{33} z + a_{34}$$

or in matrix form

$$\mathbf{V}' = \mathbf{a}\,\mathbf{V} + \mathbf{t} \qquad\qquad\qquad (2.4.2)$$

where $\mathbf{a}$ is a square matrix and $\mathbf{t}$ is a translation vector. Experience shows that it can be useful to add an identity to both sides of to yield a fourth equation that $w' = 1 \cdot w$. Thus, we change from three real coordinates to a new set of **homogeneous coordinates** $(x, y, z, w) \equiv \mathbf{V}$ so $\mathbf{V}$ now represents all four terms. Then we can combine the generalized displacement of the expanded vector into one transformation such as

$$\mathbf{V}' = \mathbf{D}\,\mathbf{V} \qquad\qquad\qquad (2.4.3)$$

where $\mathbf{D}$ denotes a partitioned "displacement matrix" given by

$$\mathbf{D} = \begin{bmatrix} \mathbf{a} & \mathbf{t} \\ \mathbf{0} & 1 \end{bmatrix} \qquad\qquad\qquad (2.4.4)$$

where $\mathbf{0}$ is a null row. The $\mathbf{t}$ partition of $\mathbf{D}$ represents a translation, and from our previous discussion we see that $\mathbf{a}$ could include the previous rotation matrices, $\mathbf{R}$. Of course, it may (and often does) include additional information. To simplify the additional identity we usually set w to unity. Of course, if we are considering only two-dimensional motion in the xy-plane we can delete the rows and columns relating to z.

Sometimes the value of **D** can be established numerically. Note that the use of homogeneous coordinates allows both finite rotations and translations to be included in a single operation of multiplication.

The partition **a** can have uses other than as rotation matrix. Most of the other uses are important mainly in computer graphics displays. Since we will not cover that subject in detail, we will consider only the most obvious use: scaling. We have already seen where **a** = **I** in pure translational. This represents a 1:1 scaling, that is, no change in shape. For general scaling we let **a** become a diagonal matrix **s**, where the diagonal terms denote relative scaling in the *x, y,* and *z* directions:

$$\mathbf{s} = \begin{bmatrix} s_x & 0 & 0 \\ 0 & s_y & 0 \\ 0 & 0 & s_z \end{bmatrix}. \tag{2.4.5}$$

If we want to execute a "zoom" of constant scale, *s*, we could employ **s** = *s***I**. The concepts of rotation, translation, and scaling in two dimensions are illustrated in Figures 2.4.1-3, respectively. Figure 2.4.4 shows all three operations in series. For rigid body dynamics we will not need scaling matrices.

From those figures we see that objects usually have several vertices associated with them. We must displace each and every vertex. When we select a single point, then **V** in Equation (2.4.3) represents the homogeneous coordinates of that point. When we apply the same displacement, **D**, to all *n* points, then we could consider **V** to be a rectangular array **V** (4 × *n*), where column *i* contains the homogeneous coordinates of the *i*th point.

As just seen, the typical terms in the translation partition are $\mathbf{t}^T = [\Delta x \quad \Delta y \quad \Delta z]$, which are the components of translation in the *x*-, *y*-, and *z*-directions, respectively. Assuming the common case where $\mathbf{a} \equiv \mathbf{R}$, the displacement matrix is

$$\mathbf{D} = \begin{bmatrix} \mathbf{R} & \mathbf{t} \\ \mathbf{0} & 1 \end{bmatrix}. \tag{2.4.6}$$

For a pure rotation about the origin we simply set **t** = **0** and substitute any valid rotation

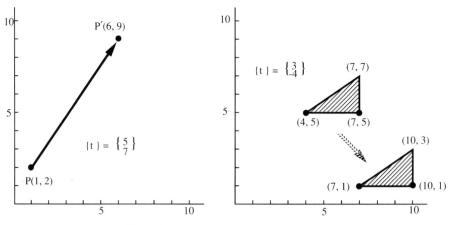

Figure 2.4.1   Two-dimensional translation.

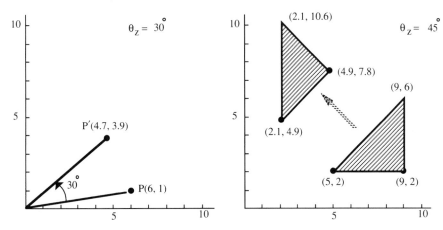

Figure 2.4.2   Rotation in two dimensions about the origin.

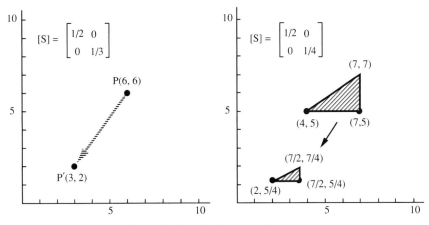

Figure 2.4.3   Scaling in two dimensions.

matrix, such as **RU**, for **R**. Conversely, if there is no rotation, then **R** = **I** and the result is the special case of pure translation. Then

$$\mathbf{D}(\mathbf{R} = \mathbf{I}) \equiv \mathbf{T} = \begin{bmatrix} \mathbf{I} & \mathbf{t} \\ \mathbf{0} & 1 \end{bmatrix} \tag{2.4.7}$$

which is a translation matrix defined by the translation vector, **t**.

With these new homogeneous coordinates, the previous procedure for combining a series of operations, such as Equation (2.2.5), is still valid. Thus, we now have the power to consider rotations about points other than the origin of the Cartesian axes. For example, to rotate an object about point A on an arbitrary axis in space, as shown in Figure 2.4.5, we must augment the previous operation:

1. Translate line from A back to origin.
2. Rotate about line through origin.
3. Translate back to point A.

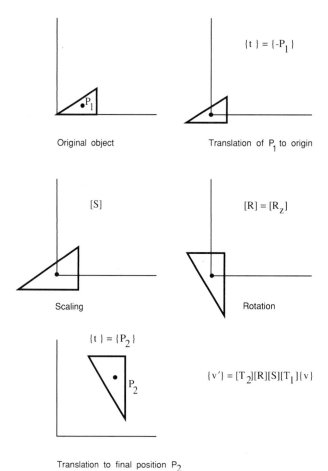

$$\{t\} = \{-P_1\}$$

Original object   Translation of P_1 to origin

$[S]$ $[R] = [R_z]$

Scaling   Rotation

$$\{t\} = \{P_2\}$$

$$\{v'\} = [T_2][R][S][T_1]\{v\}$$

P_2

Translation to final position P_2

Figure 2.4.4   A series of finite displacement operations.

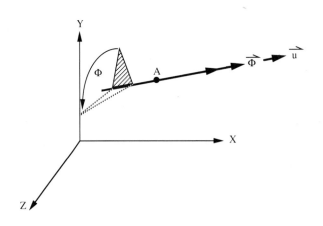

Figure 2.4.5   Rotation about a line at a point in space.

The result is

$$\mathbf{V}' = \mathbf{T}_2 \ \mathbf{RU} \ \mathbf{T}_1 \ \mathbf{V} \tag{2.4.8}$$

where

$$\mathbf{T}_1 = \begin{bmatrix} 1 & 0 & 0 & -x_A \\ 0 & 1 & 0 & -y_A \\ 0 & 0 & 1 & -z_A \\ 0 & 0 & 0 & 1 \end{bmatrix} \quad \text{and} \quad \mathbf{t}_2 = -\mathbf{t}_1 . \tag{2.4.9}$$

Again, these could be combined into a single operator.

2.5 MATRIX KINEMATICS

In mechanical engineering and computer graphics, we often consider lines on rigid bodies. By definition any two points on a rigid body always remain a constant distance apart. Often we define the motion of one point relative to the motion of the other. Let P and Q denote two points on the same rigid body. We are interested in the motion of point Q relative to the motion of point P as they move to their new positions of P' and Q', respectively. If $\mathbf{P}$ and $\mathbf{Q}$ are the position vectors to the two original points, then the relative position vector of $\mathbf{Q}$ with respect to $\mathbf{P}$ is

$$\mathbf{r} = \mathbf{Q} - \mathbf{P} . \tag{2.5.1}$$

Assume that the relative motion of the rigid link involves a translation from $\mathbf{P}$ to its new position, $\mathbf{P}'$, and a finite rotation, $\mathbf{R}$. The relative position, $\mathbf{r}$, has a constant length, but its components change as a result of the rotation. As with any vector, the new components, $\mathbf{r}' = \mathbf{Q}' - \mathbf{P}'$, are

$$\mathbf{r}' = \mathbf{R} \ \mathbf{r}$$

or

$$(\mathbf{Q}' - \mathbf{P}') = \mathbf{R} \ (\mathbf{Q} - \mathbf{P}) \tag{2.5.2}$$

so the physical components of the final point are

$$\mathbf{Q}' = \mathbf{R} \ \mathbf{Q} + (\mathbf{P}' - \mathbf{R} \ \mathbf{P})$$
$$= \mathbf{R} \ \mathbf{Q} + \mathbf{t} . \tag{2.5.3}$$

If we use homogeneous coordinates, this result can be written as a single matrix product. Then the relative motion of $\mathbf{Q}$, in homogeneous space, is

$$\mathbf{Q}' = \mathbf{D} \ \mathbf{Q} \tag{2.5.4}$$

where

$$\mathbf{D} = \begin{bmatrix} \mathbf{R} & \mathbf{t} \\ \mathbf{0} & 1 \end{bmatrix} .$$

Since the relative base point displaces an amount $\mathbf{d} = \mathbf{P}' - \mathbf{P}$, we could also write $\mathbf{t}$ in

Equation (2.5.3) as

$$t = d + (I - R)P. \tag{2.5.5}$$

This operation can be thought of in another way. That is, translate by $-P$ back to the origin, rotate Q about the origin, and translate to new positions P' so the new position of Q' is

$$Q' = (T_{P'} (RZ (T_{-P} Q))) = D \; Q$$

where

$$T = \begin{bmatrix} I & t \\ 0 & 1 \end{bmatrix}$$

so in two dimensions

$$D = \begin{bmatrix} 1 & 0 & x_2 \\ 0 & 1 & y_2 \\ 0 & 0 & 1 \end{bmatrix} \begin{bmatrix} c & -s & 0 \\ s & c & 0 \\ 0 & 0 & 1 \end{bmatrix} \begin{bmatrix} 1 & 0 & -x_1 \\ 0 & 1 & -y_1 \\ 0 & 0 & 1 \end{bmatrix}$$

and the result is

$$D = \begin{bmatrix} c_z & -s_z & (x_2 - cx_1 + sy_1) \\ s_z & c_z & (y_2 - sx_1 - cy_1) \\ 0 & 0 & 1 \end{bmatrix}$$

$$\tag{2.5.6}$$

$$= \begin{bmatrix} R & t \\ 0 & 1 \end{bmatrix}, \qquad t = P' - R \; P$$

which is the same result as in Equation (2.5.3). These three operations are illustrated in Figure 2.5.1.

Relative kinematics often employs vector operators that can also be expressed in matrix form. For example, the scalar or dot product of two vectors

$$c = \vec{a} \cdot \vec{b} = a_x b_x + a_y b_y + a_z b_z$$

$$= |a| \; |b| \; \cos \theta_{ab}$$

can also be written as one vector transposed times the other

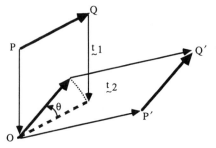

Figure 2.5.1   Relative motion of a fixed length vector.

$$c = \vec{a} \cdot \vec{b} = \mathbf{a}^T \mathbf{b} = \mathbf{b}^T \mathbf{a}. \qquad (2.5.7)$$

The vector cross product

$$\vec{c} = \vec{a} \times \vec{b} = (\,|a|\ \ |b|\ \sin \theta_{ab})\,\vec{n}_{ab}$$

has components defined in a cyclic xyz order of

$$c_x = a_y b_z - a_z b_y$$

$$c_y = a_z b_x - a_x b_z$$

$$c_z = a_x b_y - a_y b_x$$

which can be expressed as a skew-symmetric matrix

$$\begin{Bmatrix} c_x \\ c_y \\ c_z \end{Bmatrix} = \begin{bmatrix} 0 & -a_z & a_y \\ a_z & 0 & -a_x \\ -a_y & a_x & 0 \end{bmatrix} \begin{Bmatrix} b_x \\ b_y \\ b_z \end{Bmatrix} \qquad (2.5.8)$$

or

$$\mathbf{c} = \mathbf{X}(\mathbf{a})\mathbf{b}$$

where $\mathbf{X}(\mathbf{V})$ denotes a cross product operator employing vector $\mathbf{V}$. Thus, we can translate common vector kinematic expressions like

$$\vec{a} = \vec{\alpha} \times \vec{r} + [\,\vec{\omega} \times (\,\vec{\omega} \times \vec{r}\,)\,]$$

as

$$\mathbf{a} = \mathbf{X}(\alpha)\mathbf{r} + \mathbf{X}(\omega)\mathbf{X}(\omega)\mathbf{r}$$

$$= [\mathbf{X}(\alpha) + \mathbf{X}(\omega)\mathbf{X}(\omega)]\mathbf{r}$$

or we could convert the common double vector product into a single 3×3 operator

$$\mathbf{XX}(\omega) = \mathbf{X}(\omega)\mathbf{X}(\omega)$$

$$= \begin{bmatrix} -(\omega_z^2 + \omega_y^2) & \omega_y \omega_x & \omega_z \omega_x \\ \omega_x \omega_y & -(\omega_z^2 + \omega_x^2) & \omega_z \omega_y \\ \omega_x \omega_z & \omega_y \omega_z & -(\omega_y^2 + \omega_x^2) \end{bmatrix}. \qquad (2.5.9)$$

In two-dimensional formulations it is common for the vector associated with the cross-product operator to be the only one with a component normal to the plane of interest. For an angular velocity vector normal to the plane, $\omega_x = 0 = \omega_y$, so the matrix operator simplifies to

$$\mathbf{X}(\omega) = \begin{bmatrix} 0 & -\omega_z & 0 \\ \omega_z & 0 & 0 \\ 0 & 0 & 0 \end{bmatrix}$$

and the double vector product reduces to

$$\mathbf{XX}(\omega) = \begin{bmatrix} -\omega_z^2 & 0 & 0 \\ 0 & -\omega_z^2 & 0 \\ 0 & 0 & 0 \end{bmatrix}.$$

In each case the null row and column associated with the z-component of the result means that the resulting vector lies in the original xy plane. Thus, for some planar problems we can drop these items and use only 2×2 matrix operators for vector products.

For a relative position vector $\mathbf{r}$ on a rigid body we can combine the angular velocity and angular acceleration cross products into a single acceleration operator, $\mathbf{A}$:

$$\mathbf{a} = \mathbf{X}(\alpha)\mathbf{r} + \mathbf{X}(\omega)\mathbf{X}(\omega)\mathbf{r}$$

$$= [\mathbf{X}(\alpha) + \mathbf{XX}(\omega)]\mathbf{r} \equiv \mathbf{A}\ \mathbf{r}.$$

When $\mathbf{r}$ is planar with components of x and y, we can combine the preceding two-dimensional forms to give

$$\mathbf{A} = \begin{bmatrix} -\omega^2 & -\alpha \\ \alpha & -\omega^2 \end{bmatrix}. \tag{2.5.10}$$

In scalar form we obtain

$$\begin{Bmatrix} a_x \\ a_y \end{Bmatrix} = \begin{bmatrix} -\omega^2 & -\alpha \\ \alpha & -\omega^2 \end{bmatrix} \begin{Bmatrix} x \\ y \end{Bmatrix} = \begin{Bmatrix} -\omega^2 x - \alpha y \\ \alpha x - \omega^2 y \end{Bmatrix}.$$

As expected we see that the centripetal term is always directed toward the relative motion origin and is proportional to ω^2, whereas the transverse term is normal to the position vector, proportional to α, and in the "sense" of α. These familiar results are sketched in Figure 2.5.2.

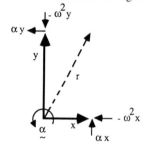
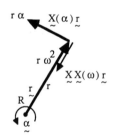

Figure 2.5.2   The relative acceleration operator, $a = Ar$.

2.6 PLANAR LINKAGE DESIGN

Consider the problem of designing a mechanism to pick up an object and move it through a set of points while rotating it a given amount at each point. This can be expressed in various ways. One approach employs matrix kinematics with constraints. The most common mechanism is the four-bar linkage. It has three moving links and considers the fourth link to be the rigidly linked ground connection. The moving rigid body coupler is attached to two links, which are each connected to the ground pins. There are three points of interest on the rigid coupler: the two pin connections to the base links and the point that is to be moved from the initial position to later points. The latter is called the "motion point." We will denote the input, or driving, link as Link A, while the output link is Link B. This system is shown in its initial configuration in Figure 2.6.1.

All lines on a rigid body undergo the same rotation. Assume the object to be moved is attached to the rigid coupler. Then when we prescribe the motion of the object we also prescribe the same rotation for the coupler, C, and the same displacement of the attachment point, P. In other words, the coupler line segments $P_1\vec{a}_1$, $P_1\vec{b}_1$ and $\vec{a_1b}_1$ have the same rotation as the object to be moved. To design this mechanism we first select (guess) the initial position of the input and output links. That is, we select the coordinates of $\vec{a}_0$, $\vec{a}_1$, $\vec{b}_0$ and $\vec{b}_1$. Next we compute the error associated with the desired motion. Then we search for another initial assembly that produces less error.

As the system moves we can find all the locations relative to the prescribed motion point. Knowing (guessing) the pin point $\vec{a}_1$ relative to the object point, $\vec{P}_1$, we compute the later position, $\vec{a}_j$, relative to the later object point, $\vec{P}_j$, with the relative rotation change, γ_j. This relative motion of point a_j with respect to the prescribed motion point, P_j, in homogeneous coordinates, follows from Equation (2.5.4):

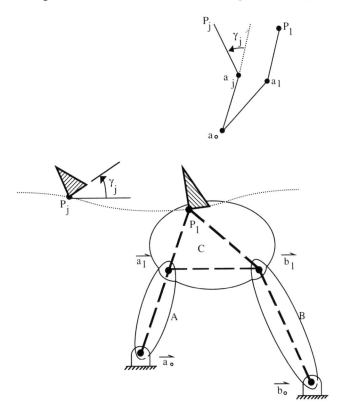

Figure 2.6.1   A motion generation four bar linkage.

$$\mathbf{a}_j = \mathbf{D}_j\,\mathbf{a}_1 \qquad\qquad (2.6.1)$$

where

$$\mathbf{D} = \begin{bmatrix} \mathbf{R}\,(\gamma_j) & \mathbf{t}_j \\ \mathbf{0} & 1 \end{bmatrix}$$

$$\mathbf{t}_j = \vec{P_j} - \mathbf{R}\,(\gamma_j)\vec{P_1}.$$

The coordinates of $\mathbf{b}_j$ are obtained by replacing $\mathbf{a}_1$ with $\mathbf{b}_1$. An alternative is to place $\mathbf{a}_1$ and $\mathbf{b}_1$ in columns of a rectangular array. When $\mathbf{D}$ operates on that array it produces an array whose columns contain the new positions, $\mathbf{a}_j$ and $\mathbf{b}_j$, for other points on the same rigid body. Note that the displacement matrix $\mathbf{D}$ involves only the given motion data, γ_j and $\vec{P_j}$. For rigid links we have constant lengths, so

$$(\vec{a}_1 - \vec{a}_0)^2 = (\vec{a}_j - \vec{a}_0)^2, \qquad (\vec{b}_1 - \vec{b}_0)^2 = (\vec{b}_j - \vec{b}_0)^2. \qquad (2.6.2)$$

Since we can now compute $\vec{a_j}$ and $\vec{b_j}$, we can check this constraint at every given motion point. Only in the most trivial cases will our design satisfy this condition exactly. Usually we will have some length error

$$L - L_j = \varepsilon.$$

A non-zero ε could still lead to an acceptable design if it is less than the tolerance to which the linkage joints are to be built. In any event, we select the square of input and output length errors as the quantities to be minimized. We do not have to check the length of any lines on the coupler since the rotation matrix, $\mathbf{R}$, preserves the constant lengths.

For a four-bar **motion generator** as just described, our trial vector, $\mathbf{x}$, simply needs to contain the eight Cartesian coordinates of the four joints in their original position. Often there are several local minima, and we may want to consider other aspects of the mechanism design to aid us in selecting which feasible design to retain. Auxiliary output can help in this respect. We may want to see the error in the lengths of each link at each motion point or the transmission angle at each coupler joint. We also need to drive the driver link to its proper angular position, say θ_j, at each point. Thus, that value should also be provided in the design output.

The above procedure can lead to mechanisms that can be assembled at each motion point but that cannot be continuously moved to each point in consecutive order. That is, one or more singular positions may exist in the range of motion of the driver angles, θ_j. To help avoid this case the designer may wish to assure that the change in drive angle, $(\theta_j - \theta_{j-1})$, has a constant sign and increases monotonically. Often a mechanism must act in (or outside) a restricted space. Then it is necessary to check the location of each pin at each motion point. If we violate the region constraints, then the amount of overrun must be penalized. For a rectangular region this check is simple. For a polygon-shaped region we must utilize one of several algorithms for determining if a point is inside a polygon. Figure 2.6.2 lists a typical subroutine, INSIDE, for such a purpose. A typical simplex merit function for the design of a four-bar motion generator is shown in Figure 2.6.3. The procedure it employs is as follows:

```
      SUBROUTINE   INSIDE (N, NPLUS1, INCODE, X, Y, ALFA,
    1                      BETA, COORD)
C     ----------------------------------------------------
C     FIND IF PT (X,Y) IS INSIDE POLYGON WITH N VERTICES
C     ----------------------------------------------------
C     REFER: IEEE TRAN EL COMP, EC-16, NO-6, DEC, 67
CDP   IMPLICIT REAL*8 (A-H,O-Z)
      DIMENSION  COORD(N,2), ALFA(NPLUS1), BETA(NPLUS1)
C     FOR RIGHT HAND SYSTEM ORDER VERTICIES IN CCW MANNER
      DATA HALF, ONE, TWOPI / 0.5D0, 1.D0, 6.283185308D0 /
C     COORD = COORD OF VERT., ALFA,BETA = WORKING ARRAYS
C     INCODE = 0 IF PT. OUTSIDE, INCODE = 1 IF PT INSIDE
C     NPLUS1 = N+1
CDP   ATAN2(Z1,Z2) = DATAN2(Z1,Z2)
      INCODE = 0
      DO 10  I = 1,N
   10 ALFA(I) = ATAN2((COORD(I,2)-Y),(COORD(I,1)-X))/TWOPI
      ALFA(NPLUS1) = ALFA(1)
      BETA(1) = ALFA(1)
      DO 20  I = 2,NPLUS1
      DA = ALFA(I) - ALFA(I-1)
      IF ( DA .EQ. HALF )  GO TO 30
      BETA(I) = BETA(I-1) + DA
      IF ( DA .GT. HALF )   BETA(I) = BETA(I) - ONE
      IF ( DA .LT. -HALF )  BETA(I) = BETA(I) + ONE
   20 CONTINUE
      IF ( BETA(NPLUS1) .EQ. (BETA(1) + ONE) )  INCODE = 1
      RETURN
   30 INCODE = 1
      RETURN
      END
```

Figure 2.6.2 Test for a point inside a polygon.

1. Input the desired motion data $\vec{P_j}$ and γ_j, in Figure 2.6.1.

2. Generate and store the relative rotation and translation operators

$$\mathbf{R}(\Delta\gamma_j), \qquad \vec{t_j} = \vec{P_j} - \mathbf{R}(\Delta\gamma_j)\,\vec{P_1}$$

to build

$$\mathbf{D}(\gamma_j, \vec{P_j}, \vec{P_1}), \quad j \geq 2.$$

3. Accept the trial vector initial assembly,

$$\mathbf{x}^T = [\vec{a_1} \ \ \vec{b_1} \ \ \vec{a_0} \ \ \vec{b_0}].$$

4. Compute the relative coupler positions

$$[\mathbf{a}_j \ \ \mathbf{b}_j] = \mathbf{D}(\gamma_j, \vec{P_j}, \vec{P_1})\,[\mathbf{a}_1 \ \ \mathbf{b}_1], \ j \geq 2.$$

5. Minimize the change in lengths of links A and B at $\mathbf{a}_j$ and $\mathbf{b}_j$.

6. Penalize any lengths that violate any design limits.

```
      FUNCTION  FN( N, X)
C     -----------------------------------------------------
C        4 BAR LINKAGE SYNTHESIS FOR MOTION GENERATOR
C     -----------------------------------------------------
      IMPLICIT REAL*8 (A-H,O-Z)
      PARAMETER ( MAXP = 9, ONE = 1.D0, ZERO = 0.D0 )
      PARAMETER ( BIG = 1.D9, D2R = 57.295779515662D0 )
      DIMENSION  X(N), XP(MAXP), YP(MAXP), ANGP(MAXP),
     1           AE(MAXP), BE(MAXP), AX(MAXP), AY(MAXP),
     2           BX(MAXP), BY(MAXP), D(2,3,MAXP)
      COMMON /USER/ D, AE, BE, AX, AY, BX, BY, AL, BL,
     1              SIZ1, SIZ2, SIZE, AX1, AY1, BX1, BY1,
     2              AX0, BX0, AY0, BY0, NPTS
      DATA KALL / 1 /
C     TRIAL VECTOR, X: 1=A1X, 2=A1Y, 3=B1X, 4=B1Y,  AND
C       OPTIONALLY 5=AX0, 6+AY0, 7=BX0, 8=BY0
C     AX, AY, AE, AL = X-Y COORD, ERROR, LENGTH OF A, ETC B
C     XP, YP, ANGP = X-Y MOTION COORD AND ROTATION (DEG)
C     AX0-BY0 = PIN PTS, SIZ1-2 ARE MIN AND MAX LENGTHS
      IF ( KALL .EQ. 0 ) GO TO 15
C - -> FIRST CALL CALCULATIONS ONLY
      KALL = 0
      AE(1) = ZERO
      BE(1) = ZERO
C        READ MOTION POINT DATA
      CALL  GETDAT ( N, MAXP, XP, YP, ANGP, NPTS,
     1               AX0, AY0, BX0, BY0, SIZ1, SIZ2 )
      SIZE = ( SIZ1 + SIZ2 )/2.
C        COMPUTE DISPLACEMENT MATRICES, D-J, AND STORE
      XP1 = XP(1)
      YP1 = YP(1)
      DO 10 J = 2,NPTS
      DIFF = ( ANGP(J) - ANGP(1) )/D2R
      CZ = DCOS(DIFF)
      SZ = DSIN(DIFF)
      D(1,1,J) = CZ
      D(2,1,J) = SZ
      D(1,2,J) = -SZ
      D(2,2,J) = CZ
      D(1,3,J) = XP(J) - XP1*CZ + YP1*SZ
 10   D(2,3,J) = YP(J) - XP1*SZ - YP1*CZ
C - - > CALCULATIONS ON EVERY TRY
C        CHANGE NOTATION
 15   AX1 = X(1)
      AY1 = X(2)
```

```
      BX1 = X(3)
      BY1 = X(4)
      IF ( N .EQ. 8 )  THEN
       AX0 = X(5)
       AY0 = X(6)
       BX0 = X(7)
       BY0 = X(8)
      ENDIF
C        LOCATE PT A-J RELATIVE TO PT 1, AJ = DJ*A1
      DO 20 J = 2,NPTS
       AX(J) = AX1*D(1,1,J) + AY1*D(1,2,J) + D(1,3,J)
       AY(J) = AX1*D(2,1,J) + AY1*D(2,2,J) + D(2,3,J)
       BX(J) = BX1*D(1,1,J) + BY1*D(1,2,J) + D(1,3,J)
   20  BY(J) = BX1*D(2,1,J) + BY1*D(2,2,J) + D(2,3,J)
C        GET INITIAL LENGTHS FOR THIS TRY
      AL = (AY1 - AY0)**2 + (AX1 - AX0)**2
      BL = (BY1 - BY0)**2 + (BX1 - BX0)**2
C        GET LENGTH SQUARED RATIO AT NEW POINT
      SUM = ZERO
      DO 25 J = 2,NPTS
       AE(J) = ((AX(J) - AX0)**2 + (AY(J) - AY0)**2 ) - AL
       BE(J) = ((BX(J) - BX0)**2 + (BY(J) - BY0)**2 ) - BL
   25  SUM = SUM + DABS(AE(J)/AL) + DABS(BE(J)/BL)
C        PENALTY ON VIOLATION OF SIZE LIMITS
      P = ZERO
      IF ( AL .LT. SIZ1 .OR. AL .GT. SIZ2 ) P = P + (AL - SIZE)**2
      IF ( BL .LT. SIZ1 .OR. BL .GT. SIZ2 ) P = P + (BL - SIZE)**2
      FN = (SUM*100.D0)**2 + P*BIG
      RETURN
      END
```

Figure 2.6.3a A four-bar motion generator function.

```
      SUBROUTINE  SUMMARY ( N, X)
C     ----------------------------------------------------------------
C            MOTION GENERATOR DESIGN RESULTS
C     ----------------------------------------------------------------
      IMPLICIT REAL*8 (A-H,O-Z)
      PARAMETER ( MAXP = 9, ONE = 1.D0, ZERO = 0.D0 )
      DIMENSION  X(N),
     1           AE(MAXP), BE(MAXP), AX(MAXP), AY(MAXP),
     2           BX(MAXP), BY(MAXP), D(2,3,MAXP)
      COMMON /USER/ D, AE, BE, AX, AY, BX, BY, AL, BL,
     1              SIZ1, SIZ2, SIZE, AX1, AY1, BX1, BY1,
     2              AX0, BX0, AY0, BY0, NPTS
C     USE XMIN FOR BEST VALUES IN COMMON
      UPDATE = FN (N, X)
      WRITE (6, * ) ' ---  MOTION GENERATOR SUMMARY ---'
```

```
        RAL = DSQRT(AL)
        RBL = DSQRT(BL)
        WRITE (6, 15) RAL, RBL
15      FORMAT (' LENGTHS: A & B = ', 1PE12.3, 1X, 1PE12.3)
        WRITE (6, * ) 'J, AX, AY, BX, BY, AE, BE, A%E, B%E'
        AX(1) = X(1)
        AY(1) = X(2)
        BX(1) = X(3)
        BY(1) = X(4)
        DO 8  J = 1,NPTS
         AE(J) = DSQRT(DABS( AE(J) + AL )) - RAL
         BE(J) = DSQRT(DABS( BE(J) + BL )) - RBL
         AP = 100.*AE(J)/RAL
         BP = 100.*BE(J)/RBL
8        WRITE (6,9) J,AX(J),AY(J),BX(J),BY(J),AE(J),BE(J),AP,BP
9        FORMAT (I2, 8F8.3 )
        RETURN
        END
```

Figure 2.6.3b A motion generator summary.

When we fix $\mathbf{a}_0$ and $\mathbf{b}_0$ and impose narrow limits on the member lengths, we obtain a design like the one listed in Figure 2.6.4. The summary program generates the coordinates of each linkage motion, $\mathbf{a}_j$ and $\mathbf{b}_j$, to aid in plotting the motion. It also gives the contributions to the merit function: the error in each link length. The same information is displayed in an alternate form as a percentage of the corresponding length. Link B has a relatively small percent error, but the actual length error at point 4, -0.129 in., would probably be more than the slack in the two joints can absorb. Thus, the motion generator may bind at that position. This design, and several others, has reached the maximum allowed length for member B. Thus, we must decide if that restriction on the design is really necessary. The generated mechanism is listed in Figure 2.6.5.

To improve the design we need to find a better local minimum or enhance our options by letting the algorithm select the pin points, $\mathbf{a}_0$ and $\mathbf{b}_0$. If we do this and also allow a wider range of allowable member lengths, we can get a design such as the one in Figure 2.6.6. There a similar length error occurs in link B at point 2. Since the member is longer, the percent error is smaller than before. Having this tentative design we could refine it by using a root mean square value for the lengths of links A and B. In any case, we should utilize a kinematic analysis program to verify the range of motion, transmission angle, and so on. We could also continue the current iterations to reduce further the error in the members lengths.

The simplex problem of making a **path generator** to fit the given points $\vec{P_j}$ is actually more expensive to compute by this approach. This is true because the $(n-1)$ coupler rotations, γ_j, are no longer given and must be added to the end of our trial vector, $\mathbf{x}$, so that it contains $(n+7)$ design variables for the n path points. Experience shows that when mechanism angles are used in the trial vector, their initial step sizes should be relatively large, say 30° to 45°.

```
      SUBROUTINE  GETDAT (N, MAXP, XP, YP, ANGP, NPTS,
     1                    AX0, AY0, BX0, BY0, SIZ1, SIZ2 )
C     ----------------------------------------------------
C         GET DESIRED MOTION DATA
C     ----------------------------------------------------
      IMPLICIT REAL*8 (A-H, O-Z)
      DIMENSION  XP(MAXP), YP(MAXP), ANGP(MAXP)
      WRITE (6, * ) 'ENTER NUMBER OF PRECISION POINTS'
      READ  (5, * ) NPTS
      IF ( NPTS .GT. MAXP ) GO TO 99
      WRITE (6, * ) 'ENTER X,Y, ANGLE FOR EACH PT.'
      DO 7 I = 1,NPTS
    7   READ  (5, * ) XP(I), YP(I), ANGP(I)
      WRITE (6, * ) 'ENTER MIN AND MAX CRANK LENGTHS'
      READ  (5, * ) SIZ1, SIZ2
      SIZ1 = SIZ1*SIZ1
      SIZ2 = SIZ2*SIZ2
      IF ( N .EQ. 8 )  RETURN
C     READ PIN LOCATIONS
      WRITE (6, * ) 'ENTER PINS: AX0,AY0 & BX0,BY0'
      READ  (5, * ) AX0, AY0, BX0, BY0
      RETURN
   99 WRITE (6, * ) 'MAX. NO. PRECISION PTS. = ', MAXP
      STOP
      END
```

Figure 2.6.3c Application input program.

The following figures illustrate several common mechanisms. The procedures for designing such linkages are not unique. Here we will outline a possible procedure for motion generators. If a path generator is desired, then the angles, γ_j, become additional unknowns. For a Stephenson mechanism, as shown in Figure 2.6.7, we would proceed as follows. Given $\vec{P_j}, \gamma_j$ compute and store $\mathbf{D}(\gamma_j, \vec{P_j}, \vec{P_1})$. Select a trial vector of $\vec{a}, \vec{b}, \vec{c}, \vec{d}, \vec{e}, \vec{f}, \vec{g}, \beta_j$. Then for motion point $j > 2$, compute:

1. With respect to $\vec{P_j}$: $[\mathbf{g} \quad \mathbf{d}]_j = \mathbf{D}(\gamma_j, \vec{P_j}, \vec{P_1})[\mathbf{g} \quad \mathbf{d}]_1$
   Merit: L_{ad}.
2. With respect to $\vec{g_j}$: $[\mathbf{f} \quad \mathbf{e}] = \mathbf{D}(\beta_j, \vec{g_j}, \vec{g_1})[\mathbf{f} \quad \mathbf{e}]_1$
   Merit: L_{cf}, L_{be}.
   Output: θ, α, ϕ for motion analysis and verification.

```
      ENTER MIN AND MAX CRANK LENGTHS
       0.200000   9.000000

      Motion.generator.design
       842   TRIALS USED, RESULTS ARE:
```

```
ENTER NUMBER OF PRECISION POINTS
9
ENTER X,Y, ANGLE FOR EACH PT.
 1.000000    2.600000    0.
 0.900000    2.100000    12.00000
 0.600000    1.500000    21.00000
 0.100000    1.000000    22.00000
-0.300000    1.100000    15.00000
-0.500000    1.500000    7.000000
-0.400000    2.000000   -1.000000
-0.100000    2.500000   -6.000000
 0.600000    2.800000   -7.000000
ENTER MIN AND MAX CRANK LENGTHS
 0.700000    5.000000
ENTER PINS: AX0,AY0 & BX0,BY0
0.   0.    4.000000   0.


Motion.generator.design
  DESIGN VARIABLE      NEXT TO BEST        BEST
  ax1                  5.629710d-01     5.629710d-01
  ay1                  7.159690d-01     7.159690d-01
  bx1                  2.629987d+00     2.629997d+00
  by1                  4.808645d+00     4.808645d+00

   ---  MOTION GENERATOR SUMMARY ---
LENGTHS: A & B =     9.108e-01    5.000e+00
J     AX      AY      BX      BY      AE      BE      A%E      B%E
1   0.563   0.716   2.630   4.809   0.000   0.000   0.000    0.000
2   0.864   0.166   2.035   4.599  -0.031   0.001  -3.372    0.028
3   0.867  -0.416   1.330   4.146   0.051  -0.069   5.576   -1.374
4   0.401  -0.911   0.784   3.658   0.084  -0.129   9.220   -2.579
5  -0.235  -0.833   0.703   3.655  -0.046  -0.077  -4.992   -1.547
6  -0.704  -0.423   0.849   3.891  -0.089   0.007  -9.796    0.139
7  -0.870   0.124   1.268   4.180  -0.032  -0.007  -3.533   -0.133
8  -0.732   0.672   1.752   4.526   0.083   0.054   9.064    1.074
9  -0.063   0.983   2.487   4.794   0.075   0.027   8.182    0.533
```

Figure 2.6.4 A typical four-variable design.

```
  DESIGN VARIABLE      NEXT TO BEST          BEST
  ax1                  1.091310d+00      1.091310d+00
  ay1                  8.747762d-01      8.747762d-01
  bx1                  3.611239d+00      3.611240d+00
  by1                  3.387822d+00      3.387823d+00
  ax0                  5.187697d-01      5.187697d-01
  ay0                  2.472727d-01      2.472726d-01
  bx0                  6.433012d+00      6.433013d+00
  by0                 -4.450221d+00     -4.450221d+00
```

```
    ---  MOTION GENERATOR SUMMARY  ---
LENGTHS: A & B =      8.494e-01    8.331e+00
 J      AX       AY       BX       BY       AE       BE      A%E      B%E
 1    1.091    0.875    3.611    3.388    0.000    0.000    0.000    0.000
 2    1.348    0.431    3.290    3.414   -0.000    0.138   -0.000    1.656
 3    1.304   -0.078    2.755    3.171   -0.000    0.132   -0.000    1.583
 4    0.831   -0.565    2.226    2.709    0.021   -0.027    2.486   -0.324
 5    0.235   -0.543    2.018    2.537   -0.010   -0.066   -1.161   -0.788
 6   -0.199   -0.201    1.996    2.600   -0.003   -0.000   -0.350   -0.000
 7   -0.339    0.273    2.225    2.742    0.009    0.003    1.005    0.031
 8   -0.190    0.775    2.579    3.011    0.034    0.067    3.960    0.802
 9    0.480    1.077    3.288    3.264   -0.019   -0.000   -2.275   -0.000
```

Figure 2.6.5 A typical eight-variable design.

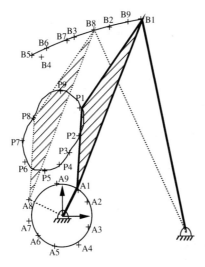

Figure 2.6.6   Mechanism for nine point motion generator.

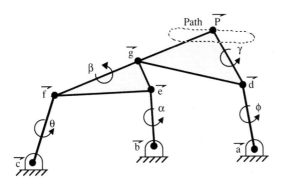

Figure 2.6.7   Stephenson mechanism motion synthesis.

For a two-point Stephenson mechanism (shown in Figure 2.6.8), we follow a similar approach. Given $\vec{P_j}, \gamma_j$, compute and store $\mathbf{D}(\gamma_j, \vec{P_j}, \vec{P_1})$. Select trial vector $\vec{a}, \vec{b}, \vec{c}, \vec{d}, \vec{e}, \vec{f}, \vec{g}, \phi_j, \theta_j$. Compute:

1. With respect to $\vec{P_j}$: $[\mathbf{g} \quad \mathbf{f}]_j = \mathbf{D}(\gamma_j, \vec{P_j}, \vec{P_1})[\mathbf{g} \quad \mathbf{f}]_1$
2. With respect to $\vec{f_j}$: $[\mathbf{c} \quad \mathbf{a}]_j = \mathbf{D}(\phi_j, \vec{f_j}, \vec{f_1})[\mathbf{c} \quad \mathbf{a}]_1$
   Merit: $\mathbf{a}_j = \mathbf{a}_1$
3. With respect to $\vec{b_j}$: $[\mathbf{d} \quad \mathbf{e}]_j = \mathbf{D}(\theta_j, \vec{b_j}, \vec{b_1})[\mathbf{d} \quad \mathbf{e}]_1$
   Merit: L_{eg}, L_{cd}.

This approach suggests another option that may improve the design. If we allow $\mathbf{a}_j$ to move in a machined slot, we can give the designer more flexibility. We simply omit the first contribution to the merit function. We define the curved slot by using a parametric interpolation (see Chapter 3) through all the $\mathbf{a}_j$ points. The designer must decide if the resulting curve for the pin is acceptable.

For a Type II Stephenson system like that shown in Figure 2.6.9, an approach is as follows. Given $\vec{P_j}, \gamma_j$ store $\mathbf{D}(\gamma_j, \vec{P_j}, \vec{P_1})$. Set trial: $\vec{a}, \vec{b}, \vec{c}, \vec{d}, \vec{e}, \vec{f}, \vec{g}, \phi_j, \beta_j$. Compute:

1. With respect to $\vec{P_j}$: $[\mathbf{f} \quad \mathbf{g}]_j = \mathbf{D}(\gamma_j, \vec{P_j}, \vec{P_1})[\mathbf{f} \quad \mathbf{g}]_1$

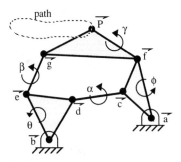

Figure 2.6.8 Two point Stephenson motion synthesis.

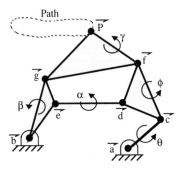

Figure 2.6.9 Type II Stephenson motion synthesis.

   2. With respect to $\vec{f_j}$: $[\mathbf{d} \quad \mathbf{c}]_j = \mathbf{D}(\phi_j, \vec{f_j}, \vec{f_1})[\mathbf{d} \quad \mathbf{c}]_1$
      Merit: L_{ac}
   3. With respect to $\vec{g_j}$: $[\mathbf{e} \quad \mathbf{b}]_j = \mathbf{D}(\beta_j, \vec{g_j}, \vec{g_1})[\mathbf{e} \quad \mathbf{b}]_1$
      Merit: L_{ed}, $\mathbf{b}_j = \mathbf{b}_1$
      Output: θ.

Figure 2.6.10 shows a Watt mechanism that can be approached in a similar fashion. Again, we have the option of letting pin point a_j enter the merit function or defining a pin guide groove to be machined in the base.

Another type of mechanism design problem is to create a function generator. There we are given an input angle θ and require an output angle $\phi = f(\theta)$. This is illustrated in Figure 2.6.11. Actually we are usually interested in having the change in the two angles satisfy a functional relationship. Thus, the starting position, θ_1, is arbitrary, and there are an infinite number of choices for it. The same is true for the initial output position, ϕ_1. The scaling that relates the independent variable, x, to input angle, θ, is usually selected to yield a Chebyshev spacing. One approach to designing the above mechanism is as follows. Given θ_j, Φ_j, $\vec{a}$, and $\vec{b}$. Store: $\mathbf{D}(\theta_j, \vec{b})$, $\mathbf{D}(\Phi_j, \vec{a})$. Set trial: $\vec{c}, \vec{d}, \vec{e}, \vec{f}, \vec{g}, \beta_j$. Compute:

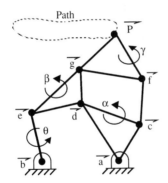

Figure 2.6.10   A Watt mechanism motion synthesis.

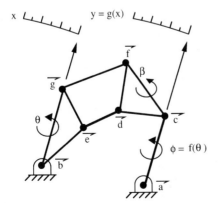

Figure 2.6.11   A six link function generator.

1. With respect to $\vec{b}$: $[\mathbf{g} \quad \mathbf{e}]_j = \mathbf{D}(\theta_j, \vec{b})[\mathbf{g} \quad \mathbf{e}]_1$
2. With respect to $\vec{a}$: $\mathbf{c}_j = \mathbf{D}(\Phi_j, \vec{a})\mathbf{c}_1$
3. With respect to $\vec{c_j}$: $[\mathbf{f} \quad \mathbf{d}]_j = \mathbf{D}(\beta_j, \vec{c_j}, \vec{c_1})[\mathbf{f} \quad \mathbf{d}]_1$
   Merit: L_{ed}, L_{gf}

For the alternate function generator, as shown in Figure 2.6.12, a design procedure is as follows. Given: $\theta_j, \Phi_j, \vec{a}$, and $\vec{b}$. Store: $\mathbf{D}(\theta_j, \vec{b}), \mathbf{D}(\Phi_j, \vec{a})$. Set trial: $\vec{c}, \vec{d}, \vec{e}, \vec{f}, \vec{g}, \beta_j$. Compute:

1. With respect to $\vec{b}$: $f_j = \mathbf{D}(\theta_j, \vec{b})\mathbf{f}_1$
2. With respect to $\vec{a}$: $\mathbf{d}_j = \mathbf{D}(\Phi_j, \vec{a})\mathbf{d}_1$
3. With respect to $\vec{f_j}$: $[\mathbf{g} \quad \mathbf{e}]_j = \mathbf{D}(\beta_j, \vec{f_j}, \vec{f_1})[\mathbf{g} \quad \mathbf{e}]_1$
   Merit: L_{ec}, L_{gd}

The displacement matrix approach used here can be extended to three dimensions. For planar mechanisms there are several other approaches. The complex number options presented by Sandor and Erdman provide useful design insights. Other applications of the matrix approach require careful description of the kinematic constraints. These often include compound joints, translational joints, spur gears, and so on. The recent work by Nikravesh illustrates how to generate these equations. They can be used as additional penalty terms in the present approach.

2.7 REFERENCES

1. Foley, J. D., and Van Dam, A. *Fundamentals of Interactive Computer Graphics.* Reading, Mass.: Addison-Wesley, 1983.

2. Greenwood, D. T. *Principles of Dynamics,* Englewood Cliffs, N. J.: Prentice-Hall, 1965.

3. Groover, M. P., and Zimmers, E. W., Jr. *Computer-Aided Design and Manufacturing,* Englewood Cliffs, N. J.: Prentice-Hall, 1984.

4. Kim, H. S., Hamid, S., and Soni, A. H. "Synthesis of Six-Link Mechanisms for Point Path Generation." *J. Mechanisms* 6 447-461, 1971.

5. Myers, R. E. *Microcomputer Graphics.* Reading, Mass.: Addison-Wesley, 1982.

6. Nikravesh, P.E. *Computer Aided Analysis of Mechanical System.* Englewood Cliffs, N. J.: Prentice-Hall, 1988.

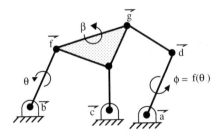

Figure 2.6.12　Alternate function generator.

7. Sandor, G. N., and Erdman, A. G. *Advanced Mechanism Design.* Englewood Cliffs, N. J.: Prentice-Hall, 1984.

8. Soni, A. H. *Mechanism Synthesis and Analysis.* New York: McGraw-Hill, 1974.

9. Suh, C. H., and Radcliffe, C. W. *Kinematics and Mechanism Design.* Melbourne, Fla.: R. E. Krieger, 1983.

2.8 EXERCISES

1. A mechanical screw couples the translation and rotation of a nut or link moving on the screw axis. Let **U** be a unit vector defining the screw axis. The displacement, $\mathbf{d} = d \cdot \mathbf{U}$, along the screw axis also introduces a rotation about the screw axis of $\mathbf{RU}(\phi)$, where the angle of rotation, ϕ, is related to the pitch of the screw axis. Let the relation be $S = k\phi$. Extend the relative motion displacement transformation in Equation (2.4.13) to include this common special case.

2. A displacement matrix such as Equation (2.4.6) can be viewed as the product

$$\mathbf{D} = \begin{bmatrix} \mathbf{I} & \mathbf{t} \\ \mathbf{0} & 1 \end{bmatrix} \begin{bmatrix} \mathbf{R} & \mathbf{0} \\ \mathbf{0} & 1 \end{bmatrix}$$

Recall that the inverse of the translation matrix in Equation (2.4.7) is

$$\mathbf{T}^{-1} = \begin{bmatrix} \mathbf{I} & -\mathbf{t} \\ \mathbf{0} & 1 \end{bmatrix}$$

Use matrix algebra to find the expression for $\mathbf{D}^{-1}$. Is this also valid for Equation (2.4.4)? Why?

3. Simplify the relative motion operator in Equation (2.5.4) for the case of pure translation.

4. Verify the triple product in (a) Equation (2.2.6), and (b) Equation (2.2.9).

5. Verify that **RU** reduces to **RZ** when $U_z \equiv 1$.

6. Simplify Equations (2.2.1) and (2.2.3) when $\theta_z = d\theta_z$ and $\theta_y = d\theta_y$ are infinitesimal rotations. For this case compare the products **RZ RY** and **RY RZ**.

7. Verify that the product of **T** and $\mathbf{T}^{-1}$ in Exercise 2 yields the identity matrix.

8. A four-bar linkage is to be designed for a "timed" path generation. The timing is described by giving the angle, ϕ, of the driving link A. In this case the path is defined in polar coordinates, (r, θ). The data are

j	r_j (in.)	θ_j (deg)	ϕ_j (deg)
1	3.86	71.57	161
2	5.87	56.53	101
3	6.93	35.85	41
4	6.26	22.14	−19
5	3.43	25.22	−79
6	2.27	58.13	−139

Design such a mechanism. Sketch it in each odd position.

9. A four-bar mechanism is to guide a rigid body through three motions. The body angle is γ and the path points are known in polar coordinates:

j	r_j	θ_j	γ_j
	(in.)	(deg)	(deg)
1	4.50	80	30
2	1.98	91	52
3	3.80	98	68

Design the mechanism. Sketch its positions.

10. Describe a motion generator design procedure for the Watt mechanism in Figure 2.6.10.

11. Check the correctness of Equation 2.6.1 for the special case of pure rigid body translation.

3

PARAMETRIC GEOMETRY

3.1 INTRODUCTION

The use of parametric geometry is at the center of many computational operations in computer-assisted mechanical design. It is employed to display, shade, contour, and shadow various surfaces and solids. It allows for the calculation of important mass and inertia properties. Parametric geometry is often used for mesh generation in finite element model builders. Even in finite element analysis (FEA) theory we find it employed to interpolate many quantities that must be integrated to enjoy the great power of FEA. Thus, we prepare for later topics by introducing the matrix algebra and calculus of parametric geometry.

3.2 REPRESENTATION OF CURVES

In two dimensions we commonly represent a curve (in a nonparametric form) as the **explicit** relation

$$y = F(x). \tag{3.2.1}$$

This gives a single value of y for each x. Thus, the explicit form cannot represent a multivalued curve that loops over itself or a closed curve. An alternate approach is to utilize the **implicit form**

$$G(x, \ y) = 0. \tag{3.2.2}$$

However, finding a point, (x, y), on the implicit curve requires computing the root of an algebraic or transcendental equation. Both of the preceding forms are axis-dependent. Alternatively, we can specify the curve in a **parametric form** as a function of a parameter, say t:

$$x = f(t)$$

$$y = g(t).$$

(3.2.3)

The parametric form has several advantages over the explicit form. Each parametric value, t, defines a unique pair of coordinates, x and y, for a point on the curve. A bounded segment of the curve can be generated by restricting the parameter to lie within a specific range. It is usually possible to express a parametric curve in a matrix form that is compatible with our previously defined matrix operators. The parametric form is also suitable for the representation of closed curves and curves with multiple values of y for each x.

In physical coordinates the position vector to a point is

$$\mathbf{P}(t) = \left\{ \begin{matrix} x \\ y \end{matrix} \right\} = \left\{ \begin{matrix} f(t) \\ g(t) \end{matrix} \right\}.$$

This concept can be extended to three-dimensional curves or surfaces. Then

$$\mathbf{P}^T(t) = [x(t) \quad y(t) \quad z(t)]$$

in physical coordinates.

For computer graphics applications, generating surfaces, and solids bounded by surfaces it is interesting to consider rational parametric expressions. A **rational form** is the ratio of two polynomials of the parameter, t. For example,

$$x = \frac{X(t)}{w(t)} \qquad y = \frac{Y(t)}{w(t)} \qquad z = \frac{Z(t)}{w(t)}$$

which can be evaluated in matrix form as

$$\left\{ \begin{matrix} wx \\ wy \\ wz \\ w \end{matrix} \right\} = \begin{bmatrix} A_{11} & A_{12} & A_{13} & A_{14} \\ A_{21} & A_{22} & A_{23} & A_{24} \\ A_{31} & A_{32} & A_{33} & A_{34} \\ A_{41} & A_{42} & A_{43} & A_{44} \end{bmatrix} \left\{ \begin{matrix} t^3 \\ t^2 \\ t \\ 1 \end{matrix} \right\}$$

(3.2.4)

so that

$$w(t) = A_{41}t^3 + A_{42}t^2 + A_{43}t + A_{44}$$

and

$$X(t) = wx(t) = A_{11}t^3 + A_{12}t^2 + A_{13}t + A_{14}.$$

Note that this reduces to a nonrational form if $w \equiv 1$ that is—when A_{41}, A_{42}, and A_{43} are 0 and $A_{44} = 1$. Otherwise we can view w as a generalized homogeneous coordinate.

3.3 PARAMETRIC CURVES

Consider a typical scalar component, x, of an entity with several components. The parametric cubic form can be expressed as

$$x(t) = \mathbf{P}(t)\mathbf{C} = \mathbf{C}^T \mathbf{P}^T \qquad (3.3.1)$$

where

$$\mathbf{P} = [t^3 \quad t^2 \quad t \quad 1] \qquad (3.3.2)$$

is a set of parametric terms and the unknown coefficients are

$$\mathbf{C}^T = [c_1 \quad c_2 \quad c_3 \quad c_4]. \qquad (3.3.3)$$

In expanded scalar notation

$$x(t) = c_1 t^3 + c_2 t^2 + c_3 t + c_4. \qquad (3.3.4)$$

For a given set of data describing x the coefficients $\mathbf{C}$ must be evaluated. We can use point and/or derivative data to do this. The choice of method may depend on the end application or the preference of the user. We begin with a point format for determining the coefficients.

3.3.1 Parametric Quadratic

To simplify our algebra we set $c_1 \equiv 0$ and begin with a parametric quadratic. Assume that our parameter lies in the **unit coordinate** space, $0 \leq t \leq 1$. To evaluate the remaining three constants we employ three points in the parametric space. They are the two endpoints and an arbitrary third interior point. The third point is usually selected at the midrange of $t = 1/2$. The corresponding x data are $x_1 = x(t = 0)$, $x_2 = x(1/2)$, and $x_3 = x(1)$. Then we can use Equation (3.3.1) to write three identities

$$x_1 = c_2 t_1^2 + c_3 t_1 + c_4$$

$$x_2 = c_2 t_2^2 + c_3 t_2 + c_4 \qquad (3.3.5)$$

$$x_3 = c_2 t_3^2 + c_3 t_3 + c_4$$

or

$$\begin{Bmatrix} x_1 \\ x_2 \\ x_3 \end{Bmatrix} = \begin{bmatrix} 0 & 0 & 1 \\ \dfrac{1}{4} & \dfrac{1}{2} & 1 \\ 1 & 1 & 1 \end{bmatrix} \begin{Bmatrix} c_2 \\ c_3 \\ c_4 \end{Bmatrix}. \qquad (3.3.6)$$

In symbolic form this is denoted as

$$\mathbf{x}^e = \mathbf{G}\ \mathbf{C}^e \qquad (3.3.7)$$

where $\mathbf{x}^e$ denotes the data defining the particular element of the curve, $\mathbf{C}^e$ denotes the corresponding constants for the parametric form, and $\mathbf{G}$ is a square matrix of constants defined by the arbitrary choice of parent reference points. For most choices of the parent points this geometry matrix will be invertible. Then we have

$$\mathbf{G}^{-1}\,\mathbf{x}^e = \mathbf{C^e}. \tag{3.3.8}$$

For the current choice of the quadratic parent segment,

$$\mathbf{G}^{-1} = \begin{bmatrix} 2 & -4 & 2 \\ -3 & 4 & -1 \\ 1 & 0 & 0 \end{bmatrix}. \tag{3.3.9}$$

In general, we can substitute Equation (3.3.8) into Equation (3.3.1) to obtain an alternate parametric form:

$$x(t) = \mathbf{P}(t)\,\mathbf{C}^e$$

$$= \mathbf{P}(t)\,\mathbf{G}^{-1}\,\mathbf{X}^e \tag{3.3.10}$$

or, combining the first product,

$$x(t) = \mathbf{H}(t)\,\mathbf{X}^e \tag{3.3.11}$$

where the H_i terms are called the **blending functions**, or **interpolation functions**, or **shape functions**. In the current example

$$\mathbf{H}(t) = [\mathbf{H}_1(t)\quad \mathbf{H}_2(t)\quad \mathbf{H}_3(t)]$$

$$= \mathbf{P}(t)\mathbf{G}^{-1}$$

$$= [t^2\quad t\quad 1] \begin{bmatrix} 2 & -4 & 2 \\ -3 & 4 & -1 \\ 1 & 0 & 0 \end{bmatrix}$$

$$\mathbf{H}(t) = [(2t^2 - 3t + 1)\ (-4t^2 + 4t)\ (2t^2 - t)]. \tag{3.3.12}$$

Figure 3.3.1 shows the blending function and the x approximation. Note that our current approximation

$$x(t) = \sum_{i=1}^{3} H_i(t)\,x_i^e \tag{3.3.13}$$

passes exactly through all three given data points. When two such curve elements are connected, as in Figure 3.3.1c, the function, x, is continuous at their junction but their slopes are generally not continuous. We define a function to have C^n continuity if its first n derivatives are continuous. Here only the function itself is continuous at a typical junction. Thus, this is called a C^o approximation.

In Equation (3.3.13) the x_i^e data are arbitrary. Thus, we can set them all equal to the same arbitrary constant, say X. This constant can be factored out of the summation so that

$$x(t) = X = X \sum_i H_i(t). \tag{3.3.14}$$

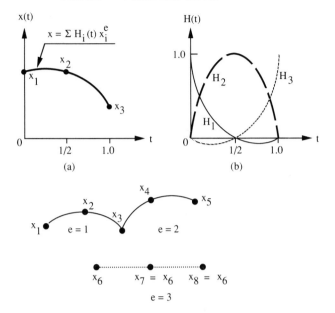

Figure 3.3.1   The C^0 parametric parabolic.

Comparing the two sides, we observe another identity that is useful in checking equations, namely,

$$1 \equiv \sum_i H_i(t) \tag{3.3.15}$$

for this type of approximation. This is true for any order C^0 parametric polynomial. Using the same procedure, it is easy to show that the parametric linear curve yields blending functions:

$$H_1(t) = (1 - t)$$
$$\tag{3.3.16}$$
$$H_2(t) = t.$$

This is also a piecewise C^o approximation. It is sketched in Figure 3.3.2.

Previously we considered slopes or derivatives when defining continuity order. Note that the parametric derivative, dx/dt, is available for all our parametric forms. One can employ either Equation (3.3.1) or (3.3.11). They give

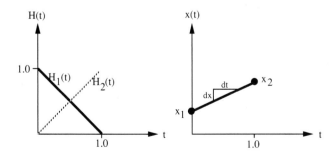

Figure 3.3.2   The parametric linear curve.

$$\frac{(dx(t))}{dt} = \frac{d}{dt}(\mathbf{P}(t)\mathbf{C}^e) \tag{3.3.17}$$

$$= \frac{d\mathbf{P}}{dt}\mathbf{C}^e$$

and

$$\frac{dx}{dt}(t) = \frac{d\mathbf{H}}{dt}\mathbf{X}^e. \tag{3.3.18}$$

In the latter case of the linear parametric form this is trivial, since from Equation (3.3.16),

$$\frac{d\mathbf{H}}{dt}(t) = \mathbf{H}' = [-1 \quad 1]$$

and

$$\frac{dx}{dt} = [-1 \quad 1]\begin{Bmatrix} x_1 \\ x_2 \end{Bmatrix}^e \tag{3.3.19}$$

$$= (x_2^e - x_1^e) = L^e$$

which is a constant. For higher-order forms the parametric derivative is also a function of t.

3.3.2 Parametric Cubic

Returning to the full parametric cubic we consider some of the most common ways to evaluate the four constants. First we examine a pair of point format approaches. Both utilize the two endpoints ($t = 0$ and $t = 1$) and two arbitrarily selected interior points on the parent. The most common choices are to employ the third points $t = 1/3$ and $t = 2/3$. Repeating the previous procedure, the parent geometry matrix is

$$\mathbf{G} = \begin{bmatrix} 0 & 0 & 0 & 1 \\ \frac{1}{27} & \frac{1}{9} & \frac{1}{3} & 1 \\ \frac{8}{27} & \frac{4}{9} & \frac{2}{3} & 1 \\ 1 & 1 & 1 & 1 \end{bmatrix} \tag{3.3.20}$$

This choice is invertible and gives

$$\mathbf{G}^{-1} = 1/2 \begin{bmatrix} -9 & 27 & -27 & 9 \\ 18 & -45 & 36 & -9 \\ -11 & 18 & -9 & 2 \\ 2 & 0 & 0 & 0 \end{bmatrix}. \tag{3.3.21}$$

This shows that the four blending functions that make x(t) go exactly through the four given values $\mathbf{x}^{e^T} = [x_1 \quad x_2 \quad x_3 \quad x_4]$ are

$$H_1(t) = (1 - t)(2 - 3t)(1 - 3t)/2$$

$$H_2(t) = 9t(1 - t)(2 - 3t)/2 \tag{3.3.22}$$

$$H_3(t) = 9t(1 - t)(3t - 1)/2$$

$$H_4(t) = t(2 - 3t)(1 - 3t)/2.$$

A sketch of this approach is shown in Figure 3.3.3. This is a C^0 approximation when employed on a piecewise basis. All the above equally spaced interpolations are known as **Lagrangian interpolation** methods. By utilizing different types of data, it is possible to generate a different four-point curve that can be made to yield C^1 continuity when joined to a similar curve. Since C^1 continuity requires matching end slopes (parametric derivatives) we need a way to bring in derivative data.

For example, we could employ four data terms, such as $x(0)$, $x'(0)$, $x(1)$, and $x'(1)$, where $(\ )' = d(\ )/dt$. When we do this later we will find that our parametric cubic is the common **Hermite cubic** polynomial. It is a C^1 function and is partially sketched in Figure 3.3.4. For the Hermite blending function we can employ Equations (3.3.1) and (3.3.17) to write two identities at each of the endpoints of a given curve element:

$$\begin{Bmatrix} x_1 \\ x_2 \\ x_1{}' \\ x_2{}' \end{Bmatrix}^e = \begin{bmatrix} [P(0)] \\ [P(1)] \\ [P'(0)] \\ [P'(1)] \end{bmatrix} \{C\}^e \tag{3.3.23}$$

or, in our previous notation,

$$\mathbf{X}^e = \mathbf{G}\ \mathbf{C}^e$$

where

$$\mathbf{G} = \begin{bmatrix} 0 & 0 & 0 & 1 \\ 1 & 1 & 1 & 1 \\ 0 & 0 & 1 & 0 \\ 3 & 2 & 1 & 0 \end{bmatrix} \tag{3.3.24}$$

and the curve element definition constants have been generalized to include parametric derivatives:

$$\mathbf{X}^{e^T} = [x_1 \quad x_2 \quad x_1{}' \quad x_2{}']^e. \tag{3.3.25}$$

As before, the inverse

$$\mathbf{G}^{-1} = \begin{bmatrix} 2 & -2 & 1 & 1 \\ -3 & 3 & -2 & -1 \\ 0 & 0 & 1 & 0 \\ 1 & 0 & 0 & 0 \end{bmatrix}$$

leads to the alternate Hermite blending functions

$$H_1 = 2t^3 - 3t^2 + 1$$

$$H_2 = -2t^3 + 3t^2$$

$$H_3 = t^3 - 2t^2 + t \tag{3.3.26}$$

$$H_4 = t^3 - t^2$$

so that

$$x(t) = H_1(t) \, x_1 + H_2(t) \, x_2 + H_3(t) \, x_1' + H_4(t) \, x_2'. \tag{3.3.27}$$

As a spot check on these equations, note that if x is a constant, X, then $x' = 0$ and we should have $H_1 + H_2 \equiv 1$ for all parametric locations, t. It is easily seen that this condition is satisfied. From Figure 3.3.4 we note that H_1 has zero slopes at the endpoints, a unit value at $t = 0$, and a zero value at $t = 1$. Conversely, the derivative blend H_3 has zero values at the ends. It has a unit derivative (slope) at $t = 0$ and a null slope at end $t = 1$.

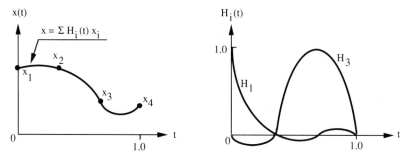

Figure 3.3.3   The Lagrangian parametric cubic.

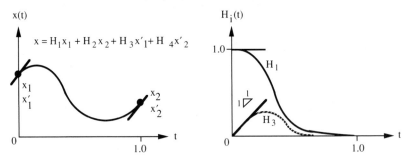

Figure 3.3.4   Hermite parametric cube.

Next we will use related concepts to find special derivative choices to generate another four-point cubic blending function that is C^0 but can be easily controlled to match similar segments with C^1 continuity at their junction. Such curves are commonly called **Bezier curves**. We have seen in Equation (3.3.19) that a parametric derivative can be viewed as a difference in x-point values. Thus, one can use four-point values to define two end derivatives. Figure 3.3.5 shows these concepts. There we employ x_1 as the first point and x_4 as the last. The interior points, x_2 and x_3, are utilized to control the parametric derivatives. Let these interior points arbitrarily be selected to be at the third points. Then we define finite difference derivatives

$$x_1' = (x_2 - x_1)/(1/3 - 0) = 3(x_2 - x_1)$$

$$x_4' = (x_4 - x_3)/(1 - 2/3) = 3(x_4 - x_3).$$

(3.3.28)

Changing notation and starting with the Hermite form, h_i:

$$x(t) = h_1 x_1 + h_2 x_2 + h_3 x_1' + h_4 x_4'.$$

We substitute these derivatives to obtain

$$x(t) = h_1 x_1 + h_2 x_4 + h_3 3(x_2 - x_1) + h_4 3(x_4 - x_3)$$

$$= (h_1 - 3h_3)x_1 + 3h_3 x_2 - 3h_4 x_3 + (h_2 + 3h_4)x_4$$

or

$$x(t) \equiv \sum_i H_i(t)x_i$$

where the resulting Bezier terms are

$$H_1 = -t^3 + 3t^2 - 3t + 1$$

$$H_2 = 3t^3 - 6t^2 + 3t$$

$$H_3 = -3t^3 + 3t^2$$

(3.3.29)

$$H_4 = t^3.$$

These Bezier blending functions are sketched in Figure 3.3.5. Part (c) of the figure illustrates a very useful property of this description, namely, that all points on the curve lie inside the polygon that defines the curve. This can be useful as a preliminary check for intersecting curves.

The preceding substitution represents a transformation or modification from Hermite data to Bezier data. These identities can be written as

$$\left\{\begin{matrix} x_1 \\ x_2 \\ x_1' \\ x_2' \end{matrix}\right\}_h^e = \begin{bmatrix} 1 & 0 & 0 & 0 \\ 0 & 0 & 0 & 1 \\ -3 & 3 & 0 & 0 \\ 0 & 0 & -3 & 3 \end{bmatrix} \left\{\begin{matrix} x_1 \\ x_2 \\ x_3 \\ x_4 \end{matrix}\right\}_b^e$$

(3.3.30)

or

$$\mathbf{X}_h^e = \mathbf{M}_{bh}\,\mathbf{X}_b^e.$$

Likewise, if we utilize Equation (3.3.27) we can find the four unique Lagrangian points that are equivalent to the usual Hermite data:

$$\left\{\begin{array}{c} x_1 \\ x_2 \\ x_3 \\ x_4 \end{array}\right\}_l^e = \frac{1}{27}\begin{bmatrix} 27 & 0 & 0 & 0 \\ 20 & 7 & 4 & -2 \\ 7 & 20 & 2 & -4 \\ 0 & 0 & 0 & 27 \end{bmatrix}\left\{\begin{array}{c} x_1 \\ x_2 \\ x_1' \\ x_2' \end{array}\right\}_h^e. \tag{3.3.31}$$

or

$$\mathbf{x}_l^e = \mathbf{M}_{hl}\,\mathbf{x}_h^e.$$

The modification operators, $\mathbf{M}$, and their inverses can be used to transform data from one parametric curve type to another.

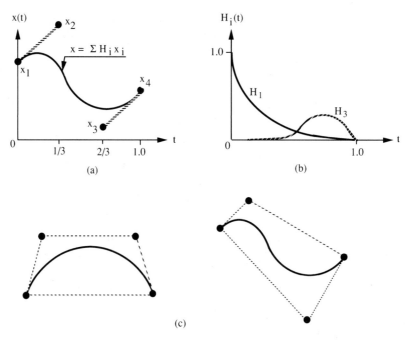

Figure 3.3.5   The Bezier cube.

Often we have to display a curve through several points. This can be done by using the Lagrangian four-point form in a piecewise display. Usually we would fit the curve through four consecutive points. Then the center third is drawn by moving through the parametric coordinates from $t = \frac{1}{3}$ to $t = \frac{2}{3}$. This approach gives a completed curve display that is aesthetically pleasing since it goes exactly through the points and looks as if it has continuous slopes. This procedure is illustrated in Figure

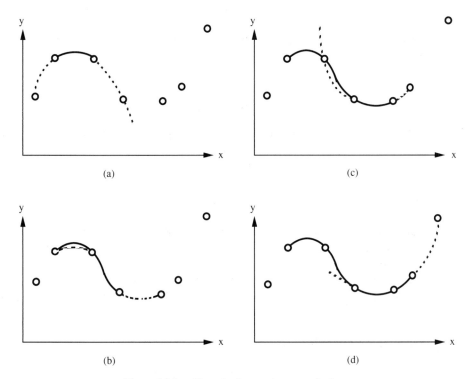

Figure 3.3.6   Piecewise Lagrangian curve displays.

3.3.6. Such a procedure would not pass through the first and the last point. To close these gaps we would also need to plot the parametric segment $t = 0$ to $t = \frac{1}{3}$ on the first segment and $t = \frac{2}{3}$ to $t = 1$ on the last segment.

We often need to have a curve with C^1 continuity. The Hermite families offer this capability directly, but the Serendipity and Lagrangian forms offer only C^0. Figure 3.3.6 showed how we could make a C^0 cubic look like it is C^1 even though it is not. The Bezier curve is a C^0 curve that can be made C^1 with another Bezier curve by simply placing the sampling points, adjacent to their common node, on the same straight line. This is illustrated in Figure 3.3.7.

The parametric cubic curve has a number of useful features. It is the lowest order curve that can yield a true space curve. The linear and quadratic parametric curves are obviously planar. The quadratic curve uses three control points. Those three points uniquely define a plane, and the curve through them lies on that plane. The parametric cubic can have a loop, or a cusp, has at most two inflection points, and can make no more than two right-angle turns with respect to a given vector. It can degenerate to quadratic or linear.

Another common use of the parametric Hermite curves is to combine them in a special way to form a C^2 **parametric spline**. Note from Equations (3.3.26-27) the second derivative (curvature) at any point is

$$x''(t) = x_1(12t - 6) + x_2(6 - 12t) + x'_1(6t - 4) + x'_2(6t - 2).$$

Thus, we can compute the curvature at either end simply by substituting $t = 0$ and $t = 1$ to yield

$$x''_1 = -6x_1 + 6x_2 - 4x'_1 - 2x'_2$$

$$x''_2 = 6x_1 - 6x_2 + 2x'_1 + 4x'_2.$$

Instead of using two points and slopes, we would like to have a single curve go through n points and still be at least C^2 at the nodes. This can be done by using the Hermite cubic on each adjacent segment pair, such as i and j in Figure 3.3.8. Since the slope data are not available, we use the preceding curvature relations to eliminate the slope input. That is, we require x''_2 of the right segment i to exactly match x''_1 of the left segment j. Since the first and last points do not have two neighbors, we arbitrarily set their curvatures to zero. This makes the curve straight at these two points.

This procedure leads to a set of n simultaneous equations that can be solved for the n slopes in terms of the n point values. These specially chosen slopes assure curvature continuity and allow the Hermite segments to be generated for display, or cutting, in a piecewise manner. This would allow a tool cutting path file to be at least C^2 everywhere on the curve defined by the n points.

3.3.3 Parametric Integration

We often find the need to execute integrations along a curve defined by our parametric representation. Consider a planar curve in the xy-plane. We may need to know its length and first moments (centroid), which are defined as

$$L = \int_L ds$$

and

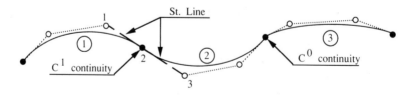

Figure 3.3.7   Bezier C^1 continuity via three points in a line.

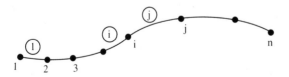

Figure 3.3.8   A piecewise cubic parametric spline.

$$\bar{x} L = \int_L x(t) \, ds$$

$$\bar{y} L = \int_L y(t) \, ds \, ,$$
(3.3.32)

respectively, where ds denotes the physical length of a segment, dt, of the parametric length. To evaluate these quantities we need to convert to an integral in the parametric space. For example,

$$L = \int_L ds = \int_0^1 \frac{ds}{dt} \, dt.$$
(3.3.33)

To relate the physical and parametric length scales, we must first recall the planar relation that

$$ds^2 = dx^2 + dy^2$$

Since both x and y are defined in terms of t we can extend this identity to the needed quantity

$$\left(\frac{ds}{dt}\right)^2 = \left(\frac{dx}{dt}\right)^2 + \left(\frac{dy}{dt}\right)^2$$

where dx/dt can be found from Equation (3.3.18), etc. for dy/dt. Thus, our physical length is defined in terms of the parametric coordinate, t, and the user-supplied data about the curve location in the xy-plane (i.e., $\mathbf{x^e}$ and $\mathbf{y^e}$):

$$L = \int_0^1 \sqrt{\left(\frac{dx}{dt}\right)^2 + \left(\frac{dy}{dt}\right)^2} \, dt$$
(3.3.34)

where

$$\frac{dx(t)}{dt} = \sum_{i=1}^N \frac{dH_i(t)}{dt} x_i^e$$

$$\frac{dy(t)}{dt} = \sum_{i=1}^N \frac{dH_i(t)}{dt} y_i^e$$

Note that this does preserve the proper units for L.

The preceding integral is trivial only when the planar curve is a straight line ($N = 2$). Then, from Equation (3.3.19),

$$\frac{dx}{dt} = x_2^e - x_1^e = \Delta x$$

$$\frac{dy}{dt} = y_2^e - y_1^e = \Delta y$$

are both constant, and the result simplifies to

$$L^e = \sqrt{(x_2^e - x_1^e)^2 + (y_2^e - y_1^e)^2} \int_0^1 dt$$

which, by inspection, is exact. For any other curve shape, these integrals become unpleasant to evaluate, and we may wish to consider their automation by means of numerical integration.

Numerical integration is simply a procedure that approximates (usually) an integral by a summation. To review this subject we refer to Figure 3.3.9. Recall that the

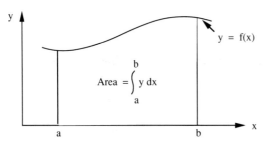

a) Exact integral equals the area

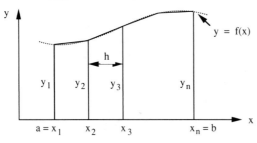

$$A \approx h(0.5 y_1 + y_2 + y_3 + \ldots + 0.5 y_n)$$

$$A \approx \sum_{j=1}^{n} w_j f(x_j), \quad w_j = h, \quad w_1 = w_n = h/2$$

b) Approximate area by Trapezoidal rule

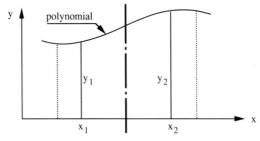

$$A \approx \sum_{j=1}^{n} w_j f(x_j), \quad \text{exact for order } (2n - 1)$$

c) Exact Guass rule for polynomials

Figure 3.3.9   Concepts of numerical integration.

integral

$$I = \int_a^b f(x)\, dx \tag{3.3.35}$$

can be viewed graphically as the area between the x-axis and the curve $y=f(x)$ in the region of the limits of integration. Thus, we can interpret numerical integration as an approximation of that area. The **trapezoidal rule** of numerical integration simply approximates the area by the sum of several equally spaced trapezoids under the curve between the limits of a and b. The height of a trapezoid is found from the integrand, $y_j = y(x_j)$, evaluated at equally spaced points, x_j and x_{j+1}. Thus, a typical contribution is $A = h(y_j + y_{j+1})/2$, where $h = x_{j+1} - x_j$ is the spacing. Thus, for n points (and $n - 1$ spaces) the well-known approximation is

$$I \approx h\left(\tfrac{1}{2}y_1 + y_2 + y_3 + \ \cdots\ + y_{n-1} + \tfrac{1}{2}y_n\right)$$

which can be expressed as a summation

$$I \approx \sum_{j=1}^{n} w_j\, f(x_j) \tag{3.3.36}$$

where

$$w_j = h, \quad \text{except} \quad w_1 = w_n = \frac{h}{2}$$

A geometrical interpretation of this is that the area under the curve, I, is the sum of the products of certain heights, $f(x_j)$ times some corresponding widths, w_j. In the terminology of numerical integration the locations of the points, x_j, where the heights are computed are called abscissae and the widths, w_j, are called weights.

Another well-known approximation is the **Simpson rule**, which uses parabolic segments in the area approximation. For most functions the above rules may require 20 to 40 terms in the summation to yield acceptable accuracy. We want to carry out the summation with the minimum number of terms, n, in order to reduce the computational cost. What is the minimum number of terms? The answer depends on the form of the integrand, $f(x)$. Since the parametric geometry usually involves polynomials we will consider that common special case for $f(x)$.

The famous mathematician Gauss posed this question: What is the minimum number of points, n, required to exactly integrate a polynomial, and what are the corresponding abscissae and weights? If we require the summation to be exact when $f(x)$ is any one of the power functions $1, x, x^2, ..., x^{2n-1}$, we obtain a set of $2n$ conditions that allow us to determine the n abscissae, x_i, and their corresponding n weights, w_j.

The n **Gaussian quadrature** points are symmetrically placed with respect to the center of the interval and will exactly integrate a polynomial of order $(2n+1)$. The center point location is included in the abscissae list when n is odd, but the end points are never utilized in a Gauss rule. The Gauss rule data are usually tabulated for a non-dimensional **unit coordinate** range of $0 \le t \le 1$, or for a **natural coordinate** range of

$-1 \leq t \leq +1$. Table 3.3.1 presents the low-order Gauss rule data. A two-point Gauss rule can often exceed the accuracy of a 20-point trapezoidal rule. A subroutine for providing those data is shown in Figure 3.3.10.

Sometimes it is desirable to have a numerical integration rule that specifically includes the two end points in the abscissae list when ($n \geq 2$). The **Lobatto rule** is

```
      SUBROUTINE  GAUSS (N, R, W)
C     - - - - - - - - - - - - - - - - - - - - - - - - - - - - - -
C     RETURN ABSCISSAE AND WEIGHTS FOR GAUSSIAN FORMULA, -1 TO +1
C     - - - - - - - - - - - - - - - - - - - - - - - - - - - - - -
      DIMENSION  R(N), W(N)
C     N = NUM. OF PTS, R = ABSCISSAE ARRAY, W = WEIGHT ARRAY
C     LIMIT N TO 1, 2, OR 3 PT RULES.  DEFAULT TO 2 PT
      DATA  NMAX / 4 /
      GO TO (1,2,3,4,5), N
C     N = 1
   1  R(1) = 0.0D0
      W(1) = 2.0D0
      RETURN
C     N = 2
   2  R(1) = 0.577350269189626D0
      R(2) = -R(1)
      W(1) = 1.D0
      W(2) = 1.D0
      RETURN
C     N = 3
   3  R(1) = 0.774596669241483D0
      R(2) = 0.D0
      R(3) = -R(1)
      W(1) = 0.555555555555556D0
      W(2) = 0.888888888888889D0
      W(3) = W(1)
      RETURN
   4  R(1) = 0.861136311594053D0
      R(2) = 0.339981043584856D0
      R(3) = -R(1)
      R(4) = -R(1)
      W(1) = 0.347854845137454D0
      W(2) = 0.652145154862546D0
      W(3) = W(1)
      W(4) = W(2)
      RETURN
   5  WRITE (*,*) N, ' COEFFICIENTS NOT IN SUBR GAUSS'
      N = 2
      IF ( N.EQ.2 )  GO TO 2
      RETURN
      END
```

FIGURE 3.3.10   Natural coordinate Gaussian data routine

such an alternate choice. Its data are included in Table 3.3.2. It is usually less accurate than the Gauss rule but it can be useful. Mathematical handbooks give tables of Gauss or Lobatto data for much higher values of n.

To complete this section we outline an algorithim to automate the calculation of the y - centroid:

1. Recover the N points describing the curve; $\mathbf{x^e}, \mathbf{y^e}$.

2. Recover the M-point quadrature data, t_j and w_j.

3. Zero the integrals: $L = 0$, $\bar{y}\,L = 0$

4. Loop over all the quadrature points: $1 \le j \le M$. At each local quadrature point, t_j:

   a. Find the length scales (i.e., Jacobian):

      (i) Compute local derivatives of the N interpolation functions

$$\mathbf{DH}_j \equiv \frac{\partial \mathbf{H}}{\partial t}\Big|_{t=t_j}$$

      (ii) Get x- and y-derivatives from curve data

$$\frac{dx}{dt}_j \equiv \mathbf{DH}_j\,\mathbf{x^e} = \sum_{i=1}^{N} \frac{\partial H_i(t_j)}{\partial t}\,x_i^e$$

$$\frac{dy}{dt_j} \equiv \mathbf{DH}_j\,\mathbf{y^e}$$

      (iii) Length scale at point t_j

$$\frac{ds}{dt_j} = \sqrt{(\frac{dx}{dt})_j^2 + (\frac{dy}{dt})_j^2}$$

   b. Evaluate the integrand at point t_j:

      (i) Evaluate the N interpolation functions:

$$\mathbf{H}_j \equiv \mathbf{H}(t_j)$$

      (ii) Evaluate y from curve data

$$y_j = \mathbf{H}_j\,\mathbf{y^e} = \sum_{i=1}^{N} H_i(t_j)\,y_i^e$$

   c. Form products and add to previous values

      (i)

$$L = L + \frac{ds}{dt_j}\,W_j$$

      (ii)

$$\bar{y}\,L = \bar{y}\,L + y_j\,\frac{ds}{dt_j}\,W_j\;.$$

5. Evaluate items computed from the completed integrals:

$$\bar{y} = \frac{\bar{y}\,L}{L}\,,$$

etc. for $\bar{x}$.

Note that to automate the integration we simply need: (1) storage of the quadrature data, M, t_j, and w_j, (2) access to the curve data, N, $\mathbf{x}^\mathbf{e}$, $\mathbf{y}^\mathbf{e}$, (3) a subroutine to find the parametric derivative of the N interpolation functions at any point, t, and (4) a function program to evaluate the integrand(s) at any point, t. This usually requires (see step 4b) a subroutine to evaluate the N interpolation functions at any point, t.

The evaluations of Equations (3.3.11) and (3.3.18), at a point t_j, can be thought of as a dot product of the data array $\mathbf{x}^\mathbf{e}$ and the evaluated interpolation quantities $\mathbf{H}_j$ and $\mathbf{DH}_j$. A FORTRAN program for evaluating $\bar{y}$ for a Lagrangian quadratic curve, in national coordinates, is shown in Figure 3.3.11. That program is easily extended to space curves, or other integrands, or other parametric curve definitions. Here SHAPE and DERIV are generic subroutine names for computing the arrays $\mathbf{H}$ and $\mathbf{DH}$. The supporting subroutines and functions are shown in Figure 3.3.12.

TABLE 3.3.1   GAUSSIAN QUADRATURE DATA:

$$\int_a^b f(r)\, dr = \sum_{i=1}^n f(r_i) w_i$$

n	Natural Coordinates, $a = -1, b = +1$		Unit Coordinates $a = 0, b = 1$	
	$\pm r_i$	w_i	r_i	w_i
1	0	2	$1/2$	1
2	$\pm \dfrac{1}{\sqrt{3}}$	1	$\dfrac{(\sqrt{3}\pm1)}{2\sqrt{3}}$	$\dfrac{1}{2}$
3	$\pm \dfrac{\sqrt{15}}{5}$	$\dfrac{5}{9}$	$\dfrac{(5\pm\sqrt{15})}{10}$	$\dfrac{5}{18}$
	0	$\dfrac{8}{9}$	$\dfrac{1}{2}$	$\dfrac{4}{9}$
4	$\pm\dfrac{\sqrt{(3 + \sqrt{24/\sqrt{5}})}}{7}$	$\dfrac{(18 - \sqrt{30})}{36}$		
	$\pm\dfrac{\sqrt{(3 - \sqrt{24/\sqrt{5}})}}{7}$	$\dfrac{(18 + \sqrt{30})}{36}$		

TABLE 3.3.2   LOBATTO QUADRATURE

DATA: $\displaystyle\int_a^b f(r)\, dr = \sum_{i=1}^n f(r_i) w_i$

n	Natural Coordinates $a = -1, b = +1$		Unit Coordinates $a = 0, b = 1$	
	r_i	w_i	r_i	w_i
2	± 1	1	0	$1/2$
			1	$1/2$
3	± 1	$1/3$	0	$1/6$
	0	$4/3$	$1/2$	$4/6$
			1	$1/6$
4	± 1	$1/6$	0	$1/12$
	$\pm 1/\sqrt{5}$	$5/6$	$(1 \pm 1/\sqrt{5})/2$	$5/12$
			1	$1/12$

```
        SUBROUTINE  CURVE (XE, YE, M, LENGTH, YBAR)
C       -----------------------------------------------
C       FIND LENGTH AND Y-CENTRIOD OF N POINT
C       LAGRANGIAN CURVE VIA M GAUSS POINTS
C       -----------------------------------------------
        PARAMETER ( N = 3, MMAX = 4 )
        DIMENSION  XE(N), YE(N), H(N), DH(N)
        DIMENSION  R(MMAX), W(MMAX)
        REAL  LENGTH
C       GET GAUSSIAN DATA IN NATURAL COORDINATES
        CALL  GAUSS ( M, R, W )
C       INITIALIZE INTEGRALS
        LENGTH = 0.
        YBARL  = 0.
C       LOOP OVER QUADRATURE DATA
        DO 10  J = 1, M
C         GET LOCAL DERIVATIVES AT THE POINT
          CALL  DERIV ( N, DH, R(J) )
C         FIND THE SPACE SCALE ( JACOBIAN )
          DXDR = DOT ( N, DH, XE )
          DYDR = DOT ( N, DH, YE )
          DSDRJ = SQRT ( DXDR**2 + DYDR**2 )
C          EVALUATE INTEGRANDS
           CALL  SHAPE ( N, H, R(J) )
           YJ = DOT ( N, H, YE )
C          UPDATE THE SUMMATIONS
           LENGTH = LENGTH + DSDRJ * W(J)
           YBARL  = YBARL  + YJ * DSDRJ * W(J)
 10     CONTINUE
C       USE INTEGRALS TO FIND Y-CENTROID
        YBAR = YBARL / LENGTH
        RETURN
        END
```

FIGURE 3.3.11   Numerical integration on a parametric curve

3.4 PARAMETRIC SURFACE PATCHES

To introduce the extension of parametric curves to parametric patches, we begin with a quadrilateral patch based on a bilinear blending function. The patch is shown in Figure 3.4.1. Consider a square parametric patch in unit coordinate space, $0 \leq r, s \leq 1$. Recall that our linear parametric curve had the form

$$x(t) = (1 - t)x(0) + tx(1)$$

```
      SUBROUTINE   DERIV (N, DH, X)
C     - - - - - - - - - - - - - - - - - - - - - - - - - - -
C     FIND LOCAL DERIVATIVES FOR A 3 NODE LINE SEGMENT
C     - - - - - - - - - - - - - - - - - - - - - - - - - - -
      DIMENSION   DH(N)
C     DH = LOCAL DERIVATIVES OF SHAPE FUNCTIONS, H
C     X = LOCAL COORDINATE OF POINT,     -1 TO +1
C     LOCAL NODE COORD. ARE -1,0,+1.   1----2----3 --> X
      DH(1) = X - 0.5
      DH(2) = -2.*X
      DH(3) = X + 0.5
      RETURN
      END
      FUNCTION DOT (N, A, B)
C     - - - - - - - - - - - - - - - - - - - - - - - - - - -
C     DOT PRODUCT OF TWO VECTORS OF LENGTH N
C     - - - - - - - - - - - - - - - - - - - - - - - - - - -
      DIMENSION   A(N), B(N)
      DOT = 0.0
      DO 10 I = 1,N
   10 DOT = DOT + A(I)*B(I)
      RETURN
      END
      SUBROUTINE   SHAPE (N, H, X)
C     - - - - - - - - - - - - - - - - - - - - - - - - - - -
C     CALCULATE SHAPE FUNCTIONS OF A 3 NODE LINE SEGMENT
C     - - - - - - - - - - - - - - - - - - - - - - - - - - -
      DIMENSION   H(N)
C     H = ELEMENT SHAPE FUNCTIONS, N = 3
C     X = LOCAL COORDINATE OF POINT,     -1 TO +1
C     LOCAL NODE COORD. ARE -1,0,+1.   1-----2-----3 --> X
      H(1) = 0.5*(X*X - X)
      H(2) = 1. - X*X
      H(3) = 0.5*(X*X + X)
      RETURN
      END
```

FIGURE 3.3.12   Routines for integration on a quadratic curve

We use the same concept to find $x(r, s)$ by using linear interpolation in r along lines of constant s:

$$x(r, s) = (1 - r)x(0, s) + rx(1, s) \qquad (3.4.1)$$

where in a similar manner the two end values, $x(0,s)$ and $x(1,s)$, are each obtained by linear parametric interpolation in s when $r = 0$ and $r = 1$:

$$x(0, s) = (1 - s)x(0, 0) + sx(0, 1)$$

and

$$x(1, s) = (1 - s)x(1, 0) + sx(1, 1). \tag{3.4.2}$$

Substituting the latter two relations into the previous one yields

$$x(r, s) = (1 - r)[(1 - s)x(0, 0) + sx(0, 1)] + r[(1 - s)x(1, 0) + sx(1, 1)]$$

$$= (1 - r)(1 - s)x(0, 0) + r(1 - s)x(1, 0) + rs\ x(1, 1) + s(1 - r)x(0, 1)$$

or

$$x(r, s) = \sum_i H_i(r, s)\, x_i \tag{3.4.3}$$

where, as shown in Figure 3.4.1, the supplied data values are:

$$x_1 = x(0, 0) \qquad x_2 = x(1, 0) \qquad x_3 = x(1, 1) \qquad x_4 = x(0, 1)$$

and the resulting four bilinear blending relations are

$$H_1(r, s) = 1 - r - s + rs$$

$$H_2(r, s) = \quad\quad r \quad\quad - rs$$

$$H_3(r, s) = \quad\quad\quad\quad rs$$

$$H_4(r, s) = \quad\quad\quad\quad s - rs$$

$$\tag{3.4.4}$$

and we note the property that

$$\sum_i H_i(r, s) \equiv 1. \tag{3.4.5}$$

This is called the bilinear parametric Lagrangian quadrilateral. Other scalar components defined at the nodes can be defined in a similar manner; e.g.,

$$y(r, s) = \sum_i H_i(r, s)y_i.$$

Since the (x_i, y_i) are arbitrary, the patch is a straight-sided quadrilateral in physical space even though it is always square in its so called parent form. The preceding

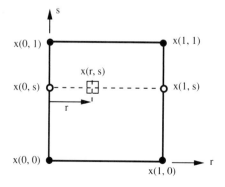

Figure 3.4.1   Bilinear patch interpolation.

parametric form is linear on any edge but is an incomplete quadratic parametric on the interior of the surface. It is missing the r^2 and s^2 terms needed for a complete quadratic. A complete polynomial requires n terms, where

$$n = \frac{(P + D)!}{P!D!} \tag{3.4.6}$$

and P is the order of the polynomial and D is the dimension of the space. This gives the numbers shown in Table 3.4.1. Complete polynomials are easy to generate only for the simplex shapes, that is, for the line, the triangle, and the tetrahedron.

TABLE 3.4.1 TERMS FOR A
COMPLETE POLYNOMIAL

P	D	n	P	D	n
1	1	2	3	1	4
1	2	3	3	2	10
1	3	4	3	3	20
2	1	3	4	1	5
2	2	6	4	2	15
2	3	10	4	3	35

We can employ another approach for triangles that is similar to the procedure used to derive the parametric curves. Assume a complete linear form

$$x(r, s) = \mathbf{P}(r, s)\, \mathbf{C}$$

$$= [1 \quad r \quad s] \begin{Bmatrix} C_1 \\ C_2 \\ C_3 \end{Bmatrix}. \tag{3.4.7}$$

Let the parametric triangle lie in the unit space, as shown in Figure 3.4.2, so that it has a right angle at the local origin. If $x_1 \equiv x(0, 0)$, $x_2 \equiv x(1, 0)$, and $x_3 \equiv x(0, 1)$, then we write these identities

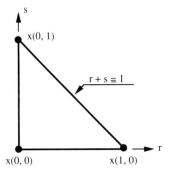

Figure 3.4.2   The linear triangle in unit coordinates.

$$\left\{\begin{matrix} x_1 \\ x_2 \\ x_3 \end{matrix}\right\}^e = \begin{bmatrix} 1 & 0 & 0 \\ 1 & 1 & 0 \\ 1 & 0 & 1 \end{bmatrix} \{C^e\} \qquad (3.4.8)$$

or

$$\mathbf{x}^e = \mathbf{G}\ \mathbf{C}^e.$$

Since the parametric geometry, $\mathbf{G}$, is invertible with

$$\mathbf{G}^{-1} = \begin{bmatrix} 1 & 0 & 0 \\ -1 & 1 & 0 \\ -1 & 0 & 1 \end{bmatrix}$$

we can substitute into Equation (3.4.7) to obtain blending functions

$$H_1(r, s) = 1 - r - s$$

$$H_2(r, s) = \quad r \qquad (3.4.9)$$

$$H_3(r, s) = \qquad\quad s$$

which also satisfy Equation (3.4.5). This form is linear on all sides (including the diagonal, r + s = 1) and is a complete linear function in the interior of the surface element.

If we add midside nodes $x_4 = x(\frac{1}{2}, 0)$, $x_5 = x(\frac{1}{2}, \frac{1}{2})$, and $x_6 = x(0, \frac{1}{2})$, then we can evaluate a complete parametric quadratic patch in exactly the same way. This results in blending functions

$$H_1 = 1 - 3r - 3s + 2r^2 + 4rs + 2s^2$$

$$H_2 = \quad -r \qquad + 2r^2$$

$$H_3 = \qquad\quad -s \qquad\qquad\quad + 2s^2$$

$$H_4 = \quad 4r \qquad - 4r^2 - 4rs \qquad\qquad\qquad (3.4.10)$$

$$H_5 = \qquad\qquad\qquad\qquad 4rs$$

$$H_6 = \qquad 4s \qquad - 4rs - 4s^2 \quad.$$

These are complete quadratics on the edges and on the interior of the triangular.

By way of comparison, if we repeat the first procedure for quadrilaterals and form a biquadratic quadrilateral from the product of two parametric edge quadratics, we generate nine points and nine blending functions. This is more than the 6 terms needed for the complete two-dimensional quadratic and less than the 10 terms needed for the two-dimensional cubic. That is, the quadrilateral is an incomplete cubic on the interior but is a complete quadratic on each of its four curved (in physical space) edges. It is also possible to remove the center node and form a quadratic quadrilateral patch that has only eight edge nodes. This is called the quadratic Serendipity quadrilateral. It is included in Table 3.4.2.

TABLE 3.4.2 SERENDIPITY QUADRILATERALS IN NATURAL COORDINATES

Type	Node Location a_i	b_i	Interpolation Functions $H_i(a, b)$, $-1 \leq a, b \leq +1$
Q4	± 1	± 1	$\dfrac{(1 + aa_i)(1 + bb_i)}{4}$
Q8	± 1	± 1	$\dfrac{(1 + aa_i)(1 + bb_i)(aa_i + bb_i - 1)}{4}$
	± 1	0	$\dfrac{(1 + aa_i)(1 - b^2)}{2}$
	0	± 1	$\dfrac{(1 + bb_i)(1 - a^2)}{2}$
Q12	± 1	± 1	$\dfrac{(1 + aa_i)(1 + bb_i)[9(a^2 + b^2) - 10]}{32}$
	± 1	$\dfrac{\pm 1}{3}$	$\dfrac{9(1 + aa_i)(1 - b^2)(1 + 9bb_i)}{32}$
	$\dfrac{\pm 1}{3}$	± 1	$\dfrac{9(1 + bb_i)(1 - a^2)(1 + 9aa_i)}{32}$

Lagrangian and Serendipity patches, of the same order, will be C^0 along a common edge, since they share common edge control nodes. They will be C^1 tangent to an edge, but not C^1 in the surface slopes normal to a common edge. A similar observation applies to two Bezier patches if they share common edge control points. On the interior of each of these patches, they are usually C^∞.

Just as it was possible to connect to Bezier curves in a C^1 fashion, we can also do the same thing with the normal derivatives on a common edge. Simply imagine the curves in Figure 3.3.7 as sections taken through the two patches in a plane normal to their common edge. This can be very useful if we want the surface to "look good" and are satisfied with passing it exactly through only the patches corners. Bezier surfaces can be made C^1 by careful selection of the control points.

If we are employing a computer numerically controlled (CNC) cutting tool to move on the surface, then the resulting cutting path file (CPF) will be C^1, and the machined surface will "look good" and be void of kinks in the surface slopes. A Bezier bicubic quadrilateral patch can be formed from the tensor product of the Bezier curves. We previously illustrated this concept for the bilinear Lagrangian patch. This means that the Bezier patch is defined by a net of 16 points of which only the four corner values actually lie on the surface. By way of contrast, the Lagrangian and Serendipity patches pass exactly through their control points. These patches are shown in Figure 3.4.3. The edge continuity of typical surfaces are sketched in Figure 3.4.4.

The term **linear blending** often has special mathematical interpretation. It is viewed as an exact matching of any smooth functions on each of the edges and an approximate description on the interior of the patch. Assuming that each edge function is known, it takes three operations to produce the blending of the approximate interior surface. These are sketched for a parametric rectangle in Figure 3.4.5. First we take the edges parallel to the r-axis and execute a linear interpolation, in s, between those two

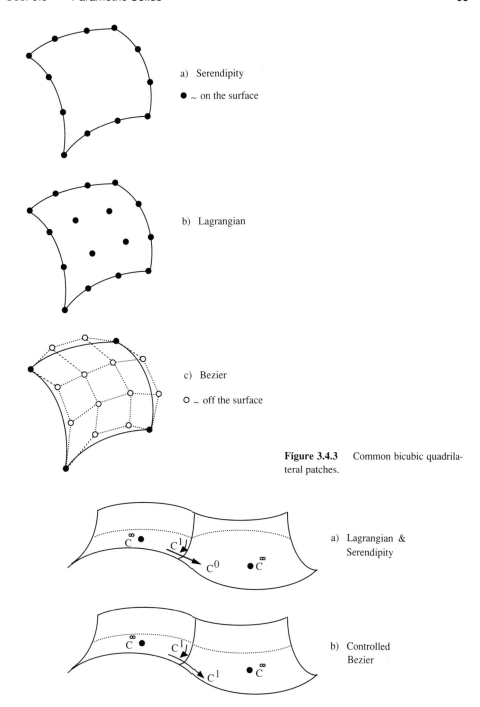

a) Serendipity

● ~ on the surface

b) Lagrangian

c) Bezier

○ ~ off the surface

Figure 3.4.3   Common bicubic quadrilateral patches.

a) Lagrangian &
    Serendipity

b) Controlled
    Bezier

Figure 3.4.4   Normal edge slope continuity between patches.

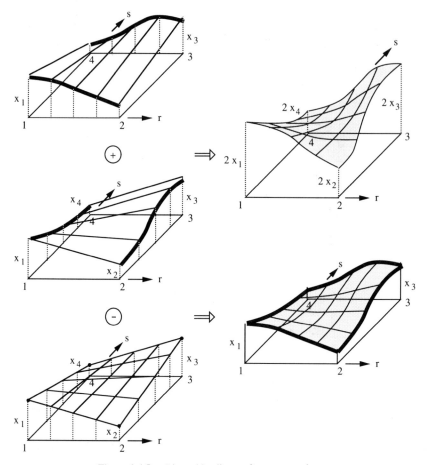

Figure 3.4.5   Linear blending surface construction.

functions. Next we carry out a linear interpolation between the edges parallel to the s-axis. If we add these two surfaces, we obtain a smooth result. However, it gives exactly twice the corner values with which we started. We also note that each edge of the approximate surface is now the sum of the original edge function and a bilinear interpolation between the corner values. We can restore the desired surface by subtracting the surface resulting from the bilinear interpolation (see Equation (3.4.4)) between the four corner values.

3.5 PARAMETRIC SOLIDS

We will have more use for parametric solids later in Chapter 5. For completeness at this point, we simply note that the previous methods can extend to parametric solids. For example, the four-noded tetrahedron in Figure 3.5.1 has linear interpolations in the unit coordinate space, $0 \leq (r, s, t) \leq 1$, of

$$H_1(r,s,t) = 1 - r - s - t$$

$$H_2(r,s,t) = \quad r$$

$$H_3(r,s,t) = \qquad s$$

$$H_4(r,s,t) = \qquad\qquad t \ .$$

Thus, we have

$$z(r,s,t) = \sum_i H_i(r,s,t)\, Z_i \ .$$

By inspection, we see that each of its four faces (like t = 0) reduces to a linear parametric surface like Equation (3.4.9) and each of its six edges (like r = s = 0) reduces to a

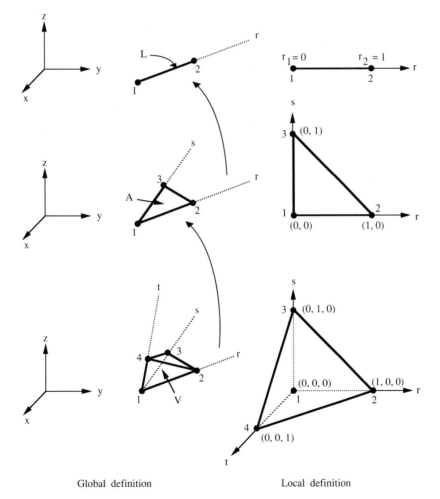

Global definition   Local definition

Figure 3.5.1   The parametric simplex family.

linear parametric like Equation (3.3.16). This solid always has straight edges and flat faces. Thus, its Jacobian is constant and equals six times the physical volume.

Similar observations apply to the faces and edges of other parametric solids like the wedge and brick (hexahedron), as shown in Figure 3.5.2. The natural coordinate interpolations for Serendipity hexahedron are given in Table 3.5.1. Their face interpolations reduce to the forms in Table 3.4.2 and their edges are simply parametric Lagrangian curves. The faces are generally nonflat surfaces, even if the edges are straight. Thus, the Jacobian in a parametric brick usually is a function of the local coordinates.

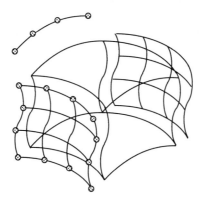

Figure 3.5.2   The compatable parametric cubic solid, surface, and edge.

TABLE 3.5.1   SERENDIPITY HEXAHEDRA IN NATURAL COORDINATES

Type	Node Location			Interpolation Functions
	a_i	b_i	c_i	$H_i(a, b, c), -1 \le a, b, c \le +1$
H8	± 1	± 1	± 1	$(1 + aa_i)(1 + bb_i)(1 + cc_i)$
H20	± 1	± 1	± 1	$\dfrac{(1 + aa_i)(1 + bb_i)(1 + cc_i)(aa_i + bb_i + cc_i - 2)}{8}$
	0	± 1	± 1	$\dfrac{(1 - a^2)(1 + bb_i)(1 + cc_i)}{4}$
	± 1	0	± 1	$\dfrac{(1 - b^2)(1 + aa_i)(1 + cc_i)}{4}$
	± 1	± 1	0	$\dfrac{(1 - c^2)(1 + aa_i)(1 + bb_i)}{4}$
H32	± 1	± 1	± 1	$\dfrac{(1 + aa_i)(1 + bb_i)(1 + cc_i)[9(a^2 + b^2 + c^2) - 19]}{64}$
	$\dfrac{\pm 1}{3}$	± 1	± 1	$\dfrac{9(1 - a^2)(1 + 9aa_i)(1 + bb_i)(1 + cc_i)}{64}$
	± 1	$\dfrac{\pm 1}{3}$	± 1	$\dfrac{9(1 - b^2)(1 + 9bb_i)(1 + aa_i)(1 + cc_i)}{64}$
	± 1	± 1	$\dfrac{\pm 1}{3}$	$\dfrac{9(1 - c^2)(1 + 9cc_i)(1 + bb_i)(1 + aa_i)}{64}$

3.6 GEOMETRIC AND MASS PROPERTIES

The important calculation of geometric or mass properties of a solid, surface, or curve can be executed in various ways. One approach for solids is based on the use of elementary calculus combined with a surface representation. The most useful techniques involve integral identities that convert volume integrals to surface integrals or convert surface integrals to closed-path integrals. These include Green's (divergence) theorem, and Stokes theorem. The transformation from parametric coordinates to physical coordinates also requires that we review the calculus concept of the **Jacobian** of a transformation. To automate the integrations we eventually require the use of numerical integration rules, such as **Gaussian quadratures**. These rules replace integrations with summations.

As an example of these concepts recall the **divergence theorem** of Green,

$$\iiint_V \vec{\nabla} \cdot \vec{A} \ dV = \iint_S \vec{A} \cdot \vec{n} \ dS \qquad (3.6.1)$$

where $\vec{A}$ is an arbitrary vector, $\vec{\nabla}$ is the divergence vector, $\vec{n}$ is the unit outward normal vector on S, and S is the closed surface that bounds the volume, V. To illustrate the usefulness of this theorem, let $\vec{A} = \vec{R}$, where $\vec{R}$ is the position vector. Previously we saw how to define the coordinates (x,y,z) of any point on the surface by the use of parametric blending functions. Thus, we will assume it is known. In this special case

$$\iint_S \vec{R} \cdot \vec{n} \ dS = \iiint_V \vec{\nabla} \cdot \vec{R} \ dV \qquad (3.6.2)$$

$$= \iiint_V \left(\frac{\partial}{\partial x}\, \hat{i} + \frac{\partial}{\partial y}\, \hat{j} + \frac{\partial}{\partial z}\, \hat{k}\right) \cdot (x\hat{i} + y\hat{j} + z\hat{k}) \ dV$$

$$= \iiint_V (1 + 1 + 1) \ dV = 3V. \qquad (3.6.3)$$

Therefore, we observe that we can compute the volume by integrations over the surface of the dot product of the position and normal vectors. If we can exactly represent the surface by the union of several surface patches, then

$$S \equiv \bigcup_e S^e \qquad (3.6.4)$$

and for a closed surface

$$3V \equiv \iint_S \vec{R} \cdot \vec{n} \ dS$$

$$\equiv \sum_e \iint_{S^e} \vec{R} \cdot \vec{n} \ dS. \qquad (3.6.5)$$

If the patches do not exactly match the surface or if there are approximations in $\vec{R}$ or $\vec{n}$, then this expression is not exact and the result contains an approximation error, ε:

$$3V + \varepsilon = \sum_e \iint_{S^e} \vec{R} \cdot \vec{n} \, dS.$$

Usually we simply compute the volume approximation;

$$V \approx \frac{1}{3} \sum_e \iint_{S^e} \vec{R} \cdot \vec{n} \, dS. \tag{3.6.6}$$

Often the analyst will have some option for reducing the error, ε, at the expense of additional computational effort.

Many solids have bounding surfaces that are flat. Thus, they can be exactly represented by flat patches. A flat patch will have a surface area, S^e, and a constant outward normal vector, $\vec{n}^e$. In that case a typical contribution is

$$\iint_{S^e} \vec{R} \cdot \vec{n} \, dS = \vec{n} \cdot \iint_{S^e} \vec{R} \, dS. \tag{3.6.7}$$

Recalling the definition of the centroid or first moment of an area, we can write

$$\iint_{S^e} \vec{R} \, dS \equiv \vec{R}_c \, S^e = \vec{R}^e \, S^e \tag{3.6.8}$$

where $\vec{R}^e$ denotes the position vector to the centroid of the area:

$$\vec{R}^e = (\bar{x} \, \hat{i} + \bar{y} \, \hat{j} + \bar{z} \, \hat{k}) \tag{3.6.9}$$

$$\bar{x} \, S^e \equiv \iint_{S^e} x \, dS. \tag{3.6.10}$$

Therefore, we can conclude that if the surface can be exactly represented by flat patches, we can exactly compute the volume from

$$V = \frac{1}{3} \sum_e \vec{R}^e \cdot \vec{n}^e \, S^e \tag{3.6.11}$$

where the surface area of a typical patch is

$$S^e = \iint_{S^e} dS. \tag{3.6.12}$$

For simple shapes, such as rectangles and triangles, the surface area, S^e, can be computed without resorting to integration. Table 3.6.1 gives some examples of the vector $\vec{A}$ in Equation (3.6.1) that can be chosen to generate the most common integral properties. These choices for $\vec{A}$ are not unique but are among the most useful. Since mass density, ρ, is usually piecewise constant, we can usually convert integral properties to mass properties directly. For example, the mass, m, is

$$m = \iiint \rho \, dV = \rho_c \iiint dV = \rho_c \, V.$$

These observations suggest the so-called divide and conquer approach. If we approximate a nonflat (generally curved) surface with a large number of flat triangular patches, this approach can yield a reasonable approximation to V. One can reduce the approximation error, ε, by increasing the number of patches and/or by using nonflat patches. Of course, the limiting case of an infinite number of flat patches yields the exact result.

TABLE 3.6.1   INTEGRAL PROPERTIES FROM $P = \iint\limits_{S} \vec{A} \cdot \vec{n} \ dS$

Property	A_x	A_y	A_z
$V = \iiint dV$	$\dfrac{x}{3}$	$\dfrac{y}{3}$	$\dfrac{z}{3}$
$\bar{X}V = \iiint x \ dV$	$\dfrac{x^2}{2}$	0	0
$\bar{Y}V = \iiint y \ dV$	0	$\dfrac{y^2}{2}$	0
$\bar{Z}V = \iiint z \ dV$	0	0	$\dfrac{z^2}{2}$
$I_{xx} = \iiint (y^2 + z^2) \ dV$	0	$\dfrac{y^3}{3}$	$\dfrac{z^3}{3}$
$I_{yy} = \iiint (x^2 + z^2) \ dV$	$\dfrac{x^3}{3}$	0	$\dfrac{z^3}{3}$
$I_{zz} = \iiint (x^2 + y^2) \ dV$	$\dfrac{x^3}{3}$	$\dfrac{y^3}{3}$	0
$I_{yz} = \iint yz \ dV$	0	$y^2 \dfrac{z}{4}$	$\dfrac{yz^2}{4}$
$I_{xz} = \iiint xz \ dV$	$x^2 \dfrac{z}{4}$	0	$\dfrac{xz^2}{4}$
$I_{xy} = \iiint xy \ dV$	$x^2 \dfrac{y}{4}$	$\dfrac{xy^2}{4}$	0

Even if our patch is flat we begin to have difficulties if one or more of its edges is curved. Then we must complete the integration

$$S^e = \iint\limits_{S^e} dS$$

and integrations like Equation (3.6.10). The difficulty arises because we may only know the integrand, x, as a function of the patch parametric coordinates, e.g., $x(r,s)$. In that case we must return to our introductory calculus and recall the use of Jacobians to transform (or map) from one coordinate system to another. For a solid we recall that the differential volume is

$$dV = dx \ dy \ dz = |J| \ dr \ ds \ dt \qquad (3.6.13)$$

whereas for a flat surface of z = constant

$$dA = dx \ dy = |J| \ dr \ ds. \qquad (3.6.14)$$

For a straight line the differential length is

$$dL = dx = |J| \ dr \qquad (3.6.15)$$

where in each case |J| denotes the determinant of the Jacobian of the transformation. Usually |J| is a function of the local parametric coordinates.

The Jacobian can be thought of as relating the derivatives in the physical (or global) space to those in the parametric (or local) space. The chain rule of differentiation gives

$$\frac{\partial f}{\partial r} = \frac{\partial f}{\partial x} \frac{\partial x}{\partial r} + \frac{\partial f}{\partial y} \frac{\partial y}{\partial r}$$

$$\frac{\partial f}{\partial s} = \frac{\partial f}{\partial x} \frac{\partial x}{\partial s} + \frac{\partial f}{\partial y} \frac{\partial y}{\partial s}.$$

In matrix form

$$\left\{ \begin{array}{c} \dfrac{\partial f}{\partial r} \\[2ex] \dfrac{\partial f}{\partial s} \end{array} \right\} = \left[\begin{array}{cc} \dfrac{\partial x}{\partial r} & \dfrac{\partial y}{\partial r} \\[2ex] \dfrac{\partial x}{\partial s} & \dfrac{\partial y}{\partial s} \end{array} \right] \left\{ \begin{array}{c} \dfrac{\partial f}{\partial x} \\[2ex] \dfrac{\partial f}{\partial y} \end{array} \right\} \qquad (3.6.16)$$

or

$$\{ \partial_l \ f(r,s) \} = [J(r,s)] \ \{ \partial_g f(r,s) \} \qquad (3.6.17)$$

$$\partial_l \ f = \mathbf{J} \partial_g f.$$

Here [J] is the Jacobian matrix, while the subscripts l and g denote local and global derivatives, respectively. Of course, the terms in the Jacobian are known if we have used blending functions to define the patch. We previously assumed, in Equation (3.4.3), that

$$x(r,s) = \mathbf{H}(r,s) \ \mathbf{x}^e$$

and

$$\frac{\partial x}{\partial r} (r,s) = \frac{\partial \mathbf{H}}{\partial r} (r,s) \ \mathbf{x}^e \qquad (3.6.18)$$

and so on for y and for $\partial/\partial s$. For the preceding two-dimensional system,

$$|J| = (\frac{\partial x}{\partial r} \frac{\partial y}{\partial s} - \frac{\partial x}{\partial s} \frac{\partial y}{\partial r}). \qquad (3.6.19)$$

For a straight line along the x-axis, the one-dimensional form of this can be seen by inspection, namely,

$$\frac{\partial f}{\partial r} = \frac{\partial x}{\partial r} \frac{\partial f}{\partial x} \tag{3.6.20}$$

so

$$[J(r)] = \frac{\partial x}{\partial r} = |J(r)|. \tag{3.6.21}$$

Returning to typical integrals over flat curved areas, such as Equation (3.6.10), we can substitute Equation (3.6.14) to convert them to integrals in the local parametric coordinates:

$$\iint_{S^e} x \; dS = \iint_{S_p} x(r,s) \; |J(r,s)| \; dr \; ds \tag{3.6.22}$$

where S_p denotes the region in the parametric space that corresponds to (is mapped to) the physical region, S^e. That is, S_p is the unit triangle or unit square in the unit parametric coordinates. For the natural coordinates, $-1 \leq a, b \leq +1$, it could represent the 2 x 2 square.

Even if $|J|$ were constant, this integral could still be awkward to evaluate. We would like to automate this procedure and still obtain exact results. If our blending functions are polynomials, then we can still get exact results, in theory, by utilizing the Gaussian quadrature numerical integration procedure. All such procedures replace the integration over the parent space, S_p, by a summation over certain tabulated quadrature points. Thus,

$$\int_{-1}^{1} \int_{-1}^{1} x \; |J| \; dr \; ds = \sum_q x(r_q, s_q) \; |J(r_q, s_q)| W_q \tag{3.6.23}$$

where the points (r_q, s_q) and the weights W_q are tabulated in mathematical handbooks. The tabulated values depend on the type of parent space, S_p, and the type of integrand function. The Gauss rules can exactly integrate polynomials. Table 3.6.2 shows tabulated data for integrating polynomials in the natural coordinate square, whereas Table 3.6.3 shows similar data for polynomial integration on the unit triangle.

In conclusion, the exact volume of an object bounded by flat patches with curved edges can be obtained by extending Equation (3.6.6) as

$$V = \frac{1}{3} \sum_e [\sum_q \vec{R}^e(r_q, s_q) \cdot \vec{n}^e(r_q, s_q) \; |J^e(r_q, s_q)| W_q]. \tag{3.6.24}$$

Since these calculations depend heavily on the unit normal vector, we may wish to get an estimate of its accuracy. The integral identity

$$\iint_S \vec{n} \; dS = \vec{0} \tag{3.6.25}$$

may serve as a useful measure of potential error in the approximations.

TABLE 3.6.2 WEIGHTS AND ABSCISSAE
FOR NATURAL COORDINATE GAUSSIAN
QUADRATURE ON A QUADRILATERAL

$$\int_{-1}^{1} \int_{-1}^{1} f(r,s) \ dr \ ds \ = \ \sum_{i=1}^{n} f(r_i, s_i) W_i$$

n	i	r_i	s_i	w_i
1	1	0	0	4
4	1	$-\dfrac{1}{\sqrt{3}}$	$-\dfrac{1}{\sqrt{3}}$	1
	2	$+\dfrac{1}{\sqrt{3}}$	$-\dfrac{1}{\sqrt{3}}$	1
	3	$-\dfrac{1}{\sqrt{3}}$	$+\dfrac{1}{\sqrt{3}}$	1
	4	$+\dfrac{1}{\sqrt{3}}$	$+\dfrac{1}{\sqrt{3}}$	1
9	1	$-\sqrt{\dfrac{3}{5}}$	$-\sqrt{\dfrac{3}{5}}$	$\dfrac{25}{81}$
	2	0	$-\sqrt{\dfrac{3}{5}}$	$\dfrac{40}{81}$
	3	$+\sqrt{\dfrac{3}{5}}$	$-\sqrt{\dfrac{3}{5}}$	$\dfrac{25}{81}$
	4	$-\sqrt{\dfrac{3}{5}}$	0	$\dfrac{40}{81}$
	5	0	0	$\dfrac{64}{81}$
	6	$+\sqrt{\dfrac{3}{5}}$	0	$\dfrac{40}{81}$
	7	$-\sqrt{\dfrac{3}{5}}$	$+\sqrt{\dfrac{3}{5}}$	$\dfrac{25}{81}$
	8	0	$+\sqrt{\dfrac{3}{5}}$	$\dfrac{40}{81}$
	9	$+\sqrt{\dfrac{3}{5}}$	$+\sqrt{\dfrac{3}{5}}$	$\dfrac{25}{81}$

As an example, consider a solid brick (hexahedron) whose lengths parallel to the Cartesian axes are 2, 3, and 1 m each, as shown in Figure 3.6.1. We wish to compute its product of inertia,

$$I_{xy} = \iiint_{V} xy \ dV.$$

We can do this from Equation (3.6.1) by arbitrarily selecting

$$\vec{A} = \frac{1}{2} x^2 y \ \hat{i} \tag{3.6.26}$$

so that the surface product is

$$\vec{A} \cdot \vec{n} = \frac{1}{2} x^2 y \ n_x.$$

But for this object $n_x \equiv 0$ on four of the six faces. On the front face, $x = 2$ we have $n_x = +1$, whereas on the back face, $x = 0$, we have $n_x = -1$. But, on the latter face our product is zero because $x = 0$. Thus, only one of our six surface integrals is not zero.

TABLE 3.6.3 SYMMETRIC QUADRATURE
DATA FOR THE UNIT TRIANGLE

$$\int_0^1 \int_0^{1-r} f(r,s)\ dr\ ds\ =\ \sum_{i=1}^{n} f(r_i,\ s_i)w_i$$

n	p^*	i	r_i	s_i	w_i
1	1	1	$\frac{1}{3}$	$\frac{1}{3}$	$\frac{1}{2}$
3	2	1	$\frac{1}{6}$	$\frac{1}{6}$	$\frac{1}{6}$
		2	$\frac{2}{3}$	$\frac{1}{6}$	$\frac{1}{6}$
		3	$\frac{1}{6}$	$\frac{2}{3}$	$\frac{1}{6}$
	3	1	$\frac{1}{2}$	0	$\frac{1}{6}$
		2	$\frac{1}{2}$	$\frac{1}{2}$	$\frac{1}{6}$
		3	0	$\frac{1}{2}$	$\frac{1}{6}$
4	3	1	$\frac{1}{3}$	$\frac{1}{3}$	$\frac{-9}{32}$
		2	$\frac{3}{5}$	$\frac{1}{5}$	$\frac{25}{96}$
		3	$\frac{1}{5}$	$\frac{3}{5}$	$\frac{25}{96}$
		4	$\frac{1}{5}$	$\frac{1}{5}$	$\frac{25}{96}$
4	3	1	$\frac{1}{3}$	$\frac{1}{3}$	$\frac{-9}{32}$
		2	$\frac{11}{15}$	$\frac{2}{15}$	$\frac{25}{96}$
		3	$\frac{2}{15}$	$\frac{2}{15}$	$\frac{25}{96}$
		4	$\frac{2}{15}$	$\frac{11}{15}$	$\frac{25}{96}$
7	4	1	0	0	$\frac{1}{40}$
		2	$\frac{1}{2}$	0	$\frac{1}{15}$
		3	1	0	$\frac{1}{40}$
		4	$\frac{1}{2}$	$\frac{1}{2}$	$\frac{1}{15}$
		5	0	1	$\frac{1}{40}$
		6	0	$\frac{1}{2}$	$\frac{1}{15}$
		7	$\frac{1}{3}$	$\frac{1}{3}$	$\frac{9}{40}$

$^*p$ = degree of polynomial for exact integration

$$I_{xy} = \int\int_{S_{x=2}} \frac{1}{2}x^2 y\ n_x\ dS = +2 \int\int_{S_{x=2}} y\ dS. \tag{3.6.27}$$

We can see the answer by inspection, but we use numerical integration over triangular patches on that surface. We use two flat, straight triangular patches, as shown. Since

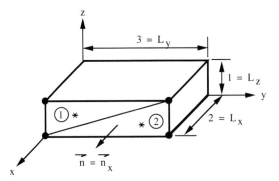

Figure 3.6.1   A model rectangular parallelepiped.

the integrand is linear we can employ a one-point quadrature rule and expect exact results. In the unit triangle coordinates of Table 3.6.2, the values are given as

$$r_q = \frac{1}{3}, \qquad s_q = \frac{1}{3}, \qquad W_q = \frac{1}{2}.$$

For flat, straight triangles it is easily shown that the determinant of the Jacobian is constant and equals twice the physical area of the triangle. Thus,

$$|J^e| = 2A^e$$

and the nonzero surface integral is

$$\iint_S y \, dS = \sum_{e=1}^{E} [\sum_{q=1}^{Q} y^e(r_q, s_q)W_q \mid J_q^e \mid]$$

$$= \sum_{e=1}^{2} A^e \, y^e(r_q, s_q) \tag{3.6.28}$$

where, from Equation (3.4.9),

$$y^e(r, s) = \mathbf{H}(r, s)\mathbf{Y}^e.$$

For the first and second patches in Figure 3.6.1, y_q takes on values of 1 and 2 m, respectively. Each patch has an area of $\frac{3}{2}$ m^2. Therefore, our numerical evaluation of the surface integral is

$$\iint_S y \, dS = (1 \, m)(\frac{3}{2} \, m^2) + (2 \, m)(3/2 \, m^2) = \frac{9}{2} \, m^3$$

and the final result is

$$I_{xy} = (+2 \, m^2)(\frac{9}{2} \, m^3) = 9 \, m^5$$

which is the exact result.

This same problem could also be solved directly by a volume integration over parametric solids. We could employ eight tetrahedra, two wedges, or a single hexahedron. The hexahedron would have the local natural coordinates (a, b, c) parallel to the physical axes (x, y, z) and they remain orthogonal. Here

$$x = \frac{L_x(1 + a)}{2}$$

$$y = \frac{L_y(1 + b)}{2}$$

$$z = \frac{L_z(1 + c)}{2}$$

so that

$$\frac{\partial x}{\partial a} = \frac{L_x}{2} = 1 \; m, \qquad \frac{\partial x}{\partial b} = \frac{\partial x}{\partial c} = 0$$

$$\frac{\partial y}{\partial b} = \frac{L_y}{2} = \frac{3}{2} \; m, \qquad \frac{\partial y}{\partial a} = \frac{\partial y}{\partial c} = 0$$

$$\frac{\partial z}{\partial c} = \frac{L_z}{2} = \frac{1}{2} \; m, \qquad \frac{\partial z}{\partial a} = \frac{\partial z}{\partial b} = 0.$$

Thus, in this special case the Jacobian will be constant. Generalizing Equation (3.6.16), the Jacobian is

$$\mathbf{J} = \frac{1}{2} \begin{bmatrix} 2 & 0 & 0 \\ 0 & 3 & 0 \\ 0 & 0 & 1 \end{bmatrix}, \qquad |\mathbf{J}| = \frac{3}{4} \; m^3.$$

If we employ a one point quadrature rule, the tabulated point is the local centroid $(0, 0, 0)$ and the weight is 8. Interpolating, the x y values at the centroid, from Table 3.5.1, are

$$x_q = 1 \; m, \qquad y_q = \frac{3}{2} \; m, \qquad z_q = \frac{1}{2} \; m$$

and the integral becomes

$$I_{xy} = \iiint_V xy \; dV$$

$$= \iiint_{abc} xy \; |J| \; da \; db \; dc$$

$$= \sum_q x_q \; y_q \; |J_q| \; W_q$$

$$= (1 \; m)(\frac{3}{2} \; m)(\frac{3}{4} \; m^3)(8)$$

$$= 9 \; m^5$$

as before. For a curvilinear solid, $|J|$ would be a variable, and thus 8 to 27 quadrature points could be needed for an accurate volume integral.

3.7 DIFFERENTIAL GEOMETRY

To employ nonflat parametric surfaces accurately for mechanical design purposes, it is necessary to utilize the subject of **differential geometry**. This is covered in texts on vector analysis or calculus. It is also an introductory topic in most books on the mechanics of thin shell structures. Here we cover most of the basic topics except for the detailed calculation of surface curvatures.

Every surface in a three-dimensional Cartesian coordinate system (x, y, z) may also be expressed by a pair of independent parametric coordinates (r, s) that lie on the surface. In our parametric form we have defined the x-coordinate as

$$x(r, s) = \mathbf{H}(r, s)\mathbf{x}^e \tag{3.7.1}$$

The y- and z-coordinates are defined similarly. The components of the **position vector** to a point on the surface

$$\vec{R}(r, s) = x(r, s)\hat{i} + y(r, s)\hat{j} + z(r, s)\hat{k}, \tag{3.7.2}$$

where $\hat{i}, \hat{j}, \hat{k}$ are the constant unit base vectors, could be written in array form as

$$\mathbf{R}^T = [x \ y \ z] = \mathbf{H}(r, s)[\mathbf{x}^e \ \mathbf{y}^e \ \mathbf{z}^e] \tag{3.7.3}$$

when we use our parametric blending definition of the surface. The local parameters (r, s) constitute a system of curvilinear coordinates for points on the physical surface. Equations (3.7.2) or (3.7.3) are called the parametric equations of a surface. If we eliminate the parameters (r, s) from Equation (3.7.2), we obtain the familiar implicit form of the equation of a surface, $f(x, y, z) = 0$. Likewise, any relation between r and s, say $g(r, s) = 0$, represents a curve on the physical surface.

In particular, if only one parameter varies while the other is constant, then the curve on the surface is called a **parametric curve**. Thus, the surface can be completely defined by a doubly infinite set of parametric curves, as shown in Figure 3.7.1. If we are going to direct a cutting tool across a surface or integrate over it to determine geometric properties, then we will need to know the relations between differential lengths, differential areas, tangent vectors, and the likes. To find these quantities we begin with differential changes in position on the surface. Since any parametric definition gives $\vec{R} = \vec{R}(r, s)$, we have

$$d\vec{R} = \frac{\partial \vec{R}}{\partial r} \, dr + \frac{\partial \vec{R}}{\partial s} \, ds \tag{3.7.4}$$

where $\partial \vec{R}/\partial r$ and $\partial \vec{R}/\partial s$ are the **tangent vectors** along the parametric curves. The physical distance, dl, associated with such a change in position on the surface is found from

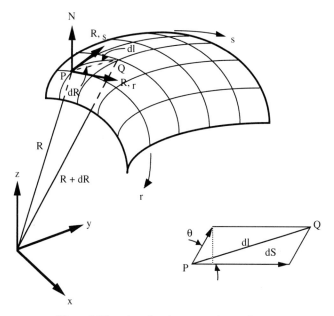

Figure 3.7.1   A surface in parametric coordinates.

$$(dl)^2 = dx^2 + dy^2 + dz^2 = d\vec{R} \cdot d\vec{R}. \tag{3.7.5}$$

From Equation (3.7.4) this gives three contributions from the parametric curves:

$$(dl)^2 = \left(\frac{\partial \vec{R}}{\partial r} \cdot \frac{\partial \vec{R}}{\partial r}\right) dr^2 + 2\left(\frac{\partial \vec{R}}{\partial r} \cdot \frac{\partial \vec{R}}{\partial s}\right) dr\ ds + \left(\frac{\partial \vec{R}}{\partial s} \cdot \frac{\partial \vec{R}}{\partial s}\right) ds^2.$$

In the common notation of differential geometry this is called the **first fundamental form** of a surface and is usually written as

$$(dl)^2 = E\ dr^2 + 2F\ dr\ ds + G\ ds^2 \tag{3.7.6}$$

where

$$E = \frac{\partial \vec{R}}{\partial r} \cdot \frac{\partial \vec{R}}{\partial r}$$

$$F = \frac{\partial \vec{R}}{\partial r} \cdot \frac{\partial \vec{R}}{\partial s} \tag{3.7.7}$$

$$G = \frac{\partial \vec{R}}{\partial s} \cdot \frac{\partial \vec{R}}{\partial s}$$

are called the first **fundamental magnitudes** (or metric tensor) of the surface. For future reference we will use Equation (3.7.7) to note that the magnitudes of the surface tangent vectors are

$$\left| \frac{\partial \vec{R}}{\partial r} \right| = \sqrt{E}$$

$$\left| \frac{\partial \vec{R}}{\partial s} \right| = \sqrt{G}.$$

Of course, these magnitudes can be expressed in terms of the parametric derivatives of the surface coordinates, (x, y, z). For example, from Equation (3.7.7),

$$F = \frac{\partial x}{\partial r} \frac{\partial x}{\partial s} + \frac{\partial y}{\partial r} \frac{\partial y}{\partial s} + \frac{\partial z}{\partial r} \frac{\partial z}{\partial s} \tag{3.7.8}$$

can be evaluated for a blended parametric surface by utilizing Equation (3.6.18). Define a surface gradient array given by

$$\mathbf{g} = \begin{bmatrix} \dfrac{\partial x}{\partial r} & \dfrac{\partial y}{\partial r} & \dfrac{\partial z}{\partial r} \\[2ex] \dfrac{\partial x}{\partial s} & \dfrac{\partial y}{\partial s} & \dfrac{\partial z}{\partial s} \end{bmatrix} \tag{3.7.9}$$

The rows contain the components of the tangent vectors along the parametric r and s curves, respectively. In the parametric blending notation of Equations (3.6.16) and (3.7.3), this becomes

$$\mathbf{g}(r, s) = [\partial_l R]$$

$$\mathbf{g} = [\partial_l \; \mathbf{H}(r, s)] \; [\mathbf{x}^e \; \mathbf{y}^e \; \mathbf{z}^e]. \tag{3.7.10}$$

In other words, the surface gradient array at any point is the product of the blending function derivatives evaluated at that point and the array of nodal data for the patch of interest. We define the **metric array, m**, as the product of the surface gradient with its transpose:

$$\mathbf{m} \equiv \mathbf{g} \; \mathbf{g}^T$$

$$\mathbf{m} = \begin{bmatrix} (x_{,r}^2 + y_{,r}^2 + z_{,r}^2) & (x_{,r}x_{,s} + y_{,r}y_{,s} + z_{,r}z_{,s}) \\ (x_{,r}x_{,s} + y_{,r}y_{,s} + z_{,r}z_{,s}) & (x_{,s}^2 + y_{,s}^2 + z_{,s}^2) \end{bmatrix} \tag{3.7.11}$$

where the subscripts denote partial derivatives with respect to the parametric coordinates. Comparing this relation with Equation (3.7.7) we note that

$$\mathbf{m} = \begin{bmatrix} E & F \\ F & G \end{bmatrix} \tag{3.7.12}$$

contains the fundamental magnitudes of the surface. This surface metric has a determinant that is always positive. It is useful in later calculations and is usually denoted in differential geometry as

$$| \mathbf{m} | \equiv H^2 = EG - F^2 > 0. \tag{3.7.13}$$

We can degenerate the differential length measure in Equation (3.7.6) to the common special case where we are moving along a parametric curve, that is, $dr = 0$ or $ds = 0$. In the first case of r = constant, we have

$$(dl)^2 = G \ ds^2$$

where dl is a physical differential length on the surface and ds is a differential change in the parametric surface. Then

$$dl = \sqrt{G} \ ds \qquad\qquad (3.7.14)$$

and for the parametric curve s = constant,

$$dl = \sqrt{E} \ dr. \qquad\qquad (3.7.15)$$

The quantities $\sqrt{G}$ and $\sqrt{E}$ are known as the **Lame parameters**. They convert differential changes in the parametric coordinates to differential lengths on the surface when moving on a parametric curve. This information is important when generating cutting tool paths, which usually use the relations in Equations (3.7.14) and (3.7.15). The concept of a CNC cutting tool path is illustrated in Figure 3.7.2. There the tool is moved to the initial position on the curved surface in such a way that it does not cut any other surfaces. Then it follows a series of local parametric paths that are converted to the actual physical cutting path by use of the blending functions for that patch. The selection of the local path depends on the size of the surface, the tool width, and the preceding relation between parametric lengths and physical lengths. This fundamental magnitude is used to select the spacing between the parametric paths.

From Figure 3.7.1 we note that the vector tangent to the parametric curves r and s are $\partial\vec{R}/\partial r$ and $\partial\vec{R}/\partial s$, respectively. While the parametric coordinates may be orthogonal, they generally will be nonorthogonal when displayed as parametric curves on the surface. The angle θ between the parametric curves on the surface can be found by using these tangent vectors and the definition of the dot product. Thus,

$$F \equiv \frac{\partial\vec{R}}{\partial r} \cdot \frac{\partial\vec{R}}{\partial s} = \sqrt{E} \ \sqrt{G} \ \cos\theta$$

and the angle at any point comes from

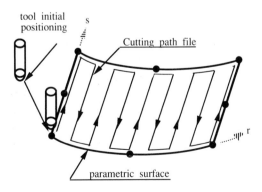

tool initial
positioning   s

Cutting path file

r

parametric surface

Figure 3.7.2   Cutting tool path on a parametric surface..

$$\cos\theta = \frac{F}{\sqrt{E}\ \sqrt{G}}.$$ (3.7.16)

Therefore, we see that the parametric curves form an orthogonal curvilinear coordinate system only when $F = 0$. Only in that case does Equation (3.7.6) reduce to the orthogonal form

$$(dl)^2 = E\ dr^2 + G\ ds^2.$$

Denote the parametric curve tangent vectors as $\vec{t}_r = \partial\vec{R}/\partial r$ and $\vec{t}_s = \partial\vec{R}/\partial s$. We have seen that the differential lengths in these two directions on the surface are $\sqrt{E}\ dr$ and $\sqrt{G}\ ds$. In a vector form those lengths are $\vec{t}_r dr$ and $\vec{t}_s ds$ and are separated by the angle θ. The corresponding differential surface area is the product

$$dS = (\sqrt{E}\ dr)(\sqrt{G}\ ds\ \sin\theta)$$
$$= \sqrt{E}\ \sqrt{G}\ \sin\theta\ dr\ ds.$$ (3.7.17)

By substituting the relation between $\cos\theta$ and the surface matrix, Equation (3.7.16), this simplifies to

$$dS = H\ dr\ ds.$$ (3.7.18)

We also note that this calculation can be expressed as a vector cross product of the tangent vectors:

$$dS\ \vec{N} = \vec{t}_r \times \vec{t}_s\ dr\ ds$$ (3.7.19)

where $\vec{N}$ is a vector normal to the surface. We also note that the **normal vector** has a magnitude of

$$|\vec{N}| = |\vec{t}_r \times \vec{t}_s| = H.$$ (3.7.20)

Sometimes it is useful to note that the components of $\vec{N}$ are

$$\vec{N} = (y_{,r}\ z_{,s} - y_{,s}\ z_{,r})\ \hat{i} + (x_{,r}\ z_{,s} - x_{,s}\ z_{,r})\hat{j} + (x_{,r}\ y_{,s} - x_{,s}\ y_{,r})\hat{k}.$$

We often want the unit vector, $\vec{n}$, normal to the surface. It is

$$\vec{n} = \frac{\vec{N}}{H} = \frac{\vec{t}_r \times \vec{t}_s}{|\vec{t}_r \times \vec{t}_s|}.$$ (3.7.21)

If we need to move a CNC milling tool in order to move the normal to the surface while following the cutting path, we would need to compute continuously the unit normal. An alternative is to interpolate parametrically the components of $\vec{n}$ between points on the cutting path. We also need the unit surface normal to compute surface lighting shades, to determine surface visibility, and so on. There are times when we need curvature data in the design or CAM process. For example, hypervelocity fluid flow over a body is quite sensitive to a lack of continuity in the surface curvature of the body. In another case a car designer may be concerned with unpleasing reflections off a surface due to its curvature. Thus, we will summarize some of the data about surface curvatures.

By combining derivatives of the zero dot products of the normal and tangent vectors, we can derive relations about the **principal radii of curvature**, ρ_1 and ρ_2. They involve the scalars

$$L = \frac{1}{H} \begin{vmatrix} x_{,rr} & y_{,rr} & z_{,rr} \\ x_{,r} & y_{,r} & z_{,r} \\ x_{,s} & y_{,s} & z_{,s} \end{vmatrix}$$

$$M = \frac{1}{H} \begin{vmatrix} x_{,rs} & y_{,rs} & z_{,rs} \\ x_{,r} & y_{,r} & z_{,r} \\ x_{,s} & y_{,s} & z_{,s} \end{vmatrix} \tag{3.7.22}$$

$$N = \frac{1}{H} \begin{vmatrix} x_{,ss} & y_{,ss} & z_{,ss} \\ x_{,r} & y_{,r} & z_{,r} \\ x_{,s} & y_{,s} & z_{,s} \end{vmatrix}$$

to define the **total curvature**, K,

$$K \equiv \frac{1}{\rho_1 \rho_2} = \frac{LN - M^2}{H^2}. \tag{3.7.23}$$

We define the surface at the point to the elliptic if the radii are of the same sign, $K > 0$, and hyperbolic if their signs are different, $K < 0$. It is parabolic when one or both of the principal curvatures is zero, $K = 0$. These three cases are illustrated in Figure 3.7.3. These second fundamental magnitudes also define the **mean** curvature of the surface

$$\frac{1}{\rho_1} + \frac{1}{\rho_2} = \frac{EN + GL - 2FM}{H^2}. \tag{3.7.24}$$

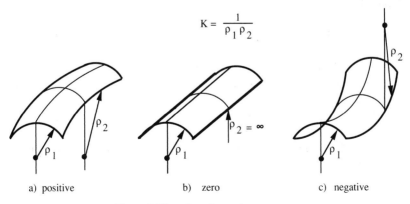

$$K = \frac{1}{\rho_1 \rho_2}$$

a) positive   b)   zero   c)   negative

Figure 3.7.3   Gaussian surface curvatures.

TABLE 3.7.1   QUANTITIES FOR DIFFERENTIAL GEOMETRY*

1. Position and tangent vectors

$$\mathbf{R} \quad, \quad \mathbf{R}_{,r} \quad, \quad \mathbf{R}_{,s} \quad, \quad \cos\theta_{rs} = F/\sqrt{EG}$$

$$E \equiv \mathbf{R}_{,r} \cdot \mathbf{R}_{,r}, \quad F \equiv \mathbf{R}_{,r} \cdot \mathbf{R}_{,s}, \quad G = \mathbf{R}_{,s} \cdot \mathbf{R}_{,s}$$

2. Arc lengths and surface area

$$dl = \sqrt{E}\ dr, \quad dl = \sqrt{G}\ ds, \quad dl^2 = E\ dr^2 + 2F\ dr\ ds + G\ ds^2$$

$$dA = H\ dr\ ds, \quad H^2 = EG - F^2$$

3. Normal vectors

$$\mathbf{N} = \mathbf{R}_{,r} \times \mathbf{R}_{,s}, \quad \mathbf{n} = \mathbf{N}/H$$

4. Curvatures

$$L \equiv \mathbf{R}_{,rr} \cdot \mathbf{N}, \quad M \equiv \mathbf{R}_{,rs} \cdot \mathbf{N}, \quad N = \mathbf{R}_{,ss} \cdot \mathbf{N}$$

$$(LN - M^2)\rho_n^2 - (EN + GL - 2FM)\rho_n + (EG - F^2) = 0$$

$$\frac{1}{\rho_1\rho_2} = \frac{LN - M^2}{EG - F^2} = K$$

$$\frac{1}{\rho_1} + \frac{1}{\rho_2} = \frac{EN + GL - 2FM}{EG - F^2}$$

* Commas denote partial differentiation

3.8 REFERENCES

1. Akin, J. E. *Application and Implementation of Finite Element Methods*, New York: Academic Press, 1982.

2. Akin, J. E. *Finite Element Analysis for Undergraduates*, New York: Academic Press, 1987.

3. Bezier, P. *Numerical Control: Mathematics and Applications*, New York: John Wiley, 1972.

4. Foley, J. D., and Van Dam, A. *Fundamentals of Interactive Computer Graphics*, Reading, Mass.: Addison-Wesley, 1983.

5. Struik, D. J. *Differential Geometry*, Reading, Mass.: Addison-Wesley, 1961.

3.9 EXERCISES

1. Verify the statement that the bilinear Lagrangian patch in Equations (3.4.3) and (3.4.4) is a quadrilateral with straight sides in physical space. Evaluate all four **H** on (a) $r = 0$, (b) $r = 1$, (c) $s = 0$, and (d) $s = 1$, and describe (x, y) on the edge.

2. Verify, from Equation (3.4.9), that the linear triangle is straight along the edge $r + s = 1$.

3. From Equation (3.4.10) verify that the quadratic triangle has a shape along edge $s = 0$ that is (a) a parabola through three points and (b) reduces to a straight line if $x_4 = \dfrac{(x_1 + x_2)}{2}$ and $y_4 = \dfrac{(y_1 + y_2)}{2}$.

4. Replace Equation (3.6.26) with the value from Table 3.6.1 and repeat the example product of inertia calculation.

5. Verify that the sum of the interpolation functions is unity at any parametric point for (a) the Q4 geometry in Table 3.4.2, and (b) the H8 geometry in Table 3.5.1.

6. For the tetrahedron given in Figure 3.5.1 and Equation (3.5.1), verify that its Jacobian matrix is constant and that its determinant is six times the physical volume.

7. For the straight-sided triangle given in Figure 3.5.1 and Equation (3.4.9), verify that its Jacobian matrix is constant and that its determinant is twice the physical area:

$$2A = [x_1(y_2 - y_3) + x_2(y_3 - y_1) + x_3(y_1 - y_2)].$$

8. A natural coordinate square parametric patch is mapped onto a flat rectangle in physical space. The rectangle has a width of B, and a height H and its sides are parallel to the xy axes. Verify that the Jacobian is constant and its determinant is one-fourth the physical area.

9. Repeat Exercise 8 if the base, B, of the rectangle makes an angle of θ with the x-axis.

10. How would Exercise 8 change if we employed unit coordinates instead of natural coordinates?

11. Solve Equation (3.6.28) for the solid face in Figure 3.6.1 using a single bilinear quadrilateral patch. Verify that in this rectangular form the Jacobian is constant and $|J| = \dfrac{A^e}{4}$. Employ the Gaussian quadrature data in Table 3.6.2 and use area integration by (a) a one-point rule, and (b) a four-point rule.

12. Evaluate Equation (3.3.18) for the quadratic fit in Equation (3.3.12).

4

SOLID MODELING

4.1 INTRODUCTION

Recent advances in software, computers, and graphical displays have made it possible to use true solid representations of components being considered in the design process. These solid models can be employed in numerous ways. At times the emphasis is on creating a realistic visual display by producing a shaded visible surface image of the solid. Other applications involve the motion of the component or its interference with other solids or surfaces. Data generation programs frequently accept the solid model data base as partial input for an analysis required as part of the design process. The most common example is automatic generation of a mesh for a finite element or finite difference analysis. The same programs often accept the results from the analysis program and display the results as contours or color levels on the surface of the solid. Thus, there is a lot of interest in solid modeling capabilities.

A solid modeling system is usually an interactive computer graphics system that is intended to create true three-dimensional components and assemblies. Once a part has been created, we have the ability to rotate, shade, section, or produce almost any view required by a designer. The algorithm should be able to ensure that it represents physically possible shape that is complete and unambiguous. Then the solid modeler provides the only data base suitable for all CAD/CAM operations. A continuing problem is how to make solid modelers user-friendly. It takes a significant amount of time to input a typical engineering component. Usually it takes much longer than the old graphical standard of defining three to six two-dimensional orthographic views of an object. Of course, once an object has been stored in the data base it can be combined with other parts, perturbed to create a new use, and so on.

104

Solid modeling allows a designer to see exactly what has been created. Modern engineering workstations have only recently provided the extensive memory size and processing power in a cost effective package that allows almost any designer to have access to the powerful design aid of solid modeling. Thus, it is no longer necessary to rely on a dense collection of lines and curves to represent the two-dimensional projection of an object. We can now actually see true shaded visible surface displays of the object and cut away sections of its interior. We can even make an object translucent to better see its internal components.

A goal behind solid modeling is to integrate all design, analysis, manufacturing, and documentation operations. Almost all information needed for part generation is contained in the solid model. Fabrication and manufacturing errors are significantly reduced if all the design engineers access the same current part description. It thus becomes important to restrict changes and revisions to the parts so that all design and manufacturing groups have the same model. Usually one person is given the authority to approve a recommended design change, release it to the data base, and inform the groups using that part design.

Part of the gap between two-and-a-half-dimensional and wireframe models and true solid modeling is filled by surface modeling, as described in the previous chapter. Surfaces work well in providing sophisticated images, shading, and mass properties. However, they do not provide a complete set of tools for constructing solid objects. For example, Boolean operations like checking for interfering parts or drilling holes are not included in surface models.

4.2 BOUNDARY REPRESENTATION

Several options are available for representing solids. There are classical analytical methods that cannot cope with realistic engineering geometries. In computer models the **wireframe** approach was one of the first methods employed. It has the advantage that it can be displayed faster than any other procedure. However, the resulting image can have a nonunique interpretation, as shown in Figure 4.2.1, and can become very cluttered if the component has a complex geometry. Today the two most common procedures for representing solid physical objects are **boundary representations** and solid constructive procedures. A boundary representation (BRep) can be thought of as a wireframe model with additional topological data that defines how the wireframe edges are connected to the enclosing surfaces. That is, the BRep consists of a list of all of the faces (surfaces), edges, and vertices on an object. These surfaces and edges are often defined by parametric geometry. The additional topological data are often viewed as a graph structure, as illustrated in Figure 4.2.2. Since they require surface topology data to enclose the solid, BRep methods are sometimes called surface representations. This surface concept is shown in Figure 4.2.3. Most BRep programs employ curved parametric surfaces, whereas a few utilize only a network of flat planar polygons. Some **tessellated modelers** employ only flat triangles and approximate curved surfaces with a large number of facets. When we used parametric surfaces in Chapter 3 we implied a topological structure when we numbered and drew (ordered) our nodal input points.

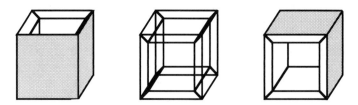

Figure 4.2.1   Wireframes are ambiguous.

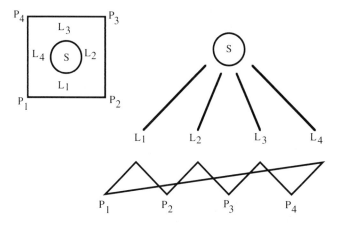

Figure 4.2.2   A graph representation of a surface.

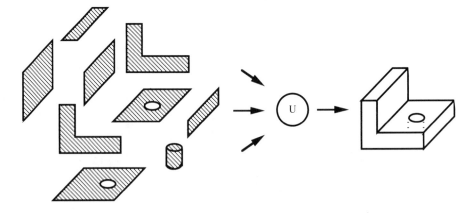

Figure 4.2.3   Boundary representation (BRep) of solids.

4.3 CONSTRUCTIVE SOLID GEOMETRY

The **constructive solid geometry** (CSG) representation utilizes a treelike data structure in which the leaves of the tree are simple **primitive solids**, such as half-spaces, blocks, or cylinders, and the nodes of the tree denote a **Boolean operation**. Thus, each node in the tree represents some intermediate object, while the root node represents the entire object. The Boolean operations applied to two objects, say A and B, are the intersection, the union, and the difference. They are defined as

Intersection, denoted by $C = A \cap B = B \cap A$, is the object, C, that contains all points that are common to both A and B.

Union, denoted by $C = A \cup B = B \cup A$, is the object, C, that contains all points originally in either A or B.

Difference, denoted by $C = A - B \neq B - A$, is the object, C, that remains when any points common to A and B are removed from A.

These basic definitions are illustrated in Figure 4.3.1. The concept of the CSG operation tree is shown in Figure 4.3.2 for the same object seen in Figure 4.2.3.

The CSG procedure employs the Boolean tree structure to describe which primitive shapes are used and how they are combined. The primitive solid typically include the half-space, block, cylinder, sphere, cone, torus, tetrahedron, and hexahedron. Some CSG systems include extruded solids or solids formed by placing a bounding "skin" over a series of cross sections that are placed along an arbitrary path.

Extruded or sweep primitives are formed by moving a given area along a curve while maintaining a given angle between the curve and the surface normal. Usually the paths are straight lines or circular arcs, but today parametric cubic paths are also

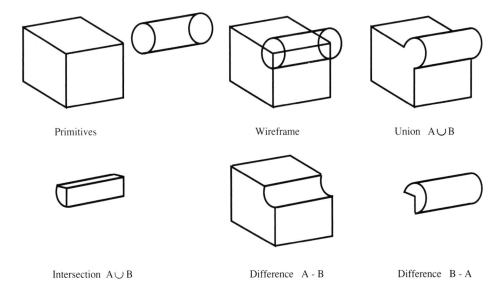

Primitives   Wireframe   Union A∪B

Intersection A∪B   Difference A - B   Difference B - A

Figure 4.3.1   Boolean operations on primitives.

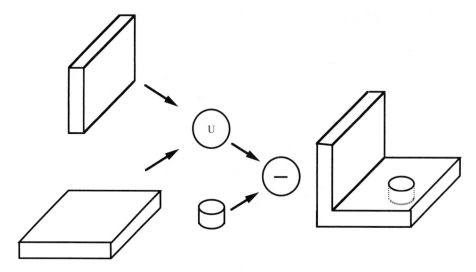

Figure 4.3.2   Constructive solid geometry (CSG) procedure.

common. Such solids are also called tabulated cylinders. Figure 4.3.3 shows two such
tabulated cylinders and the solid formed by gluing them together (taking their union).
The CSG primitives are positioned, orientated, and combined or removed in a building-
block fashion. A new part is created by the proper Boolean logic operation. Figure
4.3.4 shows a typical complicated piston constructed in this fashion. In some cases a
macro or parametric dimension is used in the definition. Later the designer can input a
specific value for one or more of the parametric dimensions to create several physical
models from one solid model. For example, the connecting rod and piston for a small
lawn mower or a large truck engine could come from a common parametric solid
model.

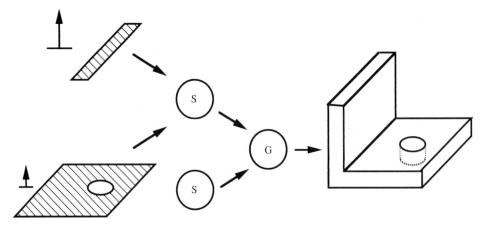

Figure 4.3.3   Solid generated by sweep and glue.

We can also create and store other primitive models by Boolean operations, as shown in Figure 4.3.5. These parts can be given names and retrieved at a later time for use in increasing the speed and ease of construction of other parts. Building such a library of parts or operations common to a particular industry is one way to significantly increase productivity by computer assisted design.

Today the trend seems to be toward using the CSG approach to input or generating an initial solid model. This is because the use of Boolean operations with simple primitives, like drill bits or milling tools, is the way that many components are actually constructed. However, there are more things of interest than simply defining an object. For example, we may need to calculate volume properties, mass properties, visible surfaces, normals to the surface, or surface curvatures. Some of these operations are best suited to BRep procedures, whereas others may be more efficient in CSG or in a third completely different formulation. Thus, a practical solid modeller may actually contain both the BRep and the CSG options. In some cases the data base is converted from one form to another as the result of a user selecting to execute some particular option. Usually these conversions are hidden from the user. The part resulting from a Boolean operation, or a series of operations, can be given a name and stored for later use. Thus,

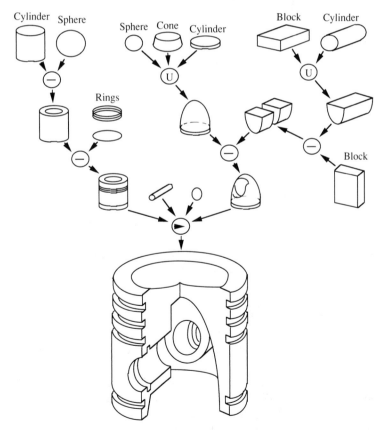

Figure 4.3.4   Boolean CSG tree for a piston.

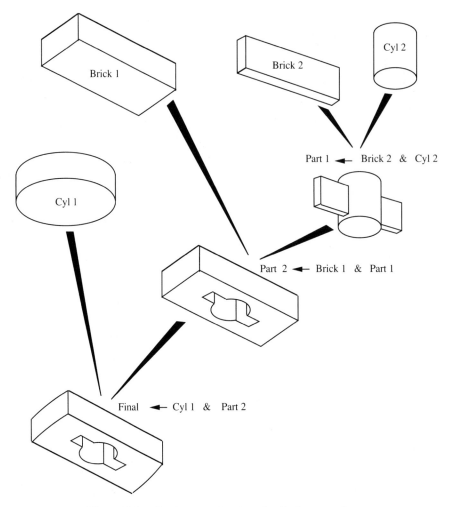

Figure 4.3.5   Naming new primatives after Boolean operations.

its construction tree can be used to start a new part or to be combined with another part. Figure 4.3.5 shows several parts named by combining previous parts.

4.4 OPERATIONS ON CELLS

An early approach to solid modeling was to divide the space into a uniform grid of cells and to locate the object in the space. Then the object was approximated by those cells that lay inside the object. The cells were identical and thus, their local geometric properties were identical. It is relatively simple to operate on such an approximation. For example, to calculate the area we simply counted the number of inside cells and multiplied that number by the area of a typical cell, A_c:

$$A = \sum_{i=1}^{n} A_i = n \ A_c \, .$$

Likewise, we could use the composite area theorem to calculate the centroid

$$\bar{x}A = \int x \ dA = \sum_{i=1}^{n} \bar{x}_i \ A_i = A_c \sum_{i=1}^{n} \bar{x}_i$$

where the centroid of a typical cell is directly related to the subscripts locating the cell. Other properties are approximated in a similar fashion. This is illustrated in two dimensions in Figure 4.4.1, where each cell has a unit length and area. These two objects are defined by the uniform square cells and their areas are displayed. In three dimensions the cells are identical cubes often called **voxels**.

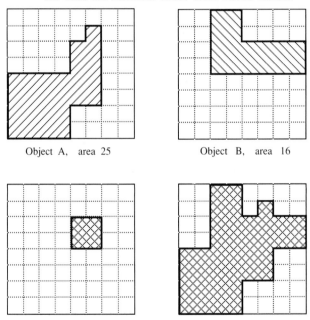

Object A,   area 25

Object B,   area 16

C = A ∩ B,   area 4

D = A ∪ B,   area 37

Figure 4.4.1   Uniform cell Boolean operations.

Boolean operations are also made simple by the use of uniform cells, as shown in the same figure. For example, to find the intersection of A and B we scan over the cells of grid A. If a cell is inside A, then we check the corresponding cell in grid B. If it is occupied by B, then the two objects intersect at that cell and we can flag that occurrence in a new grid for that operation. Similar procedures are employed for the union and difference operators. The same concepts work on three-dimensional cells as well.

This approach is somewhat wasteful, since many of the grid cells may be empty. For geometric calculations we need only one grid, but for Boolean operations we need at least three for each active pair of objects. This approach also employs uniform accuracy everywhere. For common engineering shapes the boundaries will not match a course grid, and we would like a finer resolution on the edges and a coarser one on the interior.

This observation leads to an organization structure that has several levels. Each cell level is a factor of two smaller, in each spatial dimension, than the parent cell from which it was obtained. The structures for representing these forms in one dimension, two dimensions, and three dimensions are called bintrees, quadtrees, and octrees, respectively. Figure 4.4.2 shows this concept for the same objects used in the previous figure. We begin with a single cell that completely encloses the object. This cell will be partially filled by the object. Thus, to get more detail we divide it into four equal cells. If one of these cells is completely full or empty, we note that information and stop its division. A partially occupied cell is flagged for additional division. This continues until all cells have stopped dividing (are full or empty) or until we reach the final level of division. The latter limit is usually governed by the word length of the computer or by the amount of available storage. The preceding three cell options are also

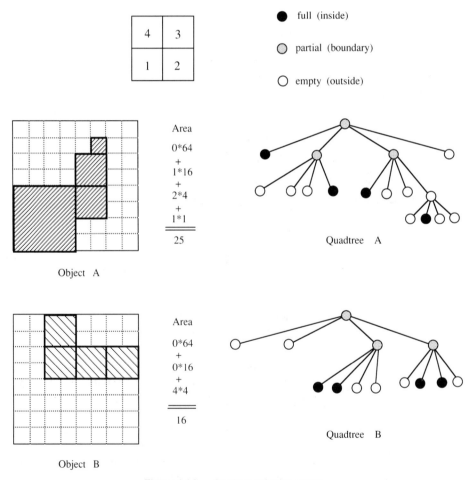

Figure 4.4.2   Quadtree objective models.

referred to as inside, outside, and boundary cells, or as black, white, and gray cells. This alternate procedure of tree division can give much more accurate boundary resolutions than a uniform grid. For example, an octree with 32 levels of division and a cell width of 0.001 in. at the bottom level would contain more than 300,000 cubic miles in the original cell. The original cell would be more than 67 mi long on each edge.

Figure 4.4.2 shows the node structure of the quadtrees. The nodes are full, empty, or partly filled (inside, outside, or boundary). In that figure the smallest cell is $2^0 = 1$ unit on each side, whereas the original cell is $2^3 = 8$ units on a side. To find the area of the object we sum the contributions from each level. The area at each level is the product of the number of completely full cells (inside cells) and the area of a typical cell, $2^m \times 2^m$. These calculations are shown in the figure.

The Boolean set operations are performed by simultaneously traversing two trees while generating a third one. Nodes examined at a common tree level represent the same region of space. Boolean operations on the tree nodes are like the operations on cells in the previous uniform cell structure. This is illustrated in Figure 4.4.3.

Once a tree structure has been completed, it is simple to determine if a specified point is interior or exterior to an object or on its surface. This fundamental test is often needed when processing a solid. The answer is obtained by traversing down the tree by always selecting the branch that contains the coordinates of the point. When the final leaf node is reached its type (e.g., inside or outside) specifies the status of the point. If

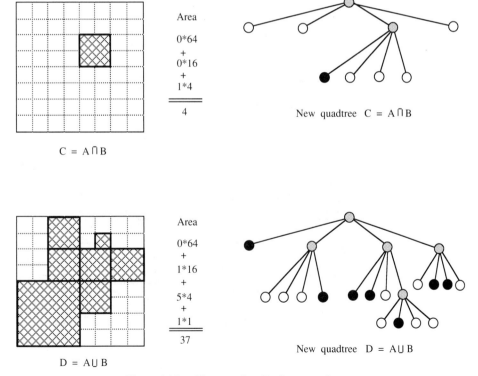

Figure 4.4.3   New trees from Boolean operations.

it is a partially full, or boundary cell, then we can consider the point to be on the surface, within a tolerance equal to the cell size.

Regardless of how small the cells are, most practical shapes will still have some cells that are only partially filled by the object. These are the boundary (partial) cells. The others are either full (inside) or empty (outside) cells. Algorithms have been developed that count these partial cells to arrive at the perimeter (or surface area) of the object. Since the object boundary can fall exactly on a cell boundary, the perimeter calculation should also check for full cells adjacent to one or more empty cells. These concepts are shown in Figure 4.4.4 for both uniform and hierarchical cell structures. The extension of the above concepts to octrees for solids is illustrated in Figure 4.4.5. Figure 4.4.6 shows how the volume and centroid calculations proceed.

The cells used in a solid modeler often have potential use in a finite element or finite difference analysis. The trend is toward having the quadtree or octree automatically generate an FEA mesh. The partial cells offer a significant challenge if we are also generating a mesh. We must decide how to place elements in these cells in a way that avoids badly distorted elements. There are limits on the ratio of long to short sides (aspect ratio) and the corner angles of these elements. The inside cells are often identical for homogeneous linear analysis problems. The element matrices of the smaller cells can be obtained by multiplying that of the parent by a constant. This economy results from the fact that the parent has a constant Jacobian. The application of quadtree structures for automatic finite element mesh generation is illustrated in Figure 4.4.7.

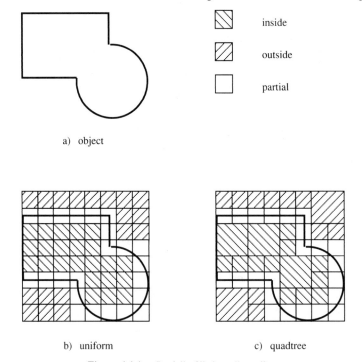

a) object

inside

outside

partial

b) uniform   c) quadtree

Figure 4.4.4   Partially filled smaller cells.

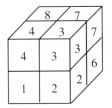

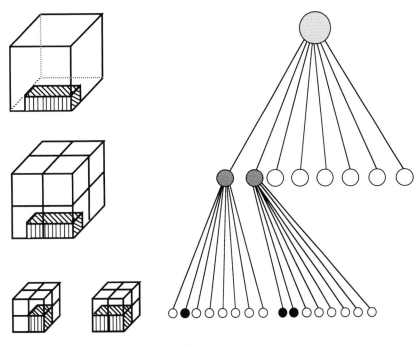

Figure 4.4.5   A sample octree.

The bottom level of the tree can be modified to give nonstandard cells in order to generate elements that exactly lie on the perimeter of the original object.

4.5 REFERENCES

1. Allen, G. "An Introduction to Solid Modeling" *Computer Graphics World* 11 (1982): 32–38.

2. Boyse, J. W., and Gilchrist, J. E. "GM Solid: Interactive Modeling for Design and Analysis of Solids," *Computer Graphics and Applications* (March 1982) 27–42, March, 1982.

3. Brown, C. M. "PADL-2: A Technical Summary," *Computer Graphics and Applications,* (March 1982): 69–85.

4. Brunet, P., and Navazo, I. "Geometric Modelling Using Exact Octree Representation of Polyhedral Objects," In *Eurographics 85*, C. E. Vandoni, (ed.), Elsevier Science Pub., 1985, 159–69.

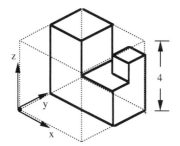

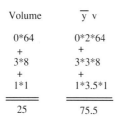

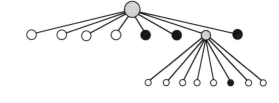

Volume	$\overline{y}$ v
0*64	0*2*64
+	+
3*8	3*3*8
+	+
1*1	1*3.5*1
25	75.5

$$\overline{y} = 75.5 / 25 = 3.02$$

Figure 4.4.6   Centroid calculations with an octree.

5. Krouse, J. K. "Sorting Out the Solid Modelers," *Machine Design* 55 (February 10, 1983): 94–101.

6. Meagher, D. J. "A New Mathematics for Solids Processing," *Computer Graphics World* (October 1984): 75–88

7. Requicha, A. A. G., and Voelcker, H. B. "Solid Modeling: A Historical Summary and Contemporary Assessment," *Computer Graphics and Applications* 2 no. 3 (March 1982): 9–26.

8. Sharpe, R. J., Thomas, P. J., and Thorne, R. W. "Constructive Geometry in Three Dimensions for Computer Aided Design," *J. Mechanical Design* ASME 104, no. 4, (October 1982): 813–16.

9. Shneier, M. "Calculations of Geometric Properties Using Quadtrees," *Computer Graphics and Image Processing* 16 (1981): 296–302.

10. Yerry, M. A., and Shephard, M. S. "A Modified Quadtree Approach to Finite Element Mesh Generation," *IEEE Computer Graphics and Applications* 3, no. 1 (January 1983): 39–46.

11. Yerry, M. A., and Shephard, M. S. "Automatic Three Dimensional Mesh Generation by the Modified Octree Technique," *Intern. J. for Num. Mech. Engr.* 20 (1984): 1965–90.

4.6 EXERCISES

1. List the CSG tree of Boolean operations used to form the Final part in Figure 4.3.5.

2. For the objects A and B shown in Figure 4.4.2, develop the quadtree, compute the area, and sketch the object formed as (a) $C = A - B$, and (b) $D = B - A$.

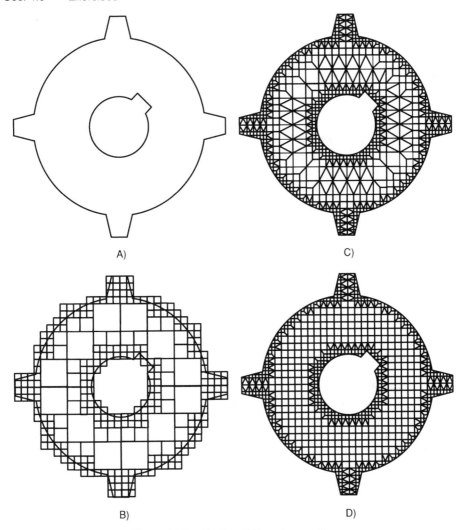

Figure 4.4.7   Quadtree FEA mesh generation.

3. Compute the first moment, $\overline{X}A$, for object B in Figs. 4.4.1 and 4.4.2. Use both the uniform cell method and quadtree method.

4. Compute the centroid, $\overline{X}$, $\overline{Y}$, and $\overline{Z}$, for the solid shown in Figure 4.4.6.

5. For fluid flow models we are often interested in the domain external to a solid. An interior quadtree is converted to an exterior one by filling the completely empty cells and voiding the full ones. Sketch the exterior domain and create its quadtree or octree for the objects in (a) Figure 4.4.2, (b) Figure 4.4.3, and (c) Figure 4.4.6.

6. For uniform mesh generation we can refine upper full cells to the size of the bottom cell. Extend the quadtree of object D in Figure 4.4.3 to create a uniform mesh.

7. Let the largest parent cell (level 0) have a side length of $L = 1$. Determine the side length and area ratios in a cell in a quadtree at level 1, 2, 4, 8, and 16.

5

FINITE ELEMENT ANALYSIS

5.1 INTRODUCTION

In modern mechanical design it is rare to find a project that does not require some type of finite element analysis (FEA). When not actually required, FEA can usually be utilized to improve a design. The practical advantages of FEA in stress analysis and structural dynamics have made it the accepted design tool for the last decade. It is also heavily employed in thermal analysis, especially in connection with thermal stress analysis.

Clearly the greatest advantage of FEA is its ability to handle truly arbitrary geometry. Probably the next important feature is the ability to include nonhomogeneous materials. These two features alone mean that we can treat systems of arbitrary shape that are made up of numerous different material regions. Each material could have constant properties or the properties could vary with spatial location. To these very desirable features we can add a large amount of freedom in prescribing the loading conditions, support conditions, and the postprocessing items such as the stresses and strains. For elliptical boundary value problems the FEA procedures offer significant computational and storage efficiencies that further enhance its use. These classes of problems include stress analysis, heat conduction, electrical fields, magnetic fields, ideal fluid flow, etc. FEA also gives us an important solution technique for other problem classes such as the nonlinear Navier-Stokes equations for fluid dynamics.

There are several good texts on the theory, application, and computational aspects of FEA. Here we will show what FEA has to offer the designer and illustrate some of its one-dimensional theoretical formulations. The modern mechanical designer should study finite element methods in more detail than we can consider here. It still is an active area of research. The current trends are toward automatic adaptive FEA procedures that give the maximum accuracy for the minimum computational cost. This is also closely tied to shape modification and optimization procedures.

5.2 CAPABILITIES OF FEA

There are several commercial and public-domain finite element systems that are available to the mechanical designer. To summarize the typical capabilities, several of the most widely used software systems have been compared to identify what they have in common. Often we find about 90% of the options are available in all the systems. Some offer very specialized capabilities such as aeroelastic flutter or hydroelastic lubrication. The mainstream capabilities to be listed here are found to be included in the majority of the commercial systems of ABACUS, ANSYS, MARC, NASTRAN, PAFEC, and SUPERB. Most of these systems are available on engineering workstations and personal computers as well as mainframes and supercomputers.

To conserve space the most important capabilities have been broken into 10 subject areas or classes. First we begin with the general capabilities of most FEA systems:

Free format input	Cyclic symmetry
Interface to CAD system	Equation renumbering
Mesh generation	Restart capability
Passive graphics	Generalized constraints
Interactive graphics	User supplied subroutines
Static structural analysis	Stress file editor
Natural frequencies and modes	Optimization interface
Direct dynamic response	Nonlinear dynamics
Modal superposition dynamics	Creep
Steady state heat transfer	Plasticity
Transient heat transfer	Buckling
Mass properties	Large deflections
Substructures	

The extent of the usefulness of a FEA system is directly related to the extent of its element library. The typical elements found within a single system usually include the following types:

Springs, masses, dashpots	Axisymmetric
Beams, bars, lines	Solids
Membranes	Shells
Linear	Nonsymmetric loads

Quadratic	Solid Elements
Cubic	Wedges
Laminated	Hexahedron
Plates	Tetrahedra
Thick	Transition
Thin	Others
Sandwich	Gaps
Shells	Crack tip
Thick	User-defined
Thin˙	
Sandwich	
Curved	

In the finite element method, the boundary and interior of the region are subdivided by lines (or surfaces) into a finite number of discrete sized subregions or finite elements. A number of nodal points are established with the mesh. These nodal points can lie anywhere along, or inside, the subdividing mesh, but they are usually located at intersecting mesh lines (or surfaces). The elements may have straight boundaries and thus, some geometric approximations will be introduced in the geometric idealization if the actual region of interest has curvilinear boundaries.

The nodal points and elements are assigned identifying integer numbers beginning with unity and ranging to some maximum value. The assignment of the nodal numbers and element numbers will have a significant effect on the solution time and storage requirements. The analyst assigns a number of generalized degrees of freedom to each and every node. These are the unknown nodal parameters that have been chosen by the analyst to govern the formulation of the problem of interest. Common nodal parameters are displacement components, temperatures, and velocity components. The nodal parameters do not have to have a physical meaning, although they usually do. This idealization procedure defines the total number of degrees of freedom associated with a typical node, a typical element, and the total system. Data must be supplied to define the spatial coordinates of each nodal point. It is common to associate an integer code to each node to indicate which, if any, of the nodal parameters at the node have boundary constraints specified.

Another important concept is that of **element connectivity**, i.e., the list of global node numbers that are attached to an element. The element connectivity data defines the topology of the mesh, which is used, in turn, to assemble the system algebraic equations. Thus, for each element it is necessary to input, in some consistent order, the node numbers that are associated with that particular element. The list of node numbers connected to a particular element is usually referred to as the element incident list for that element. We usually also associate an integer material code with each element.

Finite element analysis can require very large amounts of input data. Thus, most FEA systems, and some CAD systems, offer the user significant data generation or supplementation capabilities. The common generation and validation options include

Construction data	Replication
Points	Nodes
Lines	Elements
Arcs	Drag copies
Parametric blocks	Mirror copies
Element generation	Data validation
Mass points	Unconnected nodes
1-D Lines, bars, beams	Unconnected elements
2-D Solids	Aspect ratios
3-D Solids	Corner angles
Shells	Coincident nodes
Axisymmetric solids	Edge curvature
Data supplementation	Shell planarity
Data gap filling	Local axes
Incremental additions	For geometry input
Restraint generation	For force input
Points	For displacement output
Lines	Coordinates
Planes	Cartesian
Load generation	Cylindrical
Forces at points	Spherical
Line pressures	Edits
Surface pressures	Material properties
Acceleration loads	Coordinates
Heat flux	Boundary conditions
Temperature distribution	Load conditions
Swelling loads	Element topology

The verification of such extensive amounts of input and generated data is greatly enhanced by the use of computer graphics. The common interactive and batch graphics capabilities let the designer display

Nodes	Mesh information
Add, delete	Node numbers
Label	Node points
List coordinates	Element numbers
Change coordinates	Front order
Replicate	Property number
Elements	DOF vectors
Add, delete	Load vectors
Label	Line pressure
Display topology	Surface pressure
Modify topology	Restraint vectors
Select type or range	Axes used

Generate from blocks   Dynamic masters
Replicate   Plot limits
Rotations   By element group
   Screen axes   By element types
   Model axes   Elements inside region
   User-selected axes   Nodes inside region
   Line in space   Elements outside region
Views   Nodes outside region
   Perspective   By surface intersection
   Windows   View control
   Zoom   Given eye point
   Sections   From axis direction
   Boundary only   Perspective
   Visible surface   Hidden line removal
   Element groups   Multiple windows
Mesh plots
   Exploded elements
   Boundaries only
   Parametric blocks

Once an analysis or optimization procedure has been completed, an even larger amount of output data is generated. For example, the stress output alone can be very large. In addition to the six stress components, we compute the three principal stresses, the maximum shear stress, the Von Mises effective stress, various failure criterion, and so on. All these quantities are output at 1 to 30 points in each of thousands of elements. Thus, stress file editors are often provided to allow the designer to extract such data selectively. Most of the output options from an FEA system are available in graphical form. The most common are batch and/or interactive displays of

Graphs versus position   Contours
   Displacements   Temperatures
   Stress components   Maximum stress
   Principal stresses   Minimum stress
   Temperatures   Von Mises stress
   Failure criterion   Hoop stress
Mesh plots   Vector plots
   Displacement contours   Principal stress vectors
   Stress contours   Hoop stress
   Temperature contours   Displacement components
   Carpet plots   Heat flux
   Failure codes   Response plots
   Temperature versus time   Force versus time
   Displacement versus time   Displacement versus time
   Dynamic master points   Velocity versus time

Shape plotting
    Undeformed
    Deformed
    Mode shapes
    Mode animation
    At selected time

Acceleration versus time
Force versus frequency
Displacement versus frequency
Velocity versus frequency
Acceleration versus frequency
FFT response

The most commonly needed information in the design process is the state of stresses and displacements. Thus, almost every system offers linear static stress analysis capabilities for

Load conditions
    Nodal loads
    Pressure loads
    Gravity loads
    Thermal loads
    Swelling loads
    Centrifugal loads
    Load combinations
    Fourier harmonic loads
Support conditions
    Zero displacements
    Given displacements
    Rigid links
    Sliding interface
    Generalized constraint
    Local DOF directions
    Gaps

Material options
    Isotropic
    Orthotropic
    Anisotropic
    Temperature dependent
    Laminated
Output
    Mass properties
    Displacements
Reactions
    Stresses
    Strains
    Element forces
    Strain energy density
    Stress file editor
    Failure criterion

Linear thermal analysis capabilities for conduction and convection are often needed to provide temperature distributions for thermal stress analysis. Usually the same mesh geometry is used for the temperature analysis and the thermal stress analysis. The typical thermal analysis capabilities are

Type of analysis
    Steady-state
    Transient
    Nonlinear
    Anisotropic
Boundary conditions
    Temperature
    Temperature versus time
    Nodal flux
    Nodal flux versus time
    Convection

Initial conditions
    Uniform
    Arbitrary distribution
    Steady-state solution
Output
    Temperatures
    Reaction flux
    Nodal flux values
    Data for thermal stress
    Temperature contours
    Temperature versus path

Radiation   Temperature versus time
Thermal mass

Of course, some designs require information on the natural frequencies of vibration or the response to dynamic forces or the effect of frequency-driven excitations. Thus, dynamic analysis options are usually available. An FEA system typically offers

Type of analysis   Output
   Natural frequencies   Forces versus time
   Direct time integration   Displacements versus time
   Frequency dependent   Velocity versus time
   Nonlinear transient   Acceleration versus time
   Response spectra   Stresses versus time
Capabilities   Energy versus time
   Manual masters   Displacement versus frequency
   Automatic masters   Velocity versus frequency
   Mass elements   Acceleration versus frequency
   Discrete damping   Energy versus frequency
   Flexibility input
Damping
   Modal damping
   Mass proportional
   Stiffness proportion

Today efficient utilization of materials in the design processes often requires us to employ nonlinear material properties and/or nonlinear equations. Such resources require a more experienced and sophisticated user. The usual nonlinear stress analysis features in FEA systems include

Buckling   Element library, nonlinear
Creep   Springs
Large deflection   Dashpots
Plasticity   Beams, bars
Creep-plasticity   Axisymmetric solids
Method of solution   2-D solids
   Variable stiffness   3-D solids
   Initial stress   Shells
   Prandtl-Reuss flow

Mechanical design may also require the use of **computational fluid dynamics** (CFD). There are a small number of FEA systems that offer such analysis and design aids. For example, the FIDAP product for CFD FEA offers numerous practical incompressible flow features, such as

Isothermal Newtonian and non-Newtonian flows

Free, forced, or mixed convection

Flows in saturated porous media

Advection-diffusion problems

Periodic, separating, or recirculating flows

Swirling flows

Creeping flows

Flows with a free surface

Surface tension gradient-driven thermal flows

Solid-fluid phase change

There are certain features of finite element systems that are so important from a practical point of view that, essentially, we cannot get along without them. Basically we have the ability to handle completely arbitrary geometries, which is essential to practical engineering work. Almost all the structural analysis, whether static, dynamic, linear or nonlinear is done by finite element techniques on large problems. The other abilities provide a lot of flexibility in specifying loading and restraints (support capabilities). Typically, we will have several different materials at different arbitrary locations within an object and we automatically have the capability to handle these nonhomogeneous materials. Just as importantly, the boundary conditions that attach one material to another are automatic, and we don't have to do anything to describe them unless it is possible for gaps to open between materials. With other formulations, like finite difference techniques, we would have to supply special difference equations to invoke certain levels of compatibility across material interfaces. Most important, or practical, engineering components are made up of more than one material, and we need an easy way to handle that. What takes place less often is the fact that we have **anisotropic materials** (one whose properties vary with direction, instead of being the same in all directions). There is a great wealth of materials that have this behavior, although at the undergraduate level, anisotropic materials are rarely mentioned. Usually we give one modulus of elasticity and one Poisson's ratio, but for anisotropic materials we require a minimum of two moduli of elasticity, a shear modulus, and at least one Poisson's ratio (usually more). Many materials, such as reinforced concrete, plywood, any filament-wound material, and composite materials, are essentially anisotropic. Likewise, for heat-transfer problems, we will have thermal conductivities that are directionally dependent and, therefore, we would have to enter two or three thermal conductivities that indicate how this material is directionally dependent. Thus, these things mean that for practical use in design, finite element analysis is very important to us. It can be applied to other areas in addition to structural analysis, heat transfer, and fluid mechanics. It can be used to solve any sort of differential equations, including nonlinear problems such as the Navier-Stokes equations for fluids.

The biggest disadvantage of the finite element method is that it has so much power there is the potential that large amounts of data and computation will be required. On small problems with about two thousand unknowns, many personal computers are available that can run an FEA system. For moderate problems with 10,000 to 15,000 equations, we need an engineering workstation or superminicomputer. Above 15,000 to 20,000 unknowns, we usually need to use a mainframe. A supercomputer or mini-supercomputer is necessary when we have more than 100,000 unknowns. All these systems should provide access to good graphical displays. Nodes or grid points must be supplied to the FEA systems. A program will require several hundreds or thousands of these grid points. Grid points will be needed for certain major geometrical points, such as the control points on a parametric patch, for further division and mesh generation, and points describing the material interface locations. A large number of these sorts of activities require us to give node information. We must be able to describe the loads or forcing data. The designer will need point loads or couples, gravity, line loads or pressures, and so on. With three-dimensional solids, we must describe surfaces on which a pressure is applied. We must select a minimum number of points that are going to either describe that surface or describe some parametric patch that can be used for a surface with pressure. If interested in heat transfer we would have heat sources such as a point heat flux, a line of flux, a surface with a given heat flux, or a given convection data associated with it. Nodal information is necessary in order to be able to describe those data. These sort of data may not be convenient to input in a Cartesian coordinate system, so you might want to use different sets of axes to describe the data. It is common to need to use multiple axes for inputting either the loads, the geometry, the restraints, or all of those. There are different types of axes available. It is possible to have multiple sets of coordinate axes that are located and rotated in space for locations of the user's convenience. In addition to describing this geometry and trying to define how we are loading or forcing a system, we also have to give the geometrical data on the constraint, or support information. Restraint points have a known displacement, rotation or, in the temperature problem, temperature. Likewise, we are going to have lines or surfaces of applied constraints. Typically the user wants to minimize the input of this information. Originally, programs required the user to describe all those data for every point in the space. Today, parametric patches, or mapping domains, need to be defined for use with the mesh generation. Control points and interior subdivision information need to be given. These will describe quadratic or cubic patches to be used to generate the nodes, elements, forces, and supports.

All components employed in a design are three-dimensional but several common special cases have been defined that allow two-dimensional stress analysis studies to provide useful design procedures. The most common are the states of **plane stress** (covered in undergraduate mechanics of materials) and **plane strain**, the **axisymmetric solid** model, the **thin-plate** model, and the **thin-shell** model. The latter is defined in terms of two parametric surface coordinates even though the shell exists in three dimensions. The **thin beam** can be thought of as a degenerate case of the thin-plate model.

The states of **plane stress** and **plane strain** are interesting and useful examples of stress analysis of a two-dimensional elastic solid (in the xy-plane). These two states are illustrated in Figure 5.2.1. It is necessary to define all unknown quantities in terms of the displacements of the solid. Specifically, it is necessary to relate the strains and stresses to the displacements. Our notation will follow that commonly used in mechanics of materials. The displacements components parallel to the x- and y-axes are denoted by $u(x,y)$ and $v(x,y)$, respectively. The shear stress acting parallel to the

x- and y-axes are σ_x and σ_y, respectively. The shear stress acting parallel to the y-axis on a plane normal to the x-axis is τ_{xy}, or simply τ. The corresponding components of strain are ε_x, ε_y, and γ_{xy}, or simply γ. Figure 5.2.2 summarizes this notation. The assumption of plane stress implies that the component of all stresses normal to the plane are zero ($\sigma_z = \tau_{zx} = \tau_{zy} = 0$), whereas the plane strain assumption implies that the normal components of the strains are zero ($\varepsilon_z = \gamma_{zx} = \gamma_{zy} = 0$). The state of plane stress is commonly introduced in the first course of mechanics of materials. It was also the subject of some of the earliest finite element studies.

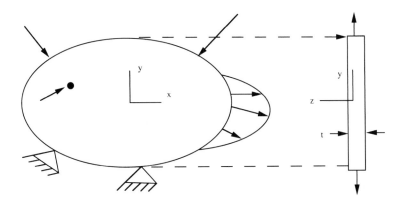

a) A plane stress solid

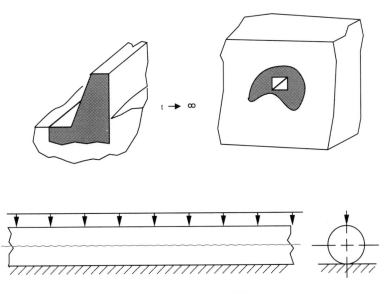

b) Common plane strain solids

Figure 5.2.1   The states of plane stress and plane strain.

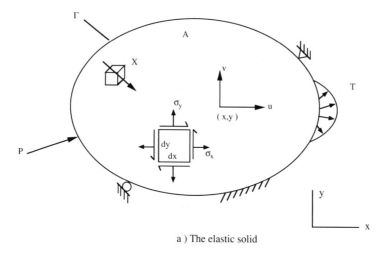

a) The elastic solid

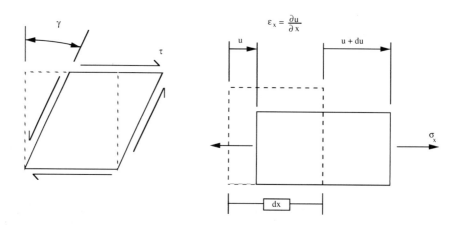

b) Typical strains

Figure 5.2.2   Notations for plane stress and plane strain.

The assumption of plane stress means that the solid is very thin and is loaded only in the direction of its plane. At the other extreme, in the state of plane strain the dimension of the solid is infinite in the z-direction. It is restrained perpendicular to the longitudinal (z-) axis, and the loads do not vary in that direction. All cross sections are assumed to be identical so any arbitrary xy section can be used in the analysis.

Another common problem is the analysis of an axisymmetric solid with axisymmetric loads and supports. This becomes a two-dimensional analysis that is very similar to the plane strain analysis considered earlier. The radial and axial displacement components are denoted by u and v. These are the same unknowns used in the plane strain study. In addition to the previous three strains there is a fourth strain known as the **hoop strain**, ε_θ. There is a corresponding hoop stress, σ_θ. The hoop strain results from the change in length of a fiber of material around the circumference of the solid. Recall the definition of strain as a change in length divided by the original length. The circumference at a typical radial position is $L=2\pi R$. When such a point undergoes a radial displacement of u, it occupies a new radial position of $(R+u)$. It has a corresponding increase in circumference. The hoop strain becomes

$$\varepsilon_\theta = \frac{\Delta L}{L} = \frac{2\pi(R+u) - 2\pi R}{2\pi R}$$

$$\varepsilon_0 = \frac{u}{R}.$$

Then our strains are denoted as

$$\varepsilon^T = [\varepsilon_R \quad \varepsilon_Z \quad \varepsilon_\theta \quad \gamma]$$

and the corresponding stress components are

$$\sigma^T = [\sigma_R \quad \sigma_Z \quad \sigma_\theta \quad \tau].$$

Thus, this is a simple extension of the plane strain model. We can use the same mesh and remember that there is a fourth stress component normal to the paper. In theory, we get a plane strain model from an axisymmetric one by letting the radius, R, approach infinity. Of course, axisymmetric models can only have positive radial coordinates. Typical axisymmetric solids are sketched in Figure 5.2.3. In a thin-plate analysis the solid is again assumed to be very thin compared to its lengths in the plane. However, in this case the loads and displacement constraints act normal to the plane. It is also possible to load the system with moment vectors that lie in the plane and to restrain the rotations about lines that lie in the plane. A thin plate model is shown in Figure 5.2.4.

5.3 OUTLINE OF FINITE ELEMENT PROCEDURES

From the mathematical point of view the finite element method is an integral formulation. Modern finite element integral formulations are usually obtained by either of two different procedures: **variational formulations** or **weighted residual** formulations. The following sections briefly outline the common procedures for establishing finite element models. It is fortunate that all these techniques use the same bookkeeping operations to generate the final assembly of algebraic equations that must be solved for the unknowns.

The earliest formulations for finite element models were based on variational techniques, which still are very important in developing elements and in solving practical problems. This is especially true in the areas of structural mechanics and stress analysis. Modern analysis in these areas has come to rely on FEA almost exclusively. Variational models find the nodal parameters that yield a minimum value of an integral known as a functional. In most cases it is possible to assign a physical meaning to the

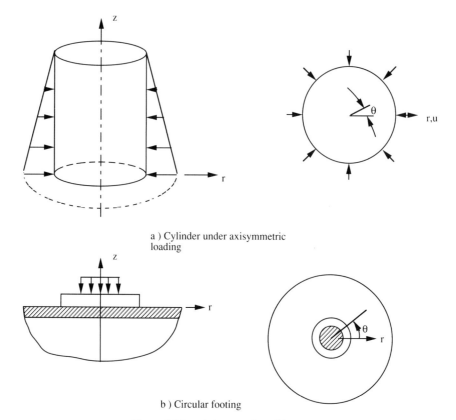

a) Cylinder under axisymmetric
loading

b) Circular footing

Figure 5.2.3   Axisymmetric problems.

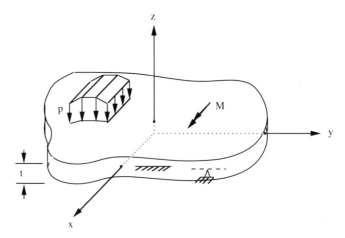

Figure 5.2.4   This plate under transverse loading.

integral. For example, in solid mechanics the integral represents the **total potential energy**, whereas in a fluid mechanics problem it may correspond to the rate of entropy production. Most physical problems with variational formulations result in quadratic forms that yield algebraic equations for the system which are symmetric and positive definite. The solution that yields a minimum value of the integral functional and satisfies the essential boundary conditions is equivalent to the solution of an associated differential equation, known as the Euler equation.

The generation of finite element models by the utilization of weighted residual techniques is increasingly important in the solution of differential equations for non-structural applications. The weighted residual method starts with the governing differential equation

$$L(\phi) = Q. \tag{5.3.1}$$

Generally we assume an approximate solution, say ϕ^*, and substitutes this solution into the differential equation. Since the assumption is approximate, this operation defines a residual error term, R, in the differential equation

$$L(\phi^*) - Q = R. \tag{5.3.2}$$

Although we cannot force the residual term to vanish, it is possible to force a weighted integral, over the solution domain, of the residual to vanish. That is, the integral of the product of the residual term and some weighting function is set equal to zero, so that

$$I = \int_V RW \ dV = 0. \tag{5.3.3}$$

Substituting blending or interpolation functions for the approximate solution, ϕ^*, and the weighting function, W, results in a set of algebraic equations that can be solved for the unknown nodal coefficients in the approximate solution. The choice of weighting function defines the type of weighted residual technique being utilized. The Galerkin criterion selects

$$W = \phi^*,$$

to make the residual error "orthogonal" to the approximate solution. Use of integration by parts with the Galerkin procedure reduces the continuity requirements of the approximating functions. If a variational procedure exists, the Galerkin criterion will lead to the same element matrices.

For both variational and weighted residual formulations, the following restrictions are accepted for establishing convergence of the finite element model as the mesh refinement increases:

1. The element interpolation functions must be capable of modeling any constant values of the dependent variable or its derivatives, to the order present in the defining integral statement, in the limit as the element size decreases.

2. The element interpolation functions should be chosen so that at element interfaces the dependent variable and its derivatives, of one order less than those occurring in the defining integral statement, are continuous.

The variables of interest and their derivatives are uniquely specified throughout the solution domain by the nodal parameters associated with the nodal points of the system. The parameters at a particular node directly influence only the elements that are connected to that particular node. An interpolation, or blending, function is assumed for the purpose of relating the quantity of interest within the element in terms of the values of the nodal parameters at the nodes that are connected to that particular element.

After the element behavior has been described by blending functions, then the derivatives of the blending functions are used to approximate the derivatives required in the integral form. The remaining fundamental problem is to establish the element matrices, S^e and C^e. This involves substituting the blending functions and their derivatives into the governing integral form. Historically, the resulting matrices have been called the element stiffness matrix and load vector, respectively. Almost all element matrix definitions involve some type of properties. A few problems require the definition of properties at the nodal points. For example, in a stress analysis we may wish to define variable thickness elements by specifying the thickness of the material at each node point.

Once the element equations have been established the contribution of each element is added, using its topology, to form the system equations. The system of algebraic equations resulting from FEA will be of the form

$$\mathbf{S} \ \mathbf{D} = \mathbf{C}. \tag{5.3.4}$$

The vector $\mathbf{D}$ contains the unknown nodal parameters, and the matrices $\mathbf{S}$ and $\mathbf{C}$ are obtained by assembling the known element matrices, S^e and C^e, respectively. In the majority of problems S^e, and thus, $\mathbf{S}$, will be symmetric. Also, the system square matrix, $\mathbf{S}$, is usually banded about the diagonal or at least **sparse**. The assembly process is graphically illustrated in Figure 5.3.1 for a three-element mesh consisting of a four-node quadrilateral and two three-node triangles, with one parameter per node. The top of the figure shows an assembly of the system $\mathbf{S}$ and $\mathbf{C}$ matrices that is coded to denote the sources of the contributing terms but not their values. A hatched area in these indicates a term that was added in from an element that has the hash code. For example, the load vector term C(6) is seen to be the sum of contributions from elements 2 and 3, which are hatched with horizontal (-) and oblique (/) lines, respectively. By way of comparison the term C(1) has a contribution only from element 2.

After the system equations have been assembled, it is necessary to apply the **essential boundary constraints** before solving for the unknown nodal parameters. The most common types of essential boundary conditions are (1) defining explicit values of the parameter at a node and (2) defining constraints equations that are linear combinations of the unknown nodal quantities. An essential boundary condition should not be confused with a forcing condition of the type that involves a flux or traction on the boundary of one or more elements. These element boundary source, or forcing, terms contribute additional terms to the element square and/or column matrices for the elements on which the sources were applied. Thus, although these (**Neumann**-type) conditions do enter into the system equations, their presence may not be obvious at the system level. There are other applications where the analyst may need to specify an

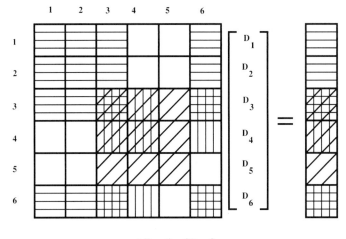

a) Equation SD = C

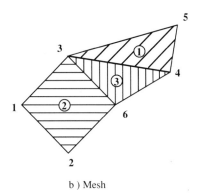

b) Mesh

Figure 5.3.1   Graphically coded assembly, **SD = C**.

input to the initial terms in the system equations column vector. For example, in structural mechanics, any applied concentrated nodal forces would be read directly into the initial system column matrix. Any additional loading terms calculated within the program would then be added to the initial set of specified loads. After all these conditions are satisfied, the system equations are solved by means of procedures that account for the sparse, symmetric nature of the problem. This greatly reduces the number of calculations that would normally be required to solve the equations.

The sparseness of the square matrix, **S**, is an important consideration. It depends on the numbering of the nodes (or the elements). If the FEA system being employed does not have an automatic renumbering system to increase sparseness, then the user must learn how to number nodes (or elements) efficiently. Figure 5.3.2 shows a typical symmetric square matrix and the bandwidth and column storage options. Note that the column mode of storage includes fewer unnecessary zero terms than the band mode. The **bandwidth**, B, depends on the difference in node numbers attached to an element.

　　　After the system algebraic equations have been solved for the unknown nodal parameters, it is usually necessary to output the parameters, **D**. In some cases the problem would be considered completed at this point, but in others it is necessary to use the calculated values of the nodal parameters to calculate other quantities of interest. For every essential boundary condition on **D**, there is a corresponding unknown **reaction** term in **C** that can be computed after **D** is known. These usually have physical meanings and should be output to help the designer check the results. Other types of postprocessing are also frequently needed. For example, in stress analysis we use the

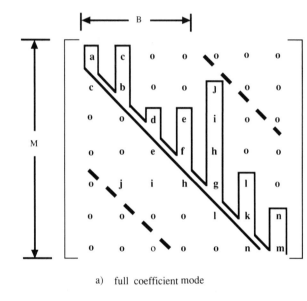

a) full coefficient mode

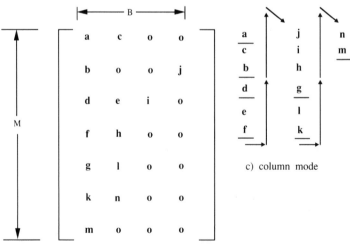

b) band mode

c) column mode

Figure 5.3.2　　Efficient storage modes.

calculated nodal displacements to solve for the strains and stresses. The preceding described data input flow and analysis steps are combined in an FEA flowchart in Figure 5.3.3. Some of the preceding concepts are also given in Tables 5.3.1 and 5.3.2.

TABLE 5.3.1   TYPICAL VARIABLES IN FINITE ELEMENT ANALYSIS

Application	Primary	Associated	Secondary
Stress analysis	Displacement, Rotation	Force, Moment	Stress, Failure criterion
Heat transfer	Temperature	Flux	Interior flux
Potential flow	Potential function	Normal velocity	Interior velocity

TABLE 5.3.2   TYPICAL GIVEN VARIABLES AND CORRESPONDING REACTIONS

Application	Given	Reaction
Stress Analysis	Displacement Rotation Force Couple	Force Moment Displacement Rotation
Heat transfer	Temperature Heat flux	Heat flux Temperature
Potential flow	Potential Normal velocity	Normal velocity Potential

There is a trade-off between the improved accuracy and increased cost associated with higher-order interpolation functions. These are illustrated in Figure 5.3.4, where the solution results for displacements and stresses from linear and cubic triangular elements are compared. The three-node linear triangles are simple to generate, since their integrals are evaluated by inspection. They have small bandwidths but usually require a large number of elements to give good accuracy. This is because their derivatives (strains and stresses) are constant. Many piecewise constant steps may be necessary to match the true solution.

By way of comparison the cubic elements connect more elements and thus, increase the bandwidth. Their integrals are complicated and require high-order numerical integration to evaluate. However, their derivatives are quadratic and they can match linear and quadratic solutions quite well. This increased accuracy allows the fewer nodal equations to be used, which helps reduce the cost. Another value of the cubic elements is that their sides can be curved through the four nodes to better match the shape of real parts. If all the elements are to be of the same order then most analysts favor the quadratic element families as the most cost-effective.

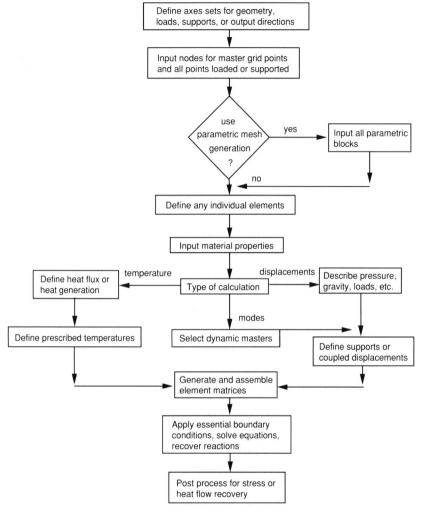

Figure 5.3.3   Data and analysis flow chart for FEA.

Current research indicates that commercial finite element codes will soon employ **self-adaptive** formulations. These programs automatically estimate the local error and then increase the order of the interpolation and/or reduce the sizes of the elements by replacing larger ones with sets of small elements.

5.4 PARTIAL MODEL ANALYSES

Many engineering problems have features that allow the analyst to reduce greatly the cost of the FEA through the use of **symmetry**, **antisymmetry**, or **cyclic symmetry** and **coupled nodes**. The system equations are sparse and can often be described by the

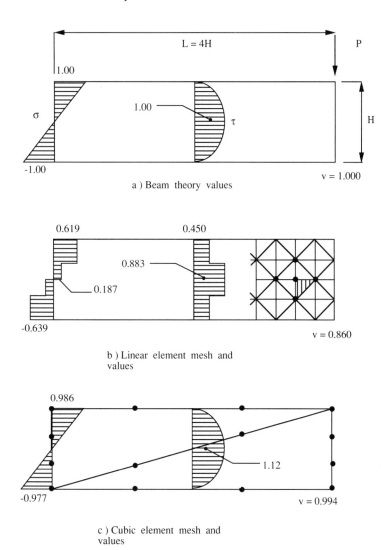

a) Beam theory values

b) Linear element mesh and
values

c) Cubic element mesh and
values

Figure 5.3.4   Cantilever beam solution via different elements.

bandwidth, say B, and the total number of equations, say M, as shown in Figure 5.3.2. Solving the equations is very expensive and is proportional to the product B^2M. The storage required by the system is proportional to BM. Whenever possible we try to reduce these two parameters. Partial models allow us to reduce them very easily and still generate all the information we require. For example, a half-symmetry model would usually reduce both B and M by a factor of two and thereby reduce the solution costs by a factor of eight and reduce the storage requirement by a factor of four.

When a model has a plane of geometric, material, and support symmetry, it is not usually necessary to analyze the whole model. Conditions of symmetry or antisymmetry in the loads or forcing terms can be applied to the planes of symmetry in order to produce a partial model that includes the effects of the other parts of the complete model. Even asymmetric loads can be treated in partial models by the superposition of results from two or more symmetric and antisymmetric partial models. The common case of cyclic symmetry can also be treated in greatly reduced partial models by careful use of the boundary conditions (coupled nodes).

In order to employ a partial analysis involving a symmetry plane, it is necessary for the following quantities to be symmetric with respect to that plane: the geometry, the material regions, the material properties, and the essential boundary conditions (on the temperature or generalized displacements). If these conditions are not quite fulfilled, then the designer will have to use engineering judgement before selecting a partial model. Even if a full model is selected for eventual use, an approximate partial model can give useful insight and aid in planning the details of the full model to be run later. Of course, the force or source terms do not have to be symmetric or antisymmetric to create a valid partial model.

In thermal models any symmetry plane has a zero heat flux and temperature gradient normal to that plane. That is because the temperatures are mirror images of each other and have the same sign when moving normal to the plane. The state of zero heat flux normal to a boundary is a natural boundary condition in a finite element analysis (but not in finite differences). We obtain that condition by default. If you desire a different type of condition to apply on a boundary, then we must prescribe either the temperature (the essential condition) or a different nonzero normal flux. We cannot give both. When you prescribe one of them, the other becomes a "reaction" to be determined from the final result. Thermal antisymmetry means the temperatures approach the plane with opposite signs but equal magnitudes. Thus, the temperature must be zero on a plane of antisymmetry. When that essential boundary condition is imposed, the necessary normal heat flow through that plane can be found as a "reaction" from the final solution. These concepts are illustrated in Figure 5.4.1.

For structural models it is somewhat more difficult to describe the necessary boundary conditions, since most FEA systems employ a displacement formulation. Thus, we must identify the essential boundary conditions in terms of the three

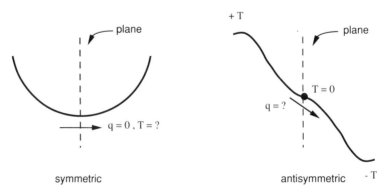

Figure 5.4.1   Normal temperature distribution.

displacement components and the three rotation components (if available in the element). Figure 5.4.2 shows the essential generalized displacements on the Cartesian planes necessary to impose symmetric or antisymmetric deformation. Note that half of the generalized displacements are zero in each case and that they reverse their roles when going from symmetric to antisymmetric planes. The rotations about the axes are drawn as double-headed arrows, where the positive sense of the rotations is defined by the right-hand rule. Figure 5.4.3 shows the same information relative to components tangent to and normal to a general plane in space. To use these conditions the analyst must usually introduce a **local coordinate axis** on the plane and associate the generalized coordinates with that coordinate set.

To illustrate these concepts, Figure 5.4.4 shows how a simply supported beam can be formulated as a one-half partial model for any of three load cases: symmetric, antisymmetric, or asymmetric. Of course, some problems are simple enough that we can afford to go directly to a full model and avoid the planning necessary to formulate a partial model. However, we will sooner or later encounter a problem that requires these extra skills.

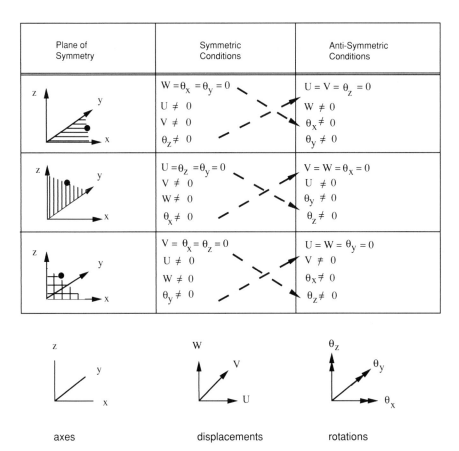

Figure 5.4.2   Three-dimensional structural boundary conditions.

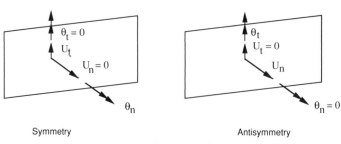

Symmetry   Antisymmetry

Figure 5.4.3   General tangential and normal components.

These concepts can also be useful in reducing the cost of natural frequency and **mode shape** calculations. Figure 5.4.5a shows a rectangular frame that vibrates in its plane. It has double symmetry of its geometry, stiffness, and mass. Thus, we could use a one-quarter partial model, say the first quadrant of the xy-plane. By applying the proper boundary conditions at points 1 and 2, it is possible to recover all the modes and frequencies (beyond the three rigid body modes). The various combinations of symmetric and antisymmetric conditions are shown in Figure 5.4.5b–e. Dynamics problems and eigenvalue problems are much more expensive than linear statics problems or thermal analysis problems. Thus, the effort required to use the one-quarter model in four different analyses really pays off.

To give some specific examples of these concepts, some typical thermal and stress problems will be represented. Figure 5.4.6 shows a planar rectangular region with homogeneous conduction properties, k, and internal and external specified edge temperatures, T_1 and T_2. In addition, it has free convection, q_h, over its face to a fluid with homogeneous convection properties, h and T_∞. Such a system has double symmetry, which allows us to employ a one-quarter model with consistent boundary conditions. Doing this cuts M by a factor of 4 and reduces B by at least a factor of 2 and possibly much more. Thus, the cost drops by at least a factor of 16. The alternate partial model form still requires the essential conditions on T_1 and T_2 and the face convection data for q_h. The change is that the heat flow is zero on the new boundary lines formed by the symmetry planes. This is a natural condition in FEA and requires no input data (other than the geometry of the new line).

Figure 5.4.7 shows a homogeneous square planar object with a circular hole at the center. Its weight is small compared to the centrifugal loads caused by high-speed angular rotation around a normal axis at the circle center. Note that we have radial loads and displacements that are symmetric with respect to both centerlines and both diagonal lines. We have at least two choices for our reduced model. If we do not have local axes and associated displacements, then we could employ the one-quarter model in Figure 5.4.7b. There the planes of radial motion coincide with the global xy-planes and the displacements normal to them are easily set to zero. Still, that approach is not as desirable as the one-eighth model in 5.47c. It utilizes the additional symmetry about the diagonal line. We know that the material must move only radially along this plane. The common approach is to assign the displacements on that line to a new coordinate system constructed normal and tangent to the plane. Then we set the normal

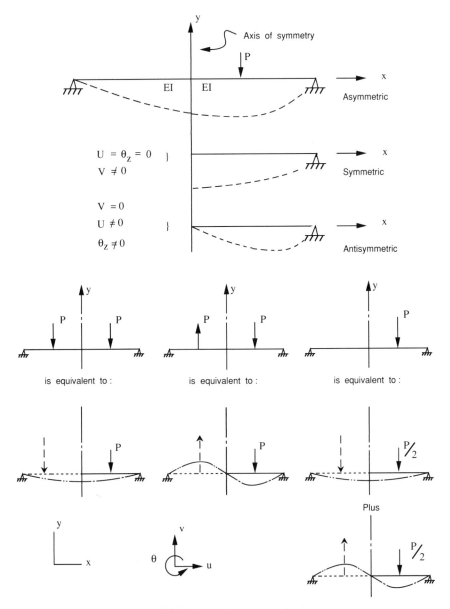

Figure 5.4.4   Employing beam half-models.

displacement, say v_2, to zero. An alternate approach, if available, is to retain the original axes and use a repeated freedom option to set $u = v$ along that line. This says that their values are unknown but equal. This is a special case of a generalized or multipoint constraint.

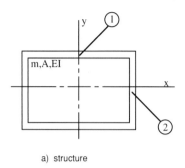

a) structure

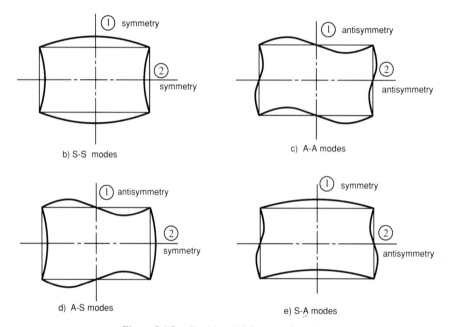

b) S-S modes   c) A-A modes

d) A-S modes   e) S-A modes

Figure 5.4.5   Partial model for natural modes.

For any point that is on more than one plane of symmetry or antisymmetry, all the constraints required for each of those planes must be applied. As an example, consider the closed thin box in Figure 5.4.8, that is subjected to a loading combination that gives symmetry (S) about planes perpendicular to the x- and z-axes (lines 2-5-3 and 1-4-2) and antisymmetry (A) about a plane perpendicular to the y-axis (line 1-6-3). The nodes on intersecting planes must satisfy all conditions. Thus, node 1 has A-S conditions, node 2 has S-S conditions and node 3 has S-A conditions, as shown in the figure.

There are many components in mechanical design problems that have **cyclic symmetry**. That is, they are made up of n parts that each occupy an angle of $\beta = 2\pi/n$ of any circumference. Thus, if we have a partial model of such a system, then any of the other $n - 1$ parts can be obtained by rotating the partial model through an angle that is a multiple of β. To illustrate these important concepts we begin with an example from heat conduction.

Consider the nonhomogeneous cyclic symmetry system shown in Figure 5.4.9. Most of the region has a conductivity of k_1, but there are four offset vanes of material having a conductivity of k_2. Thus, it has $n = 4$ typical segments. The same model could apply to a homogeneous material that has four vanes of additional thickness running across its surface. With the proper choice of the boundary conditions we can use any partial model made by two cuts along paths that have an angular separation, at any radius R, of $\beta = \pi/2$. There are an infinite number of choices, but we quickly learn which makes the mesh generation and or boundary conditions the easiest. Of the two options shown in Figure 5.4.9, the first has simpler mesh generation. There is one other choice that would be better than either of these.

For this problem the square outer boundary is maintained at a constant temperature of T_2, while the inner circle is held at T_1. We need to determine the interior temperature distribution. Due to the cyclic symmetry we know an important feature of the solution. Consider any interior point that lies on a circle of radius R measured from the center. Whatever its temperature is we know that there are $n - 1$ other points with the same temperature on that circle. They are equally spaced at an angle of β relative to each other. We must employ this knowledge to apply the boundary conditions to the two new edges created by the partial model. These two edges must be meshed in the

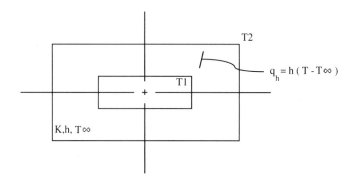

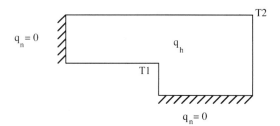

Figure 5.4.6   Rectangular region with quarter symmetry.

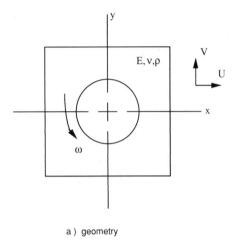

a) geometry

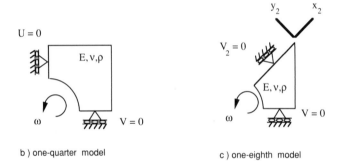

b) one-quarter model   c) one-eighth model

Figure 5.4.7   Centrifugal loads on a plate.

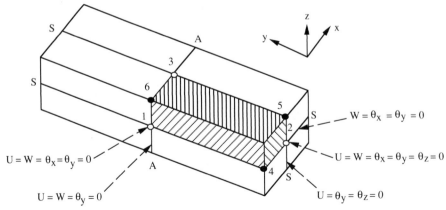

Figure 5.4.8   A box with S-S-A loads.

same manner. That is, they must have the same number of nodes and the same relative spacings between nodes on the new edges. Thus, for points *a, b, c* on one cyclic symmetry edge, there must be a corresponding set of nodes *A, B, C* on the second created edge. To account for the removed material we must use the **repeated freedom** concept and equate the unknown temperatures along the two edges. Thus, we set $T_a = T_A$, $T_b = T_B$, and so on for each node on the created edge that does not have an essential boundary condition. This tells the model that although we do not know the temperature distribution along these two edges, we do know that they are the same.

These cyclic symmetry boundary conditions on the created edges were relatively simple because the temperature is a scalar and thus, has the same value regardless of which coordinate axis system is used to describe the point. This simplicity vanishes when we go to a stress analysis model and must describe the components of displacements or stresses (vector or tensor quantities). In the displacement model it is necessary to equate components of displacements, relative to the created edge, at corresponding points along those two edges. To illustrate these concepts assume that the previous

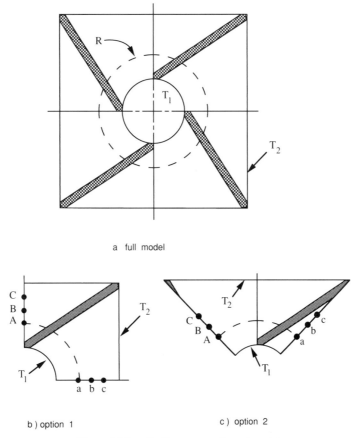

Figure 5.4.9   Cyclic symmetry thermal model.

solid with vanes is rotating about its center, with an angular speed of ω, and we wish to compute its displacements and stresses. First we have to decide which coordinate axes are to be employed to describe the directions of the displacements on the created cyclic edges. Figure 5.4.10a shows that we know that on those edges the relative displacements are the same. Thus, we may wish to employ local axes that are tangent and normal to the cyclic curve, or we may choose to use global polar coordinate components. In this example, since $\beta = \pi/2$ and the cyclic curve is straight, these happen to be the same. To use the first approach we have to work with each corresponding pair of nodes on the cyclic curve, say points a and A. At the point on the first curve we define a local tangent-normal axis system, say $x_1 - y_1$. Then at the corresponding point, A,

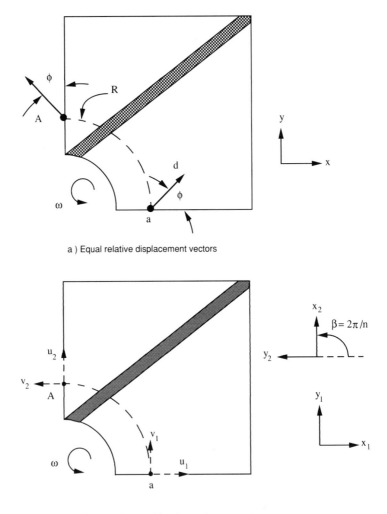

a) Equal relative displacement vectors

b) Repeated tangential and normal components, $u_1 = u_2$, $v_1 = v_2$

Figure 5.4.10   Cyclic relative displacements.

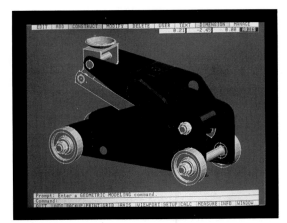

Solid model of a hydraulic jack arm.

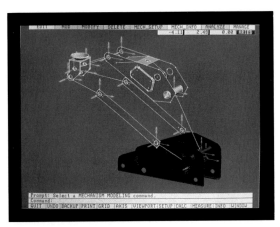

Exploded view of jack arm parts.

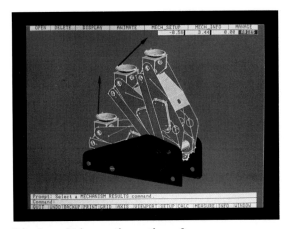

Display of kinematic motion of arm.

Finite element mesh of jack arm.

Mesh and support details.

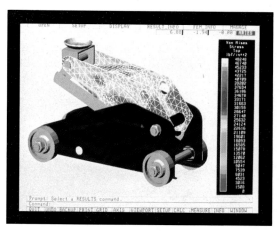

Von Mises stress distribution.

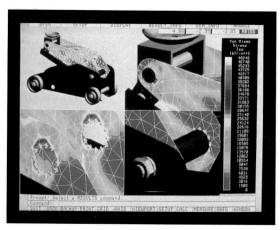

Details of stress distribution.

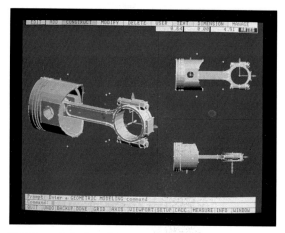

Solid model of a piston and rod.

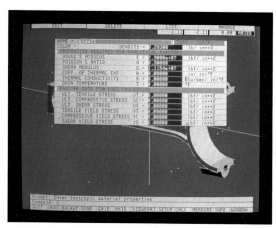

Engineering properties for connecting rod.

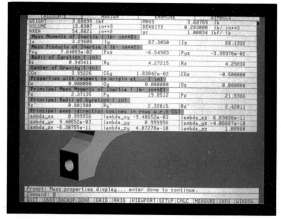

Mass properties of the connecting rod.

we establish a second axis set, say $x_2 - y_2$, that is obtained by rotating the first set by the amount, β, of the cyclic symmetry. That is shown in Figure 5.4.10b. Then we impose cyclic symmetry conditions by coupling (equating) the unknown components at point a to the corresponding component at point A:

$$u_1 = u_2$$

$$(5.4.1)$$

$$v_1 = v_2 \, .$$

Some programs can automatically generate tangent axis sets at nodes on selected curves or surfaces. If we had used polar (radial and transverse) components relative to the axis of rotation, then we again couple the pair of components:

$$u = u'$$

$$v = v' \, .$$

These relate the polar components at position (R, θ) on the first cyclic curve to those at the corresponding position at $(R, \theta + \beta)$ on the second cyclic curve.

It is also possible to retain only the original global axis and displacement components and still impose the cyclic symmetry condition. Referring to Figure 5.4.10 we could set

$$u_a = v_A$$

$$v_a = - u_A$$

or as generalized or **multipoint constraint** relations

$$1 * u_a - 1 * v_A = 0$$

$$(5.4.2)$$

$$1 * v_a + 1 * u_A = 0.$$

Here the constraints are simple because $\beta = \pi/2$. Since axis system 2 used in Figure 5.4.10 is obtained from a coordinate transformation in terms of β, Equation (5.4.1) could be written in a more general form of Equation (5.4.2) that each includes both components at point a and the sine and cosine of β.

The definition of coupled displacement components on curved cyclic symmetry lines is shown in Figure 5.4.11. It illustrates an eight-vane impeller segment that is coupled by polar components or local tangent axis pairs. Many impellers have a much larger number of vanes. Other types of repeating domains are shown in Figure 5.4.12.

5.5 ONE-DIMENSIONAL THEORY

We begin the introduction of finite element theory with the study of a typical heat transfer problem. The problem involves only a single unknown: the temperature distribution. The finite element method requires an integral form, but we begin with the more familiar differential equation. After the thermal study we will summarize the results for structural mechanics and apply them to elastic bars.

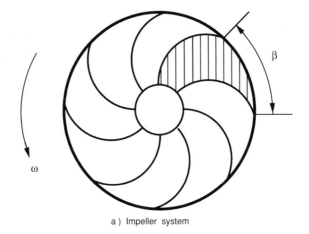

a) Impeller system

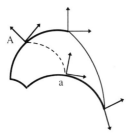

b) Tangential - Normal option

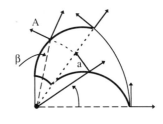

c) Global polar option

Figure 5.4.11   Coupling curved segment lines.

5.5.1 Governing Thermal Differential Equation

Consider the problem of one-dimensional, steady-state heat conduction through a thin rod, shown in Figure 5.5.1, that has convection from its surface and internal heat generation. The rod of area A, perimeter P, has a specified temperature of t_o at $x = 0$ and is insulated, $dt/dx = 0$, at $x = L$. It is surrounded by a convecting fluid. It can be shown that the governing differential equation and boundary conditions are

$$\frac{d}{dx} [k \, A \, \frac{dt}{dx}] - hP (t - t_r) + Q = 0 \tag{5.5.1}$$

$$t(0) = t_0 \tag{5.5.2}$$

$$\frac{dt}{dx} (L) = 0, \quad or \quad q = q_L \tag{5.5.3}$$

where
     k = thermal conductivity

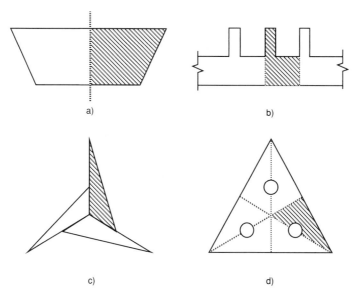

Figure 5.4.12   Tyical repeating domains..

h = convective transfer coefficient on the surface
t_r = reference temperature of surrounding media
Q = rate of internal heat generation
q = point heat flow
q_L = convective loss at the end.

Note that the area and perimeter could be functions of position, x. The same is true for the physical properties, k and h. This shows that when finished we will automatically be able to include arbitrary geometry and nonhomogeneous material properties. These equations are called the strong form.

5.5.2 Integral Formulation

The finite element model of a problem must be based on an integral formulation. This can be accomplished by a **variational statement, a weighted residuals** procedure, or a direct statement of an integral conservation law. The most common weighted residuals methods for finite element solutions are the method of least squares and the Galerkin criterion.

From the calculus of variations it can be shown that a problem equivalent to the solution of Equations (5.5.1) and (5.5.3) is to find the function $t(x)$ that satisfies the essential boundary condition, $t(0) = t_0$, and renders stationary (minimizes) the integral

$$I = \frac{1}{2} \int_0^L \left[kA \left(\frac{dt}{dx} \right)^2 + hP\,(t^2 - 2tt_r) - 2QtA \right] dx - q_o t_o + q_L t_L. \qquad (5.5.4)$$

Recall from calculus that the extreme value is obtained when $\delta I = 0$, which in turn

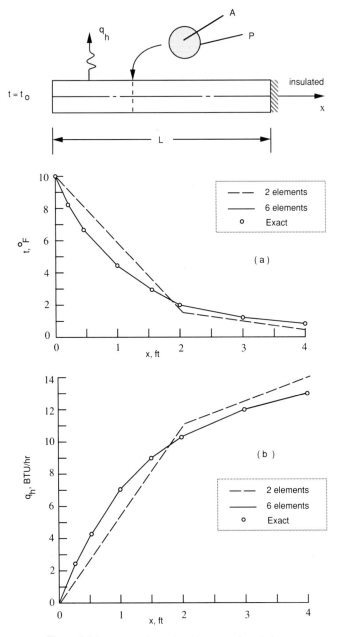

Figure 5.5.1   A one-dimensional heat transfer solution.

requires that

$$\frac{\partial I}{\partial t} = 0. \tag{5.5.5}$$

For this problem it can be shown, by considering the second derivative, that the extreme value is always the minimum value. This equivalent integral formulation is the basis for our present finite element formulation. This alternate approach is known as the weak form. Note that the first and fourth integrals are actually volume integrals, while the second and third are actually surface integrals.

5.5.3 Finite Element Model

Introduce a set of M nodal points in the region from $x = 0$ to $x = L$. Let this set of nodes divide the region into a total of NE one-dimensional elements. Assume each element has two nodes, say i and j, with coordinates x_i and x_j, respectively. We will consider the simplest possible element by letting the degrees of freedom at each node be the temperatures t_i and t_j. Since we have two constants available (t_i and t_j) in each element, let us assume that the temperature variation in a typical element is linear. That is, we assume a physical coordinate interpolation of

$$t^e(x) = \alpha_1 + \alpha_2\, x \qquad\qquad (5.5.6)$$

or, in matrix form:

$$1 \times 1 \quad\ 1\ \times\ 2 \quad\ 2\ \times\ 1$$

$$t^e(x) = [1 \ \ x]\begin{Bmatrix} \alpha_1 \\ \alpha_2 \end{Bmatrix} \qquad\qquad (5.5.7)$$

or, symbolically,

$$t^e(x) = \ \ \mathbf{M}(x) \quad \alpha^e$$
$$\qquad\qquad\qquad 1 \times 2 \quad 2 \times 1 \qquad\qquad (5.5.8)$$

Here $\mathbf{M}$ contains the spatial variation, while the α are unknown mathematical constants. This expression is valid at all points within the element, including the nodal points.

Evaluating it at each of the nodal points gives the following set of identities that relate the mathematical constants to the physical constants:

$$\begin{Bmatrix} t_i \\ t_j \end{Bmatrix} = \begin{bmatrix} 1 & x_i \\ 1 & x_j \end{bmatrix} \begin{Bmatrix} \alpha_1 \\ \alpha_2 \end{Bmatrix} \qquad\qquad (5.5.9)$$

or

$$2 \times 1 \ \ 2 \times 2 \ \ 2 \times 1$$
$$\mathbf{T}^e = \ \ \mathbf{C}^e \quad \alpha^e$$

where $\mathbf{T}^e$ denotes the unknown nodal quantities (d.o.f.) associated with the element. Solving for α^e:

$$2 \times 1 \ \ 2 \times 2 \ \ 2 \times 1$$
$$\alpha^e = \ \ \mathbf{C}^{e^{-1}} \quad \mathbf{T}^e \ \ \equiv \mathbf{CI}^e\, \mathbf{T}^e \qquad\qquad (5.5.10)$$

where

$$\mathbf{CI}^e = \frac{1}{(x_j - x_i)} \begin{bmatrix} x_j & -x_i \\ -1 & 1 \end{bmatrix}.$$

Substituting this relation between α and $\mathbf{T}$ into Equation (5.5.8) gives

$$t^e(x) = \mathbf{M}(x) \, \mathbf{CI}^e \, \mathbf{T}^e.$$

Note that $\mathbf{CI}$ introduces geometrical constants for this specific element. Simplifying the matrix product gives the element interpolation function:

$$t^e(x) = \mathbf{H}^e(x) \, \mathbf{T}^e \tag{5.5.11}$$

where

$$\begin{array}{ccc} 1 \times 2 & 1 \times 2 & 2 \times 2 \end{array}$$
$$\mathbf{H}^e(x) = \mathbf{M}(x) \quad \mathbf{CI}^e.$$

In this simple case $\mathbf{H}^e$ can be obtained in closed form and is given by

$$\mathbf{H}^e(x) = \left[\left(\frac{x_j - x}{x_j - x_i} \right) \quad \left(\frac{x - x_i}{x_j - x_i} \right) \right] \tag{5.5.12}$$

$$= [H_i(x) \quad H_j(x)].$$

The important thing to note here is that this equation defines the approximate temperature within the element in terms of the temperature at the nodes of the element. We should also note that the numerical values of $\mathbf{CI}$ could have been obtained by the computer. Also note the linear spatial variations of the two interpolation functions. For future reference, note that matrix algebra gives

$$t^e = \mathbf{H}^e \, \mathbf{T}^e = \mathbf{T}^{e^T} \, \mathbf{H}^{e^T}$$

and our approximation of the temperature gradient is

$$\frac{dt^e}{dx} = \frac{d\mathbf{H}^e}{dx} \, \mathbf{T}^e = \mathbf{T}^{e^T} \left[\frac{d\mathbf{H}^e}{dx} \right]^T. \tag{5.5.13}$$

Of course, we could directly define the interpolation function, $\mathbf{H}$, in terms of local parametric geometry introduced in Chapter 3. If the same parametric interpolation is used for both the primary unknown and the geometry, then the element is classified as **isoparametric**. The same interpolation is usually used for describing source terms that vary with location.

5.5.4 System Equations

Next we will outline the development of the algebraic equations governing the system, or domain, under study. Recall the integral over the entire domain presented in Equation (5.5.4):

$$I = \frac{1}{2} \int_0^L \left[kA \left(\frac{dt}{dx}\right)^2 + hP\,(t^2 - 2tt_r) - 2QtA \right] dx - q_o t_o + q_L t_L.$$

Assume that the integral over the total domain is the sum of the integrals over the elements, that is,

$$I = \sum_{e=1}^E I^e + I^p \qquad (5.5.14)$$

where, for future reference, the typical element integral is

$$I^e = \frac{1}{2} \int_{x_i}^{x_j} \left[k^e A^e \left(\frac{dt^e}{dx}\right)^2 + h^e P^e (t^e)^2 \right] dx - \int_{x_i}^{x_j} h^e P^e t^e t_r \; dx \qquad (5.5.15)$$

$$- \int_{x_i}^{x_j} Q^e A^e t^e \; dx$$

and at the end caps

$$I^p = q_L t_L - q_o t_o \qquad (5.5.16)$$

denotes the contribution from the boundary points. Of course, t_L will eventually be related to a nodal temperature on the end element. Recall from calculus that in order to split the integrals in Equation (5.5.14) we must have C^n continuity of t between the domains, where $n + 1$ is the highest derivative in the integrand. Here we have $n = 0$, so that t must be continuous between elements. By inspection we have satisfied this condition. Any C^0 parametric interpolation would likewise work.

It has been assumed that the temperature at any point in the domain is uniquely defined by the nodal quantities. That is,

$$t = t\,(\mathbf{T})$$

where $\mathbf{T}$ is the system array of nodal quantities,

$$\mathbf{T}^T = [t_1 \quad t_2 \quad t_3 \quad \cdots \quad t_M]. \qquad (5.5.17)$$

Therefore, the integral must also be a function of the nodal quantities

$$I\,(t) = I\,(\mathbf{T})$$

so that the minimization $\partial I / \partial t = 0$ implies that

$$\partial I / \partial t_1 = 0$$

$$\partial I / \partial t_2 = 0$$

$$.$$

$$.$$

$$.$$

$$\partial I / \partial t_M = 0$$

or symbolically, the governing system equation is

$$\begin{matrix} M \times 1 & M \times 1 \\ \dfrac{\partial I}{\partial \mathbf{T}} = & 0 \end{matrix} \tag{5.5.18}$$

Substituting Equation (5.5.14) into these relationships gives

$$\frac{\partial I^p}{\partial \mathbf{T}} + \sum_{e=1}^{E} \frac{\partial I^e}{\partial \mathbf{T}} = 0 \tag{5.5.19}$$

which is the basis for our system of algebraic equations. Note that this procedure leads to a minimum solution over the entire domain but not necessarily a minimum in each and every element. Before substituting into the preceding equation, we will utilize the interpolation equations to define I^e in terms of the nodal quantities. That is, from Equations (5.5.11) and (5.5.13):

$$I^e = \frac{1}{2} \int_{L^e} \left\{ k^e A^e \, \mathbf{T}^{e^T} \frac{\partial \mathbf{H}^e}{\partial x}^T \frac{\partial \mathbf{H}^e}{\partial x} \mathbf{T}^e + h^e P^e \mathbf{T}^{e^T} \mathbf{H}^{e^T} \mathbf{H}^e \mathbf{T}^e \right\} dx$$

$$- \int_{L^e} Q^e A^e \mathbf{T}^{e^T} \mathbf{H}^{e^T} \, dx - \int_{L^e} t_r \, h^e P^e \, \mathbf{T}^{e^T} \mathbf{H}^{e^T} \, dx.$$

Since the $\mathbf{T}^e$ are unknown constants, they move outside the integrals, and this becomes

$$I^e = \frac{1}{2} \overset{1 \times 2}{\mathbf{T}^{e^T}} \left[\int_{L^e} [k^e A^e \overset{2 \times 1}{\frac{\partial \mathbf{H}^{e^T}}{\partial x}} \overset{1 \times 2}{\frac{\partial \mathbf{H}^e}{\partial x}} + h^e P^e \overset{2 \times 1}{\mathbf{H}^{e^T}} \overset{1 \times 2}{\mathbf{H}^e} \, dx] \right] \overset{2 \times 1}{\mathbf{T}^e}$$

$$\overset{1 \times 2}{- \mathbf{T}^{e^T}} \left[\int_{L^e} [Q^e A^e \overset{2 \times 1}{\mathbf{H}^{e^T}} - t_r \, h^e P^e \overset{2 \times 1}{\mathbf{H}^{e^T}}] \, dx \right] \tag{5.5.20}$$

or symbolically

$$\overset{1 \times 1}{I^e} = \frac{1}{2} \overset{1 \times 2}{\mathbf{T}^{e^T}} \overset{2 \times 2}{\mathbf{S}^e} \overset{2 \times 1}{\mathbf{T}^e} - \overset{1 \times 2}{\mathbf{T}^{e^T}} \overset{2 \times 1}{\mathbf{C}^e} . \tag{5.5.21}$$

Thus, we find that the element contribution, I^e, is a symmetric quadratic function of the two nodal quantities, $\mathbf{T}^e$. However, to evaluate the thermal equilibrium relation

$$\sum_e \frac{\partial I^e}{\partial \mathbf{T}} = 0$$

we must express I^e as a function of all the nodal parameters, $\mathbf{T}$. This is simply a book-keeping problem since the element temperatures, $\mathbf{T}^e$, are a subset of the system temperatures $\mathbf{T}$. Therefore, define a bookkeeping (or Boolean) matrix $\mathbf{b}$ such that

$$\mathbf{T}^e \subset \mathbf{T}$$

gives

$$\underset{\mathbf{T}^e}{\overset{2\times 1}{}} \equiv \underset{\mathbf{b}^e}{\overset{2\times M}{}} \underset{\mathbf{T}}{\overset{M\times 1}{}} \cdot \tag{5.5.22}$$

The typical element contribution is then symbolically expressed as

$$I^e = \frac{1}{2}\,\mathbf{T}^T(\mathbf{b}^{e^T}\mathbf{S}^e\mathbf{b}^e)\,\mathbf{T} - \mathbf{T}^T(\mathbf{b}^{e^T}\mathbf{C}^e)$$

and

$$\underset{\dfrac{\partial I^e}{\partial \mathbf{T}}}{\overset{M\times 1}{}} = \frac{2}{2}\, \underset{\mathbf{b}^{e^T}}{\overset{M\times 2}{}}\, \underset{\mathbf{S}^e}{\overset{2\times 2}{}}\, \underset{\mathbf{b}^e}{\overset{2\times M}{}}\, \underset{\mathbf{T}}{\overset{M\times 1}{}} - \underset{\mathbf{b}^{e^T}}{\overset{M\times 2}{}}\, \underset{\mathbf{C}^e}{\overset{2\times 1}{}} \cdot$$

Similarly, we can define the single end point subset on either end as

$$t_L = \underset{\mathbf{T}_p}{\overset{1\times 1}{}} = \underset{\mathbf{b}^p}{\overset{1\times M}{}}\, \underset{\mathbf{T}}{\overset{M\times 1}{}}$$

so that, from Equation (5.5.16)

$$I^p = - \underset{\mathbf{T}^T}{\overset{1\times M}{}}\, \underset{\mathbf{b}^{p^T}}{\overset{M\times 1}{}}\, \underset{\mathbf{C}^p}{\overset{1\times 1}{}}$$

where the boundary column matrix is

$$\underset{\mathbf{C}^p}{\overset{1\times 1}{}} = q_o \quad or \quad q_L$$

so that the endpoint contribution to the system equations is

$$\frac{\partial I^p}{\partial \mathbf{T}} = - \underset{\mathbf{b}^{p^T}}{\overset{M\times 1}{}}\, \underset{\mathbf{C}^p}{\overset{1\times 1}{}} \cdot$$

Finally, substituting the preceding typical terms into the summation yields

$$-\left[\underset{\displaystyle\sum_{p=1}^{2}\mathbf{b}^{p^T}\mathbf{C}^p}{\overset{M\times 1}{}}\right] + \left[\underset{\displaystyle\sum_{e=1}^{E}\mathbf{b}^{e^T}\mathbf{S}^e\mathbf{b}^e}{\overset{M\times M}{}}\right]\underset{\mathbf{T}}{\overset{M\times 1}{}} - \left[\underset{\displaystyle\sum_{e=1}^{E}\mathbf{b}^{e^T}\mathbf{C}^e}{\overset{M\times 1}{}}\right] = \underset{0}{\overset{M\times 1}{}} \tag{5.5.23}$$

or symbolically

$$\mathbf{S}\;\mathbf{T} - (\mathbf{C}^p + \mathbf{C}^e) = 0$$

$$\underset{\mathbf{S}}{\overset{M\times M}{}}\underset{\mathbf{T}}{\overset{M\times 1}{}} = \underset{\mathbf{C}}{\overset{M\times 1}{}} \cdot \tag{5.5.24}$$

These are the governing system equations to be solved for the unknown nodal parameters **T**. Equation (5.5.23) is a symbolic definition of the assembly procedure. Recall that the "element matrix," $\mathbf{S}^e$, is symmetric. Thus, **S** will also be symmetric. With proper numbering of the nodes it will be banded as well. Thus, several computational and storage advantages are obtained with this formulation.

5.5.5 The Element Matrices

Recall that **S**, the system square matrix, is the assembled sum of the contributions of the $\mathbf{S}^e$, which are known as "the" element matrices. Returning to the definition of $\mathbf{S}^e$ we have

$$\underset{\mathbf{S}^e}{2x2} = \int_{L^e} (k^e A^e \frac{\partial \mathbf{H}^{e^T}}{\partial x} \frac{\partial \mathbf{H}^e}{\partial x} + h^e P^e \mathbf{H}^{e^T} \mathbf{H}^e)\, dx. \tag{5.5.25}$$

Generally, the interpolation functions $\mathbf{H}^e$ are too complicated to integrate analytically. Thus, many codes use numerical integration.

$$\mathbf{S}^e = \sum_{i=1}^{Q} W_i\, (k_i^e A_i^e \frac{\partial \mathbf{H}_i^{e^T}}{\partial x} \frac{\partial \mathbf{H}_i^e}{\partial x} + h_i^e P_i^e \mathbf{H}_i^{e^T} \mathbf{H}_i^e) \tag{5.5.26}$$

where Q is the number of quadrature points, W_i is the tabulated weighting function, and $k_i = k(x_i)$, where x_i are the tabulated abscissae of the quadrature point. Similarly the element convection column matrix is

$$\mathbf{C}^e = \int_{L^e} t_r^e h^e P^e \mathbf{H}^T\, dx. \tag{5.5.27}$$

Assuming constant properties and linear interpolation for t

$$\mathbf{C}_h^e = \frac{1}{2} L^e t_r h^e P^e \begin{Bmatrix} 1 \\ 1 \end{Bmatrix} \tag{5.5.28}$$

and the internal source matrix is

$$\mathbf{C}_Q^e = \frac{1}{2} Q^e L^e A^e \begin{Bmatrix} 1 \\ 1 \end{Bmatrix}. \tag{5.5.29}$$

The preceding numerical integration easily allows for variable properties. If we assume the properties are constant in a typical element, we can integrate the present linear element in closed form. The result is

$$\mathbf{S}^e = \frac{A^e k^e}{L^e} \begin{bmatrix} 1 & -1 \\ -1 & 1 \end{bmatrix} + \frac{P^e h^e L^e}{6} \begin{bmatrix} 2 & 1 \\ 1 & 2 \end{bmatrix} \tag{5.5.30}$$

where $L^e = x_j - x_i$ is the length of the element. Note that the conduction contributions vary inversely with the length of the element, whereas the convection contribution is proportional to the length (i.e., the surface area $L^e P^e$). This is what we should expect from introductory courses in heat transfer.

5.5.6 The Element Bookkeeping Matrix

Consider a system of five nodes and four elements with the following topology:

$$
\begin{array}{cc}
\text{Element} & \text{Topology} \\
1 & 1, 5 \\
2 & 5, 2 \\
3 & 2, 3 \\
4 & 3, 4
\end{array}
$$

The system level unknowns are

$$
\underset{\mathbf{T}}{5 \times 1} = \begin{Bmatrix} t_1 \\ t_2 \\ t_3 \\ t_4 \\ t_5 \end{Bmatrix}.
$$

For element 2 the element unknowns are $\mathbf{T}^{e'} = [\, t_5 \quad t_2 \,]$. The relation between the two sets can be expressed as

$$
\mathbf{T}^e = \begin{Bmatrix} t_1^e \\ t_2^e \end{Bmatrix} \equiv \begin{Bmatrix} t_5 \\ t_2 \end{Bmatrix} = \begin{bmatrix} 0 & 0 & 0 & 0 & 1 \\ 0 & 1 & 0 & 0 & 0 \end{bmatrix} \begin{Bmatrix} t_1 \\ t_2 \\ t_3 \\ t_4 \\ t_5 \end{Bmatrix}
$$

or

$$
\underset{\mathbf{T}^e}{2 \times} = \underset{\mathbf{b}^e}{2 \times 5} \underset{\mathbf{T}}{5 \times 1}.
$$

Since each typical $\mathbf{b}^e$ matrix contains only 0s and 1s, it is called the element Boolean, or binary, matrix. Note that the matrix is null except for a single unity term on each row. This makes bookkeeping operations using this matrix very inefficient. Thus, an alternate method of bookkeeping is used in practice to accomplish a fast, direct assembly of the system equations.

5.5.7 Numerical Example

Consider a numerical example where $A = 0.01389$ ft^2, $h = 2$ BTU/h ft^2, $k = 120$ BTU/h ft $^\circ$ F, $L = 4$ ft, $P = 0.5$ ft, $Q = 0$, $t_r = 0$, and the boundary conditions are $t_o = 10^\circ$ F, $q_L = 0$. Employ two identical elements along the rod so that $L^e = L/2 = 2$ ft and the element properties are the same as the homogeneous rod. Then the element matrices are $\mathbf{C}_h^e = \mathbf{0} = \mathbf{C}_Q^e$ and

$$
\mathbf{S}_k^e = 0.8334 \begin{bmatrix} 1 & -1 \\ -1 & 1 \end{bmatrix}, \quad \mathbf{S}_h^e = 0.3333 \begin{bmatrix} 2 & 1 \\ 1 & 2 \end{bmatrix}
$$

and the point source array is $\mathbf{C}_q^T = [\,+q_o \quad 0 \quad 0\,]$. The temperature array is $\mathbf{T}^T = [T_1 \ T_2 \ T_3]$. Combining these two contributions, the typical element matrix is

$$\mathbf{S}^e = \begin{bmatrix} 1.5001 & -0.5001 \\ -0.5001 & 1.5001 \end{bmatrix} \approx \frac{1}{2} \begin{bmatrix} 3 & -1 \\ -1 & 3 \end{bmatrix}$$

Substituting the element contributions into the system thermal equilibrium by using the element topology gives

$$\frac{1}{2} \begin{bmatrix} 3 & -1 & 0 \\ -1 & (3+3) & -1 \\ 0 & -1 & 3 \end{bmatrix} \begin{Bmatrix} T_1 \\ T_2 \\ T_3 \end{Bmatrix} = \begin{Bmatrix} +q_o \\ 0 \\ 0 \end{Bmatrix} + \begin{Bmatrix} 0 \\ 0+0 \\ 0 \end{Bmatrix} \qquad (5.5.31)$$

or

$$\mathbf{S}\,\mathbf{T} = \mathbf{C}.$$

Since the first temperature is known, $T_1 = t_o = 10$, the first row is not an independent equation for the temperature and we retain only the last two rows:

$$\frac{1}{2} \begin{Bmatrix} -1 \\ 0 \end{Bmatrix} T_1 + \frac{1}{2} \begin{bmatrix} 6 & -1 \\ -1 & 3 \end{bmatrix} \begin{Bmatrix} T_2 \\ T_3 \end{Bmatrix} = \{ 0 \}$$

or

$$\begin{bmatrix} 6 & -1 \\ -1 & 3 \end{bmatrix} \begin{Bmatrix} T_2 \\ T_3 \end{Bmatrix} = \{0\} - \begin{Bmatrix} -10 \\ 0 \end{Bmatrix} = \begin{Bmatrix} 10 \\ 0 \end{Bmatrix}.$$

Inverting gives:

$$\begin{Bmatrix} T_2 \\ T_3 \end{Bmatrix} = \begin{bmatrix} 6 & -1 \\ -1 & 3 \end{bmatrix}^{-1} \begin{Bmatrix} 10 \\ 0 \end{Bmatrix} = \frac{1}{17} \begin{Bmatrix} 30 \\ 10 \end{Bmatrix} = \begin{Bmatrix} 1.765 \\ 0.588 \end{Bmatrix} {}^{\circ}F.$$

Returning to the first row we now recover the value of the heat flow reaction necessary to maintain the temperature at $t_0 = 10 = T_1$:

$$\frac{3}{2} T_1 - \frac{1}{2} T_2 + 0 = q_o \rightarrow q_o = 14.12 \text{ BTU/h}.$$

We can check this by postprocessing to find the convection heat loss in each element:

$$q = \int dq_h = \int_{L^e} h^e P^e \,(t - t_r)\, dx \qquad (5.5.32)$$

which for $t_r \equiv 0$, constant properties, and linear interpolation, reduces to

$$q_h^e = \frac{1}{2} h^e P^e L^e \,[1 \quad 1]\mathbf{T}^e.$$

Thus, the losses due to convection are 11.77 and 2.35, respectively, for a total of 14.12 BTU/h. The results of this crude two-element solution are compared with the exact values in Figure 5.5.1. Note that in this case the computed nodal temperatures are not exact but are reasonably close. The convection losses are also reasonably accurate. Employing more elements improves the accuracy, as we would expect. Error analysis shows us that the local error is a product of the size of the element, L^e, and the temperature gradient (derivative of the primary variable). We know from experience where to expect the largest gradients. In those regions (near x = 0) we should use smaller elements. Figure 5.5.1 shows computed points from seven elements and eight nodes. The element lengths were selected with the spacing ratios of 1, 1, 2, 2, 2, 2, 4, 4. The accuracy of the natural boundary condition (insulated end) approximation could have been improved by making the last element smaller.

An interesting observation here is that as the convection coefficient is reduced, the finite element solution accuracy improves. If the internal source term, Q, is not zero and there is no convection, $h = 0$, then the computed nodal temperatures are *exact* at the node points. It is approximate within the element due to our linear interpolation. It is common for finite element solutions to have primary variables that are most accurate at the nodes. Their derivatives are usually more accurate on the interior of the elements.

5.5.8 Structural Mechanics

Modern structural analysis relies extensively on the finite element method. Its integral formulation is the principal of minimum total potential energy. (This is also known as the principal of virtual work.) Basically, it states that the displacement field that satisfies the essential displacement boundary conditions and minimizes the total potential energy is the one that corresponds to the state of static equilibrium. This implies that displacements are our primary unknowns. They will be interpolated in space as will their derivatives, the strains. The total potential energy, Π, is the strain energy, U, of the structure minus the mechanical work, W, done by the applied forces. Recall from introductory mechanics that the mechanical work, W, done by a force is the scalar dot product of the force vector, $\mathbf{F}$, and the displacement vector, $\mathbf{u}$, at its point of application.

To illustrate the concept of energy formulations we will review the equilibrium of the well-known linear spring. Figure 5.5.2 shows a typical spring of stiffness k that has an applied force, F, at the free end. That end undergoes a displacement of Δ. The work done by the single force is

$$W = \vec{\Delta} \bullet \vec{F} = \Delta F \quad . \tag{5.5.33}$$

Recall that the spring stores potential energy due to its deformation. Here we call that strain energy. That energy is given by

$$U = \frac{1}{2} k \Delta^2 \quad . \tag{5.5.34}$$

Therefore, the total potential energy for the loaded spring is

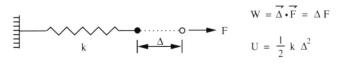

Figure 5.5.2   The linear spring.

$$\Pi\,(\Delta)\ =\ \frac{1}{2}\,k\,\Delta^2 - \Delta\,F \tag{5.5.35}$$

The equation of equilibrium is obtained by minimizing Π with respect to the displacement:

$$\frac{\partial\,\Pi}{\partial\Delta} = 0 \quad.$$

This simplifies to

$$0\ =\ \frac{2}{2}k\,\Delta - F \tag{5.5.36}$$

or

$$k\,\Delta = F$$

which is the well-known equilibrium equation for a linear spring. This example was slightly simplified, since we started with the condition that the left end of the spring had no displacement (an essential boundary condition).

The elastic bar is often modeled as a linear spring. A typical bar is shown in Figure 5.5.3. It has a length of L, an area A, and an elastic modulus of E. In introductory mechanics of materials the axial stiffness of a bar is defined as

$$k\ =\ \frac{EA}{L} \quad.$$

The bar has two end displacements, Δ_1 and Δ_2, and two associated axial forces, F_1 and F_2. The net deformation of the bar is

$$\Delta\ =\ \Delta_2 - \Delta_1 \quad. \tag{5.5.37}$$

We denote the total vector of displacements as

$$\mathbf{\Delta}^T\ =\ [\ \Delta_1\ \ \Delta_2\ ]$$

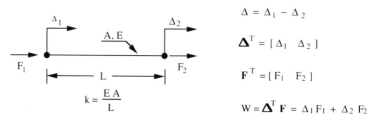

Figure 5.5.3   The elastic bar.

and the associated vector of forces as

$$\mathbf{F}^T = [\, F_1 \quad F_2\,] \quad .$$

Then the work done on the bar is

$$W = \mathbf{\Delta}^T \mathbf{F} = \Delta_1 F_1 + \Delta_2 F_2 \quad .$$

The net displacement will be expressed in matrix form to compare with later mathematical formulations. It is

$$\Delta = [\, -1 \quad 1\,]\, \mathbf{\Delta} \tag{5.5.38}$$

Then the strain energy can be written as

$$U = \frac{1}{2} k\,\Delta^2$$

$$= \frac{1}{2} \left[\frac{EA}{L} \right] \mathbf{\Delta}^T \left\{ \begin{matrix} -1 \\ 1 \end{matrix} \right\} [\, -1 \quad 1\,]\, \mathbf{\Delta}^T$$

$$= \frac{1}{2}\, \mathbf{\Delta}^T \mathbf{K}\, \mathbf{\Delta}$$

where the bar stiffness is

$$\mathbf{K} = \frac{EA}{L} \begin{bmatrix} 1 & -1 \\ -1 & 1 \end{bmatrix} \quad .$$

The total potential energy, Π, depends on all the displacements, $\mathbf{\Delta}$:

$$\Pi(\mathbf{\Delta}) = \frac{1}{2}\, \mathbf{\Delta}^T \mathbf{K}\, \mathbf{\Delta} - \mathbf{\Delta}^T \mathbf{F} \tag{5.5.39}$$

and the equation of equilibrium comes from the minimization

$$\frac{\partial \Pi}{\partial \mathbf{\Delta}} = \mathbf{0} \quad .$$

Thus,

$$\frac{2}{2}\, \mathbf{K}\, \mathbf{\Delta} - \mathbf{F} = 0$$

or simply

$$\mathbf{K}\, \mathbf{\Delta} = \mathbf{F} \tag{5.5.40}$$

represents the system of algebraic equations of equilibrium for the bar. These two equations do not yet reflect the presence of an essential boundary condition, and $|\mathbf{K}| \equiv 0$

and the system is singular. These relations were developed on physical arguments and did not involve any finite element theory. Next we will see that a one-dimensional FEA yields the same forms.

The strain energy per unit volume of an elastic solid is half the product of the stresses, σ, and the strains, ε. Thus, the integral formulation for static equilibrium states that

$$\Pi(\mathbf{u}) = \frac{1}{2}\int_V \sigma^T \varepsilon \, dV - \mathbf{u}^T \mathbf{F} \tag{5.5.41}$$

is minimum, and $\mathbf{u}$ satisfies the boundary conditions. The definition of mechanical work W can be generalized for more than one force, $\mathbf{F}$. We can allow for several point forces, $\mathbf{F}_j$, as well as **body forces** per unit volume, say $\mathbf{f}$, and surface forces (**tractions**) per unit surface area, say $\mathbf{T}$. Therefore, a more general definition of mechanical work would be

$$W = \int_V \mathbf{u}^T \mathbf{f} \, dV + \int_S \mathbf{u}^T \mathbf{T} \, dS + \sum_j \mathbf{u}_j^T \mathbf{F}_j \ . \tag{5.5.42}$$

Our previous one dimensional heat transfer example can be used to develop the corresponding elastic bar formulation by inspection. There is only one axial displacement, u, one strain component, $\varepsilon = du/dx$, and one corresponding stress component, $\sigma = E\varepsilon$, where E denotes the elastic modulus of the material. We can make the following analogies in one-dimension.

Thermal Analysis	Stress Analysis
Temperature, t	Displacement, u
Thermal gradient, dt/dx	Strain, du/dx
Heat flux, $q = -k \, dt/dx$	Stress, $\sigma = E \, du/dx$
Heat generation, Q	Body Force, f.

The element stiffness $\mathbf{K}^e$ is associated with the strain energy. If we interpolate the displacements in space as $u(x) = \mathbf{H}(x)\,\mathbf{u}^e$, then the strain is associated with $d\mathbf{H}/dx$. From Equation 5.5.12 the strain in a linear displacement bar is

$$\varepsilon^e = \frac{du}{dx} \approx \frac{1}{L^e}[-1 \quad 1]\,\mathbf{u}^e \ . \tag{5.5.43}$$

This agrees with the simple engineering definition of axial strain as the change in length divided by the original length. We see it is the same as the deformation in Equation (5.5.38) divided by the original length. Since this strain is constant, the axial stress in the element is

$$\sigma^e = E^e \varepsilon^e \approx \frac{E^e}{L^e} [\,-1 \quad 1\,]\, \mathbf{u}^e \quad .$$

This means that for constant, E and A the strain energy does not require integration and simplifies, from Equation (5.5.41), to

$$U = \frac{1}{2}\, \mathbf{u}^{e^T} \begin{Bmatrix} -1 \\ 1 \end{Bmatrix} \frac{E^e}{L^e} \frac{1}{L^e} [\,-1 \quad 1\,]\, \mathbf{u}^e A^e L^e = \frac{1}{2}\, \mathbf{u}^{e^T} \mathbf{K}^e \mathbf{u}^e$$

where for the linear displacement bar the simplified stiffness is, as before,

$$\mathbf{K}^e = \frac{E^e A^e}{L^e} \begin{bmatrix} 1 & -1 \\ -1 & 1 \end{bmatrix} \quad . \tag{5.5.44}$$

As with the thermal conduction matrix, we find the general form of the stiffness matrix to be defined as

$$\mathbf{K}^e = \int_{V^e} E^e \frac{d\mathbf{H}^T}{dx} \frac{d\mathbf{H}}{dx}\, dV \tag{5.5.45}$$

and the volumetric source term nodal resultant is defined as

$$\mathbf{C}^e = \int_{V^e} \mathbf{f}^e \mathbf{H}^T\, dV \tag{5.5.46}$$

The linear displacement element matrix has the same form as before and for constant properties yields

$$\mathbf{C}^e = \frac{f^e A^e L^e}{2} \begin{Bmatrix} 1 \\ 1 \end{Bmatrix} \quad .$$

For a bar with two nodes we again have linear displacement and constant strains. Since AL is the total volume, $\mathbf{C}^e$ lumps half the body force at each end of the bar. The total potential energy of an element is

$$\Pi^e = \frac{1}{2}\, \mathbf{u}^{e^T} \mathbf{K}^e \mathbf{u}^e - \mathbf{u}^{e^T} \mathbf{C}^e - \sum_j \mathbf{u}_j^T \mathbf{F}_j^e$$

and if we minimize the total potential energy with respect to all displacements, $\mathbf{U}$, we get the algebraic **equations of equilibrium**:

$$\mathbf{K}\, \mathbf{U} = \mathbf{P} \tag{5.5.47}$$

where $\mathbf{K}$ is the assembly of the element stiffnesses, $\mathbf{K}^e$, and $\mathbf{P}$ is the resultant of the point forces, $\mathbf{F}$, body forces, $\mathbf{C}^e$, and the like.

The preceding equilibrium equations are automatically valid for statically indeterminate structures. As a trivial example of this, consider a bar (see Figure 5.5.4), fixed at both ends and loaded in the middle by a load of P. We wish to determine the displacement at the midpoint and the two reaction forces at the ends. Number the three nodes from left to right. If the bar had a length of L, then the two elements each have $L^e = L/2$ and thus, a stiffness of

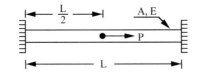

Figure 5.5.4   A statically indeterminate structure.

$$k^e = \frac{2EA}{L} \begin{bmatrix} 1 & -1 \\ -1 & 1 \end{bmatrix}$$

The three equations of equilibrium assembled from the two elements are

$$\frac{2EA}{L} \begin{bmatrix} 1 & -1 & 0 \\ -1 & (1+1) & -1 \\ 0 & -1 & 1 \end{bmatrix} \begin{Bmatrix} u_1 \\ u_2 \\ u_3 \end{Bmatrix} = \begin{Bmatrix} R_1 \\ P \\ R_2 \end{Bmatrix} \tag{5.5.48}$$

where R_1 and R_2 are the unknown end reactions. These three equations come from minimizing the total potential energy but do not yet reflect the essential boundary conditions that $u_1 = 0 = u_3$. Only the second row is an independent equation for displacement calculation:

$$\frac{2EA}{L}(2)u_2 = P + u_1 \frac{2EA}{L} + u_3 \frac{2EA}{L} = P$$

Solving gives $u_2 = PL/4EA$, which is the exact algebraic answer for this indeterminate system. Now that all the displacements are known, we can use the equation rows associated with the essential boundary conditions to determine the reactions necessary to enforce these conditions. The first row now yields

$$\frac{2EA}{L}(u_1 - u_2 + 0) = R_1$$

so

$$\frac{2EA}{L}\left[0 - \frac{PL}{4EA} + 0\right] = R_1$$

so that the left reaction is $R_1 = -P/2$, as expected. Likewise, we find the right reaction has the same value. Of course, if the load, P, had been placed at any other point, these reactions would not be equal, but their sum would be equal and opposite to the applied load.

Now that all the displacements are known, Equation (5.5.43) can be utilized to compute the strain in each element. For the first element

$$\varepsilon^e \;=\; \frac{2}{L}\,[-1 \;\; 1] \left\{ \begin{array}{c} u_1 \\ u_2 \end{array} \right\}^e \;=\; \frac{2}{L}\,[-1 \;\; 1] \left\{ \begin{array}{c} 0 \\ PL/4EA \end{array} \right\}$$

so $\varepsilon^e = P/2EA$, and the stress $\sigma^e = E^e\,\varepsilon^e$ is $\sigma^e = P/2A$. This agrees with the engineering definition that the axial stress is the force in the bar (P/2) divided by its cross-sectional area. For the current support and load conditions, the second element has the same strain and stress magnitudes but opposite signs.

5.5.9 Isoparametric Elements

The formulations, such as Equation (5.5.4), for heat transfer and structural analysis are well known. Thus, we mainly need to concentrate on the contributions made by a typical element, like Equation (5.5.25). Those calculations in turn depend on the shape of the element and how we do the interpolation within the element. The use of global coordinate interpolation, such as Equations (5.5.11) through (5.5.13), is quite restrictive and difficult to automate. However, by using the previous concepts of parametric geometry, we can employ compatible curvilinear elements and also automate the integrations necessary to form the element matrices, such as Equations (5.5.25) and (5.5.26). This provides us with the most practical FEA tools.

The most popular way to employ parametric models is through the use of **isoparametric elements**. They have that name because we use a single (iso) set of parametric interpolations to define all the quantities of interest inside the element in terms of the corresponding nodal values. Sometimes we interpolate for unknowns, like the temperature, and other times we interpolate from given data, like the global coordinates of the nodes.

For example, in two dimensions we could interpolate for the x-coordinate from Equation (3.4.3):

$$X(r,s) = \mathbf{H}(r,s)\,\mathbf{X}^e \tag{5.5.49}$$

and use the same interpolations for the temperature

$$t(r,s) = \mathbf{H}(r,s)\mathbf{T}^e. \tag{5.5.50}$$

Then the element integrals become functions of the parametric coordinates. The derivatives and differential volumes in the two systems are related by the **Jacobian, J**, as described in Equations (3.6.13) through (3.6.19). They allow us to convert the physical integrals, such as Equation (5.5.25) or (5.5.26), to a corresponding integral in the parametric space, such as Equation (3.6.22), that can then be numerically integrated, as Equation (3.6.23).

In stress analysis and heat conduction problems we can always express the element matrices in a standard matrix form:

$$\mathbf{C}^e = \int_{V^e} \mathbf{H}^{e^T} Q^e \; dV \tag{5.5.51}$$

$$\mathbf{S}^e = \int_{V^e} \mathbf{B}^{e^T} \mathbf{D}^e \mathbf{B}^e \; dV. \tag{5.5.52}$$

Here Q denotes some volumetric source or forcing term. In $\mathbf{S}$ the term $\mathbf{D}$ denotes a material property array. For conduction it contains the thermal conductivity, whereas in stress analysis it contains the elastic modulus and Poisson's ratio. The array $\mathbf{B}$ contains contributions from the physical derivatives of the interpolations, $\mathbf{H}$, and possibly the interpolations themselves. In heat conduction the rows of $\mathbf{B}$ are the components of the gradient operator (del) acting on $\mathbf{H}$. For stress analysis each row comes from the definition of a strain in terms of the displacements. Thus, it also contains the physical derivatives of $\mathbf{H}$ (and $\mathbf{H}$ itself, if axisymmetric). To illustrate the concept, generalize the previous example in Section 5.5.5 to pure orthotropic conduction in two dimensions:

$$\mathbf{S}^e = \int_{A^e} \begin{bmatrix} \mathbf{H}^e_{,x} \\ \mathbf{H}^e_{,y} \end{bmatrix}^T \begin{bmatrix} k^e_x & 0 \\ 0 & k^e_y \end{bmatrix} \begin{bmatrix} \mathbf{H}^e_{,x} \\ \mathbf{H}^e_{,y} \end{bmatrix} t^e \; dA \tag{5.5.53}$$

where the element thickness, t^e, can be assumed to be a known constant. For pure conduction ($h = 0$) this clearly reduces to the previous case if $k_y = 0$ and $k_x = k$. Since $\mathbf{H}$ is a function of the parametric coordinates, we do not yet know how to find the physical derivatives with respect to x and y. However, the parametric geometry in Section 3.6 gives us the necessary tools to form $\mathbf{B}$ and still have the integration automated. From Equations (3.6.16) and (3.6.18) we see that the Jacobian, $\mathbf{J}$, involves the product of the parametric derivatives of the interpolation, say Δ, and the input global coordinates of the element nodes, say $\mathbf{R}^e$. Here the first column of $\mathbf{R}^e$ contains the y values, and so on. Then we can always numerically form the Jacobian in an element as

$$\mathbf{J}^e = \Delta \, \mathbf{R}^e \tag{5.5.54}$$

where

$$\Delta \equiv \partial_l \, \mathbf{H} = \begin{bmatrix} \dfrac{\partial \mathbf{H}}{\partial r} \\[2ex] \dfrac{\partial \mathbf{H}}{\partial s} \end{bmatrix}. \tag{5.5.55}$$

From Equations (3.6.16) and (3.6.17) we can then carry out the inverse relation,

$$\partial^e_g \, f = \mathbf{J}^{e^{-1}} \partial_l \, f \tag{5.5.56}$$

to find the physical derivatives of the parametric interpolation functions, say $\mathbf{d}^e$, in that element that are required to substitute into $\mathbf{B}^e$. Specifically, we have

$$\mathbf{d}^e \equiv \mathbf{J}^{e^{-1}} \Delta \tag{5.5.57}$$

so

$$\mathbf{d}^e = \begin{bmatrix} \dfrac{\partial \mathbf{H}}{\partial x} \\[2mm] \dfrac{\partial \mathbf{H}}{\partial y} \end{bmatrix}^e \equiv \begin{bmatrix} \mathbf{d}_x^e \\[2mm] \mathbf{d}_y^e \end{bmatrix}.\tag{5.5.58}$$

Comparing to Equation (5.5.53) for heat conduction, we see that $\mathbf{B}^e = \mathbf{d}^e$. However, in stress analysis $\mathbf{B}$ is larger than $\mathbf{d}$. It still uses all the terms in $\mathbf{d}$ but combines them in a different way. Note that each row of $\mathbf{d}$ contains the derivatives, with respect to one physical coordinate, of all the element's interpolation functions. Similarly, the k-th column of $\mathbf{d}$ contains all the physical derivatives of the interpolation function for that node, H_k. The array $\mathbf{B}^e$ can always be written in terms of subpartitions, $\mathbf{B}_k^e$, that contain all the contributions from the interpolation function H_k and/or its physical derivatives (terms from the k-th column of $\mathbf{d}^e$). The number of columns in the partition $\mathbf{B}_k^e$ equals the number of unknowns at node k. Typical entries for $\mathbf{D}$ and $\mathbf{B}$ are in Table 5.5.1.

TABLE 5.5.1   ELEMENT SQUARE MATRIX DEFINITIONS

$$\mathbf{S} = \int_V \mathbf{B}^T \mathbf{D}\, \mathbf{B}\ dv, \quad \mathbf{B} = [\mathbf{B}_1\ \mathbf{B}_2\ \cdots\ \mathbf{B}_n]$$

A. Conduction

$$\mathbf{D} = \begin{bmatrix} k_x & 0 & 0 \\ 0 & k_y & 0 \\ 0 & 0 & k_z \end{bmatrix}^e, \quad \mathbf{B}_k^e = \begin{bmatrix} \partial H_k/\partial x \\ \partial H_k/\partial y \\ \partial H_k/\partial z \end{bmatrix}^e = \begin{bmatrix} H_{,x} \\ H_{,y} \\ H_{,z} \end{bmatrix}_k^e$$

B. Plane stress or plane strain

$$\mathbf{D} = \frac{E}{1-v^2} \begin{bmatrix} 1 & v & 0 \\ v & 1 & 0 \\ 0 & 0 & (1-v)/2 \end{bmatrix}, \quad \mathbf{B}_k^e = \begin{bmatrix} H_{,x} & 0 \\ 0 & H_{,y} \\ H_{,y} & H_{,x} \end{bmatrix}_k^e$$

For plane strain, use $E^* = E/(1-v^2)$, $v^* = v/(1-v)$.

C. Axisymmetric solids

$$\mathbf{D} = \frac{E}{1-v^2} \begin{bmatrix} 1 & v & v & 0 \\ v & 1 & v & 0 \\ v & v & 1 & 0 \\ 0 & 0 & 0 & (1-v)/2 \end{bmatrix}, \quad \mathbf{B}_k^e = \begin{bmatrix} H_{,r} & 0 \\ 0 & H_{,z} \\ H/R & 0 \\ H_{,z} & H_{,r} \end{bmatrix}_k^e, \quad R = \mathbf{H}\mathbf{R}^e$$

To illustrate the extension of our parametric geometry to the calculation of the physical derivatives necessary for FEA, consider the simple three-node triangle given in Equation (3.4.9). By inspection we can see that its local parametric derivatives are

$$\Delta = \begin{bmatrix} \mathbf{H}_{,r} \\ \mathbf{H}_{,s} \end{bmatrix} = \begin{bmatrix} -1 & 1 & 0 \\ -1 & 0 & 1 \end{bmatrix}. \tag{5.5.59}$$

In this special case they are seen to be constant. The Jacobian of this element is

$$\mathbf{J}^e = \Delta \, \mathbf{R}^e = \begin{bmatrix} -1 & 1 & 0 \\ -1 & 0 & 1 \end{bmatrix} \begin{bmatrix} x_1 & y_1 \\ x_2 & y_2 \\ x_3 & y_3 \end{bmatrix}^e$$

$$\mathbf{J}^e(r,s) = \begin{bmatrix} (x_2 - x_1) & (y_2 - y_1) \\ (x_3 - x_1) & (y_3 - y_1) \end{bmatrix}^e. \tag{5.5.60}$$

In this case, the determinant of this constant Jacobian equals twice the physical area of the element, A^e. The inverse Jacobian, Equation (3.6.16), here becomes

$$\mathbf{J}^{e^{-1}} = \frac{1}{2A^e} \begin{bmatrix} (y_3 - y_1) & -(y_2 - y_1) \\ -(x_3 - x_1) & (x_2 - x_1) \end{bmatrix}^e. \tag{5.5.61}$$

Although we do not know the $\mathbf{H}$ in terms of the physical coordinates, x and y, we can find their physical derivatives from

$$\mathbf{d}^e = \mathbf{J}^{e^{-1}} \Delta$$

which reduces to

$$\mathbf{d}^e = \begin{bmatrix} \mathbf{H}^e_{,x} \\ \mathbf{H}^e_{,y} \end{bmatrix} = \frac{1}{2A^e} \begin{bmatrix} (y_2 - y_3) & (y_3 - y_1) & (y_1 - y_2) \\ (x_3 - x_2) & (x_1 - x_3) & (x_2 - x_1) \end{bmatrix}^e.$$

A common notation is to let b_j denote the difference in y-coordinates of the two nodes opposite node j. Likewise, we denote the negative of the x-coordinate difference by c_j. Then for this three-node triangle we have

$$\mathbf{d}^e = \frac{1}{2A^e} \begin{bmatrix} b_1 & b_2 & b_3 \\ c_1 & c_2 & c_3 \end{bmatrix}^e. \tag{5.5.62}$$

For the two-dimensional conduction in Equation (5.5.53) we have $\mathbf{B}^e = \mathbf{d}^e$, which is constant for this element. Thus, no integration is required and we see by inspection that the typical entry in the square matrix is

$$S_{ij}^e = \frac{t^e}{4A^e} \, (k_x \, b_i \, b_j + k_y \, c_i \, c_j). \tag{5.5.63}$$

For any other two-dimensional element, Δ, and thus, $\mathbf{J}^e$ and $\mathbf{d}^e$, will be functions of the parametric coordinates and $\mathbf{S}^e$ must be integrated in parametric coordinates.

The complete details of automating the calculation of the element matrices, including FORTRAN source, have been presented by Akin, Hinton and Owen, Zienkiewicz, and others. Numerically integrated isoparametric elements are the foundation of most commercial and research codes for finite element analysis.

5.6 COMBINING FINITE ELEMENT ANALYSIS AND OPTIMIZATION

As we have already stated, the design optimization process frequently involves utilizing a finite element analysis. The merit function is often defined as an output from an FEA. system. Example quantities may include the maximum temperature, deflection, or stress or related items such as the natural frequency, the strain-energy density, or the weight. Thus, we note that any FEA output data or postprocessing combinations of those data can be employed in an arbitrary fashion by the designer to describe the merit function.

Many optimization software systems provide for an interface to a general analysis program that will return the merit function. However, FEA programs are generally quite large, and each merit function evaluation may be very expensive to evaluate. The merit function in a FEA system can be difficult to define and recover, since FEA systems were not originally designed with such an option in mind.

Thus, there are special considerations and trends in analysis for combining FEA and optimization procedures. Commercial FEA systems are beginning to offer optimization options to their already numerous capabilities. These options usually offer the designer a **parametric language** by which he or she can select the design variables, analysis functions, or state variables and the merit function. The parametric design language lets a designer access, manipulate, and recover almost any quantity in the data base. The availability of such a parametric design tool in an FEA system will become increasingly common and will significantly enhance the state of computer assisted mechanical design.

The expense of evaluating the merit function via an FEA system also causes the designer to utilize **approximate optimization** procedures. Since the simplex search algorithm often needs thousands of merit function evaluations, its heavy use with FEA systems may have to await the next generation of computers. Since the **ANSYS** system for FEA analysis is widely utilized, its approximate optimization capability will be described here as an example of what is commercially available today.

A parametric language lets the designer identify the design variables, the analysis functions (or state variables), and the merit or objective function. It also allows for regional or functional constraints to be defined. The characteristics of the analysis functions are determined by calculating their actual values for a given set of design variables. Usually a complete FEA is employed for each set of design variables in order to produce the preceding values for the analysis functions. The resulting data are then fit with surfaces (or curves) in the design variable space. A similar fit for the merit function is obtained by either using the values returned by the FEA system or by post-processing the returned analysis function (state variable) values. Each surface fit to the FEA results defines an approximation. An individual approximation surface, in terms of the design variables, is formed for the merit function and each analysis variable selected through the parametric design language. Thus, all these approximations are dependent quantities that act as functions of the design variables.

To construct the initial approximations the range of the design variables is usually sampled at random. The approximating surfaces are fitted to those results by a least squares technique. During each optimization loop and new FEA run, the approximations are updated or refit to account for the new data. It is the **merit function approximation** that is actually minimized. Likewise, it is the approximations to the analysis functions that are checked against the functional constraints or are modified with penalties to include the constraint data.

At this point we can envision employing the simplex search algorithm to search these approximate surfaces for a feasible minimum rather than actually calling the FEA system with the design variables at each vertex. Clearly this will be much faster (more economical) than dealing exclusively with the FEA system during the design optimization. Regardless of the optimization algorithm used, the location of the minimum merit function (e.g., the set of optimum design variables) indicated by these approximations will differ from the location of the true minimum. However, the approximation location of the minimum usually is very close to the location of the true minimum, even though the function values at the two locations may be noticeably different. The ANSYS system employs the approximations to locate the minimum, but the actual value of the merit function is calculated by returning to the FEA system with the design variables that were found at the minimum location. If the optimization loop is to proceed, then this new and accurate merit function value is used to update the approximations for the next location search. Within ANSYS the designer is allowed to select approximation surfaces in the design space that are either linear, incomplete quadratic, or quadratic. Given a trial vector, $\mathbf{x}$, with N design variables the approximating surfaces have the form

$$A(\mathbf{x}) = a_o + \sum_{j=1}^{N} a_j x_j + \sum_{j=1}^{N} b_j x_j^2 + \sum_{j=1}^{N} \sum_{k=j+1}^{N} c_{jk} x_j x_k . \tag{5.6.1}$$

The coefficients a_j, b_j, and c_{jk} are found by minimizing the weighted least squares error for the variable A:

$$E^2 = \sum_{n=1}^{S} w_n [A_n - A(\mathbf{x}_n)]^2 \tag{5.6.2}$$

where S denotes the total number of sets of design variables. The weights, w, are often selected to bias the fit in favor of sets that are closest to the previous estimate of the location of the minimum. Figure 5.6.1 illustrates a one-dimensional problem where the biased quadratic approximation of a cubic merit function gives a good prediction for the location of the minimum. The actual minimum value would be calculated by using the true cubic at that point. True design optimization often involves the concept of **design sensitivity**. These data can be very expensive to compute, especially when a large FEA is used to define the merit function. The design sensitivities are defined as the partial derivatives, with respect to the design variables, of the merit function and the analysis functions (state variables). The preceding approximation surfaces can be used to calculate those derivatives, at the local minimum location, and thus, to estimate the design sensitivities. In that case we use the approximate merit function to define the slopes at the optimal point but not the value there.

A problem used by several authors to illustrate the combination of finite element analysis and optimization is to find the optimum shape of a cantilever beam. An aluminum beam is shown in Figure 5.6.2. We would like the beam of minimum weight, w, that does not exceed the allowed tip deflection, D, nor the maximum Von Mises effective stress limit, S. The data for the beam are: $D = 0.5$ in., $L = 10$ in., $h = 0.3$ in., $t = 1$ in., $E = 1 \times 10^7$ lb/in^2, $\nu = 0.33$, $\gamma = 0.10$ lb/cu. in., $S = 3 \times 10^4$ lb/in^2, $M = 450$ in.-lb. It is assumed to have a constant width, t, normal to the plane shown. The half-thickness at the tip, h, was assigned to satisfy the stress limit there and is based on a simple Mh/I calculation. By using a parametric mesh generator, we could control the shape by specifying the location of the two free master nodes of the patch shown in the figure. By placing the master nodes at the end and midspan locations, we could use only their y-coordinates, y_3 and y_4, as design variables (see Figure 5.8.1). Thus, at this point we assume that the control node locations (thicknesses) are given, and we can concentrate on describing the FEA model.

We will employ a typical plane stress model. Since the material is homogeneous, we do not have to locate any other material interfaces. Each point in the model will have two displacements (u, v) and three stresses $(\sigma_x, \sigma_y, \tau)$ that can be reduced to a single Von Mises effective stress, σ_E, that is used as a failure criterion for ductile materials. To cut the cost of the finite element analysis by a factor of four, we look for symmetry and antisymmetry. The geometry, material properties, and supports are

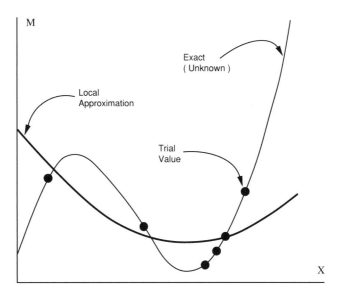

Figure 5.6.1   Merit function approximations.

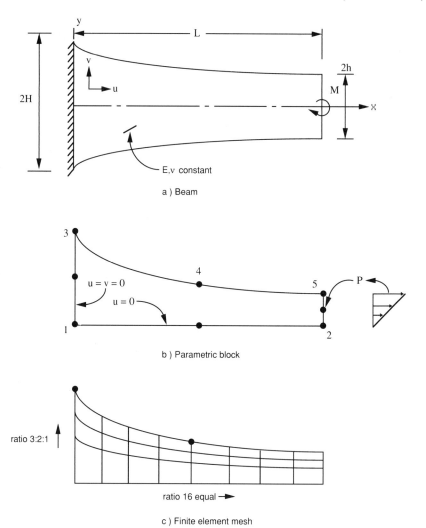

Figure 5.6.2   Optimum shape by moving modes 3 and 4.

symmetric with respect to the beam centerline. The loading (moment), deflections, and stresses are antisymmetric. Therefore, we will utilize a half-body model. The antisymmetric quantities change sign with the sign of y. Quantities of interest are

$$y > 0 \qquad u \qquad v \qquad \sigma_x \qquad \sigma_y \qquad \tau \qquad \sigma_E$$
$$y < 0 \qquad -u \qquad v \qquad -\sigma_x \qquad \sigma_y \qquad \tau \qquad \sigma_E$$

The change in sign of u with y means that it must be zero when y is zero, that is, at points along the neutral axis (centerline). Thus, in the half-body model we must impose that displacement boundary condition to account for the omitted material. The fixed, or encastre, support at the left end can be interpreted in two ways. In the classical sense we should set all displacements (u and v) to zero along that line. But if the fixity is not complete, then v could move due to a Poisson ratio contraction. Then the wall would act like another line of symmetry. In that case we would set $u = 0$ along the line. Of course, both u and v are zero at the point where the two symmetry lines intersect. Here we will follow the classical approach and encastre all points at $x = 0$. These displacement conditions assure us that our model will deform as the complete body would.

Application of the consistent loading conditions still remain. To apply a moment exactly we must have a rotational degree of freedom at a node. A plane stress model includes displacement but no rotations. Thus, the moment must be approximated by some statically equivalent method. Before doing that we should note that our model requires only half the moment. The physical moment is applied at the centerline of the body and half goes into the top material and half into the bottom.

Our half antisymmetry model will be loaded with $M/2 = 225$ in.-lb. We can apply this moment in either of two ways. The simplest approach is to convert the moment to a force couple. We could apply these two equal and opposite forces at the centerline and the top fiber. The required force magnitude is $F_x = M/2h$. That is, we select any two nodes, say 2 and 5, and divide the moment, $M/2$, by the distance between the nodes, h. This is completely arbitrary because it does not load any other nodes that may be on that end section. It has disadvantages in that the results overestimate both the displacements and stresses at those two nodes due to the local stress concentration. A short distance away the results should be fairly accurate.

The second option is to apply a statically equivalent normal pressure on the end of the beam. That has advantages, since it does not cause local stress concentration and agrees with the simple beam theory for σ_x (but not τ). The pressure would be zero at the centerline and maximum at the top fiber. The maximum pressure would be

$$\frac{M}{2} = \frac{1}{2}\ (Pht\ )(\frac{2}{3}\ h\ )$$

$$P = \frac{3}{2}\ \frac{M}{h^2\ t} = 7500\ \text{lb/in.}^2\ .$$

The application of this pressure may be automated to require the user to supply only the pressure at the two or three nodes on the master block. The program will then numerically integrate this distribution to give the proper resultant element nodal forces. Some programs require the user to input the resultant force manually at a node. For a straight-sided element the nodal resultant forces are shown in Figure 5.6.3 for both the quadratic and linear elements. Note that the three (or two) forces sum to the resultant applied force, which is $L(P_1 + P_2)/2$. The figure can be applied for triangular pressure distributions ($P_1 = 0$) and uniform distributions ($P_1 = P_2$). For quadratic elements most of the resultant goes to the midside node.

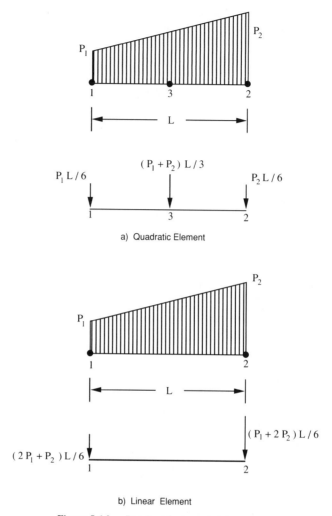

Figure 5.6.3   Resultant for trapeziodal pressure.

Having established a finite element model in terms of parameters y_3 and y_4 that can be controlled by an optimization program, the finite element analysis system is called to evaluate the merit function(s). As the optimization search (or structural design iteration) proceeds, we obtain nondimensional mass and stress changes similar to those sketched in Figure 5.6.4. Any structure can be solved in this manner. Since the FEA can be very time consuming, the merit function is quite expensive and the preceding search approximation procedures are employed to yield a better design but not a true optimum.

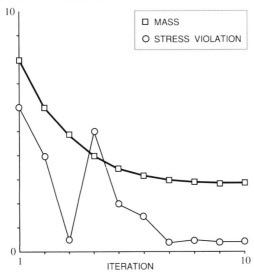

Figure 5.6.4   Typical shape optimization results.

5.7 REFERENCES

1. Akin, J. E. *Application and Implementation of Finite Element Methods.* New York: Academic Press, 1982.

2. Akin, J. E. *Finite Element Analysis for Undergraduates.* New York: Academic Press, 1986.

3. Beazley, P. K. *Design Optimization Tutorial.* Swanson Analysis Systems, Inc., 1987.

4. Cook, R. D. *Concepts and Applications of Finite Element Analysis.* New York: John Wiley, 1974.

5. Hughes, T. J. R. *The Finite Element Method.* Englewood Cliffs, N. J.: Prentice Hall, 1987.

6. Imgrund, M. C. "Design Improvements Using Finite Elements and Optimizing with Approximate Functions." ASCE, 9th Conference on Electronic Computation, February 1986, pp. 508–18.

7. Imgrund, M. C. "Using the Approximate Optimization Algorithm in ANSYS for the Solution of Optimum Convective Surfaces and Other Thermal Design Problems." "5th Intern. Conference on Thermal Problems," Montreal, 1986.

8. Imgrund, M. C., and Wheeler, M. J. "Reducing Design Cost by Integrating Finite Element and Optimization Techniques." ASME National Design Engineering Show, March 1986, pp. 79–92.

9. Irons, B. M., and Ahmad, S. *Techniques of Finite Elements,* New York: John Wiley, 1980.

10. Robinson, J. "A Single Element Test." *Comp. Math. Appl. Mech. & Eng.* 7, (1976): 191–200.

11. Vanderplaats, G. N., and Sugimoto, H. "A General Purpose Optimization Program for Engineering Design." *Intern. J. Computers and Structures* 24, no. 1, 1986.

12. Vanderplaats, G. N., Miura, H., and Chargin, M. "Large Scale Structural Synthesis." *Finite Elements in Analysis and Design,* 2, no. 2 (1985): 117–130, 1985.

13. Zienkiewicz, O. C. *The Finite Element Method.* New York: McGraw-Hill, 1978.

5.8 EXERCISES

1. Set to zero the integral, over the length, of the product of Equation (5.5.1) and t. Integrate that identity by parts. Substitute element parametric forms for H and verify that results identical to Equations (5.5.23), (5.5.25) and (5.5.27) are obtained.

2. How does the partial model in Figure 5.4.6 change if: (a) the rectangle becomes a square with a square hole, (b) the top and bottom lines of the rectangle are insulated instead of having T_2 given, (c) the top half of the rectangle is made of a different homogeneous material, and (d) the system has a homogeneous rate of internal heat generation?

3. How do the partial models in Figure 5.4.7 change if (a) the object also has a uniform temperature increase, (b) the top half is made of a different homogeneous material, (c) the rotation takes place about the x-axis instead of the z-axis, and (d) the hole is in the center of a rectangle instead of a square?

4. What modeling changes occur if the box in Figure 5.4.8 is actually a homogeneous solid loaded in the same fashion?

5. Create a cyclic symmetry model of the system in Figure 5.4.9. Let the long vane edge be one of the created partial model sides.

6. For the quadratic element in Figure 5.6.3 verify that two-thirds of the resultant goes to the midpoint node when the pressure is either uniform or triangular.

7. Name the types of repeatable domains shown in Figure 5.4.12.

8. A standard beam bending element has an equilibrium equation of

$$\frac{EI}{L^3}\begin{bmatrix} 12 & 6L & -12 & 6L \\ 6L & 4L^2 & -6L & 2L^2 \\ -12 & -6L & 12 & -6L \\ 6L & 2L^2 & -6L & 4L^2 \end{bmatrix}\begin{Bmatrix} v_1 \\ \theta_1 \\ v_2 \\ \theta_2 \end{Bmatrix} = L\begin{Bmatrix} \dfrac{(7P_1 + 3P_2)}{20} \\ \dfrac{L(3P_1 + 2P_2)}{60} \\ \dfrac{(3P_1 + 7P_2)}{20} \\ \dfrac{-L(2P_1 + 3P_2)}{60} \end{Bmatrix}$$

when subjected to transverse loads, per unit length, of P_1 and P_2. Solve for the deflection and/or rotation of a single element model with (a) node 2 fixed and $P_2 = P_1$, (b) node 2 fixed and $P_1 = 0$, (c) node 2 fixed, node 1 pinned, and $P_2 = P_1$, and (d) both node 1 and 2 pinned, and $P_1 = 0$. Compare the answers with the exact results. Compute the reactions in each case.

9. Use a commercial FEA system to solve the following thermal and stress analysis problems that refer to Figure 5.8.1.

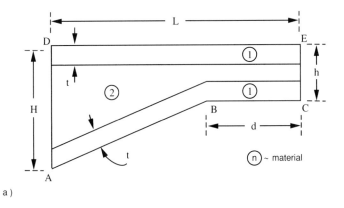

a)

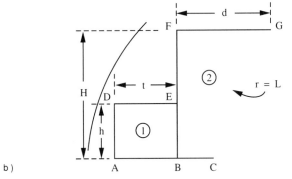

b)

Figure 5.8.1   Exercise Figures.

a. Axisymmetric thermal

Ex.	Part	Axis	Region	Material	T = 200 on	T = 10 on
1	a	AD	1	Alum	—	AB
			2	Steel	DE	—
2	a	CE	1,2	Copper	BC	AD
3	a	DE	1	Steel	CE	AB
			2	Copper		
4	b	AC	1,2	Alum	AD	FG
5	b	AD	1,2	Steel	AC	FG
6	b	AD	1	Copper	DE	—
			2	Steel	—	CG
7	b	FG	1,2	Alum	EF	AB

b. Planar thermal

Use the conditions in (a), but assume unit thickness and ignore the axis of revolution.

c. Axisymmetric stress

Replace the given temperature in (a) with a given pressure with the same numerical value. In addition, add the following displacement constraints to the exercises (for axis of revolution denoted as x-axis):

Ex.	Point Restrained	Line Restrained
1	A, C in u	AD in v
2	D in u, v	CE in v
3	—	DE in u, v
4	—	FG in u, v
5	F in v	AC in u
6	—	FG in u, v
7	F, G in u, v	—

d. Plane stress

Repeat (c) with the axis of revolution replaced by a plane of symmetry.

e. Thermal stress

Repeat Example 4 with additional loading from the temperatures obtained in the thermal analysis.

6

SIMULATION METHODS

6.1 INTRODUCTION

Any design process should involve several "what if" questions. Related to this is the concept of "test before production." **Simulation** involves experimentation with computerized models of a system or process. Thus, it allows the designer to consider a range of coefficients, or forcing functions, to test the design before it goes into production. Thus, simulation is an important part of the computer aided design process.

The two most common types of simulators are those for **discrete events** and **continuous systems**. The event simulators can be important in economic or in project planning. In mechanical engineering it is much more common to deal with the simulation of systems represented by differential equations. Design problems often involve several, if not hundreds, of differential equations that may contain nonlinear coefficients and/or nonlinear forcing functions. Clearly a computerized process is necessary to solve such a problem. Since these continuous systems are common to several areas of engineering, committees have prepared suggested guidelines for continuous system simulation languages (CSSL). These guidelines have led to the development of commercial systems for engineering simulations. One of the earliest was the Continuous System Modeling Program, CSMP, which was developed and released by IBM Corp. It and its upgrade, CSMP III, are available for batch operation on IBM mainframes. Other companies have released CSMP on other classes of machines. A version with enhanced interactive graphics, PCESP, is available for personal computers. A 1984 update of CSMP was released with the name of Dynamic Simulation Language (DSL). It has a number of improved features, such as output to modern graphics terminals. Another commonly used system is the Advanced Continuous Simulation Language, ACSL.

These two are similar in many respects. There are other systems, such as TUTSIM, that use **block diagrams** exclusively to describe the model being considered. The block diagram approach is considered at the end of this chapter.

6.2 CONTINUOUS SIMULATORS

Many of us have had experience with a continuous system simulator. The popular flight simulator game available on personal computers and workstations is an example of a well-planned mechanical simulator. It begins with the six differential equations from flight mechanics that describe its translational and rotational motion. The characteristics of the aircraft appear as parameters in the differential equations. By integrating these equations in time in response to the pilot input, we can compute the position and orientation of the craft relative to its initial position before takeoff. Such things as the continuously updated yaw, pitch, or fuel level can be combined with a graphical display to resemble the actual dials and displays on the aircraft console. The simulator also has a stored polygon surface model of the geometry of the topography and buildings surrounding the takeoff point. Having computed the position of the craft in three-dimensional space as well as its orientation, it is possible to compute and display the visible surface view that the pilot would actually see. If the computed point is inside a building polygon, then the simulator signals a crash.

More advanced simulators are used in a similar manner to train real pilots for airlines, fighters, space shuttles, and the like. One luxury car manufacturer uses an advanced simulator to test new designs before they are built. They code the equations for the new suspension and steering systems and combine them with the equations of motion. This creates a set of 20 nonlinear differential equations to solve in time. This system is combined with a parametric surface display system, MOVIE.BYU, to display a realistic road with moveable obstacle images. A human driver is placed in the simulator to drive the "new" car to see how it would respond to emergency situations.

When the continuous simulators solve an nth order differential equation, they split it into a system of n first-order differential equations. They are integrated as initial value problems. For example, a fourth-order system such as

$$\frac{d^4y}{dt^4} = f\left[y, \frac{dy}{dt}, \frac{d^2y}{dt^2}, \frac{d^3y}{dt^3}, t\right]$$

could be replaced by the system

$$\frac{da}{dt} = b$$
$$\frac{db}{dt} = c$$
$$\frac{dc}{dt} = e$$
$$\frac{de}{dt} = f[a, b, c, e, t].$$

(6.2.1)

Thus, a typical concern is the solution of a nonlinear first-order ordinary differential equation (ODE):

$$\frac{dx}{dt} = g\,[x(t),\,t]$$ (6.2.2)

which has a solution of the form

$$x = \int g\ dt + x_i$$ (6.2.3)

where x_i denotes the **initial condition** on x. The simulators carry out this integration numerically. Typically they employ Adams second-order method, a Runge-Kutta fourth-order method, or, for a **stiff system**, they may use Gears method. Since this operation is needed so often, a command for it is included in the simulation language. In CSMP and ACSL it has the format of

$$x = INTGRL\ (XI,\,G)$$ (6.2.4)

or

$$x = INTEG\ (G,\,XI)$$

respectively, where the integrand G is defined in another statement. Simulation systems are usually nonprocedural languages. Thus, the order of the statements is not important, so the definition of G can appear after the instruction to integrate it. It is possible to define procedural segments for branching or loops as in FORTRAN.

It is often necessary to define terms in the ODE by interpolating from tabulated data. The simulator gives us the choice of piecewise linear or nonlinear interpolation and a way to tabulate the given data. In CSMP this tabulation is done by following the command FUNCTION with a name assigned to the quantity and a list of pairs of independent and dependent variables. Most simulators also have a large library of function generators to describe various forcing functions. They include the Dirac impulse, a Heavyside step, a ramp, sine waves, square waves, dead spaces, sawtooth waves, and so on.

In mechanical engineering education, students are often taught how to derive the ODEs that describe the equations of motion of a system. Yet these equations are seldom carried through to find the solution that describes the motion. A continuous system simulator allows us to easily obtain numerical solutions of these equations. This frees the designer to vary the design parameters and address the "what if" aspects of the problem. There are other problems where we know in theory how to solve an ODE problem but still employ a simulator to save time or to prepare plots for a design report. The usefulness of these features will be illustrated by the solution of some relatively simple physical systems.

6.2.1 Pendulum

Consider the motion of a pendulum mass, m, that moves in a vertical plane at the end of a massless connector of length L as shown in Figure 6.2.1. We recall that velocity is tangent to the path and has a magnitude of $V = L\,d\phi/dt$. The viscous damping drag

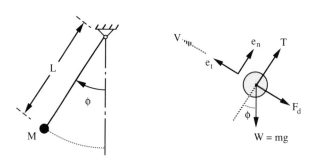

Figure 6.2.1   Motion of a pendulum in a vertical plane.

force opposes the motion and is given by $\vec{F}_D = -C\vec{V}$, where C is the damping coefficient. Applying Newton's second law to the tangential motion gives

$$F_T = ma_T$$

where the tangential acceleration is $Ld^2\phi/dt^2$. Thus, from Figure 6.2.1

$$-mg\ \sin\ \phi - CL\ \frac{d\phi}{dt} = mL\ \frac{d^2\phi}{dt^2}.$$

Thus, the tangential equation of motion can be expressed as

$$\frac{d^2\phi}{dt^2} = -(\frac{g}{L}\ \sin\ \phi + \frac{C}{m}\ \frac{d\phi}{dt}). \qquad (6.2.5)$$

subject to initial conditions on the initial position, ϕ_o, and initial angular velocity, $\dot{\phi}_o$. We know that for no damping ($C = 0$) and small angular motion ($\sin\ \phi \approx \phi$), we have an analytic solution represented by simple harmonic motion. For finite angles of un-damped motion, a solution can be obtained in terms of elliptical integrals. However, in the presence of damping, especially nonlinear damping, a numerical solution is required. Physically we know that in the presence of damping, the steady-state solution approaches static equilibrium at the bottom with the connector in the vertical position. In the mathematical sense we can represent that vertical position as $\phi = 0$ or any multiple of 2π. Thus, for large times we expect small oscillations centered about $\phi = 2\pi n$. If the initial conditions are small, then we have the common case and $n = 0$. If we give the mass a large initial velocity, then it could make one or more complete revolutions over and around the pin support before settling down near the final vertical position. Figure 6.2.2 shows typical solutions that result in $n = 0$ and $n = 1$.

Up to this point we may consider the problem completely formulated. However, the description of the connector has not been given. *What if* it is a string whose mass can be neglected compared to the attached mass? Is it still possible to obtain either or both of the complete time histories sketched in Figure 6.2.2? How could the new information change the solution? If the required tension exceeds the strength of the string at some point on the bottom half of the path, then it would break and the preceding model fails. The mass would then begin moving as a projectile, outside the original pendulum circle. On the other hand, if the force in the string goes from tension to compression, then it no longer constrains the mass to move on a circular path, and the preceding

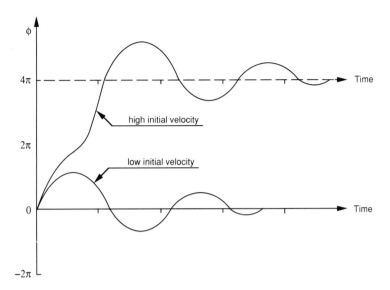

Figure 6.2.2   Typical Long time solutions.

model fails. In this case it breaks down at some point on the upper half of the path. From that point the mass moves as a projectile within the original circular region (until $R = L$ again).

To determine when the tangential motion model breaks down for a string, we must also include the equation for the normal component of motion. Newton's second law gives

$$F_n = m \; a_n$$

$$T - W \; \cos \phi = ma_n$$

where for circular motion $a_n = L \; \dot\phi^2$, and a dot denotes a time derivative. Thus, the tension is given by

$$T = m \, (L \; \dot\phi^2 + g \; \cos \phi). \qquad (6.2.6)$$

To simulate this physical problem we integrate Equation (6.2.5) in time to determine $\phi(t)$ and $\dot\phi(t)$, which are in turn used to compute the tension, $T(t)$. The solution is terminated at any time when either of the two tension limits is reached.

To build the computer model some items can be defined as constants. Other items selected as design parameters can be given in lists, and a solution is automatically obtained for each value in the list. Figure 6.2.3 shows a typical list of commands that would execute this simulation. The initial angular velocity has been selected as design parameters and are thus, included in a PARAMETER statement to produce a solution automatically for each given value. A RANGE statement is included to capture the maximum and minimum values of the tension and when they occur. A print-plot is requested to show the time history of the angle and the tension.

```
* STRING-MASS PENDULUM SIMULATION VIA CSMP
* UNITS: FT, SEC, LB, SLUG, RADIANS
CONSTANT  G=32.2, W=5.0, DAMP=0.03, BREAK=40.0
CONSTANT  L=2.0, PHI0=0.
PARAMETER PHID0 = ( 4., 6., 8., 10. )
INITIAL
   M = W/G
DYNAMIC
* INTEGRATION RULES
   PHI = INTGRL (PHI0, PHID)
   PHID = INTGRL (PHID0, PHIDD)
* TANGENTIAL MOTION
   PHIDD = -( G*SIN(PHI)/L + DAMP*PHID/M )
   SPEED = L*PHID
* STRING TENSION
   T = M*L*PHID*PHID + W*COS(PHI)
   ANGLE = PHI*57.296
* TERMINATE FOR BREAK, COMPRESSION, MAX TIME
RANGE   T
TERMINAL
 TIMER   FINTIM = 1.25, OUTDEL = 0.025
 FINISH  T = BREAK, T = 0.0
 PAGE MERGE
 OUTPUT T
 OUTPUT ANGLE
END
STOP
ENDJOB
```

Figure 6.2.3   CSMP string-mass simulation commands

Various solutions were simulated by increasing the initial angular velocity from the initial static vertical equilibrium. Since the mass starts from the lowest position and since damping is present, the maximum tension occurs at the initial position. From Equation (6.2.6) we note that the tension is proportional to the square of the angular velocity. Thus, only a small number of initial velocities were needed. The PARAMETER statement ranged over initial angular velocities of 4, 6, 8, and 10 rad/s.

The first print-plot result is shown in Figure 6.2.4. It shows the sort of response that we expect to encounter. It remains below 57° on the lower half of the circular path and gradually comes to rest at the initial angle of zero. The tension remains far below its breaking point and fluctuates about a value that asymptotically decreases toward the static value, $T = w$.

In the next case ($\dot{\phi} = 6$ rad/s), the initial tension almost doubles and the angle rapidly increases to about 91°, where the tension goes slack and the simulation terminates. At 8 rad/s the mass rises to about 124° before the string goes slack. The final initial velocity creates a tension that is 90% of the breaking point. The mass is able to pass the topmost point and begin a full loop. The tension when the top is first reached has

'*'=ANGLE
'+'=T

-60.00   90.00
2.400   10.40

ANGLE

TIME	T	ANGLE
0.00000E+00	9.9689	0.00000E+00
2.50000E-02	9.8470	5.7062
5.00000E-02	9.5829	11.328
7.50000E-02	9.1902	16.810
0.10000	8.6883	22.099
0.12500	8.1006	27.146
0.15000	7.4533	31.908
0.17500	6.7734	36.343
0.20000	6.0873	40.415
0.22500	5.4196	44.096
0.25000	4.7923	47.360
0.27500	4.2245	50.184
0.30000	3.7317	52.554
0.32500	3.3261	54.456
0.35000	3.0169	55.881
0.37500	2.8102	56.823
0.40000	2.7096	57.280
0.42500	2.7160	57.250
0.45000	2.8282	56.738
0.47500	3.0424	55.747
0.50000	3.3527	54.285
0.52500	3.7506	52.364
0.55000	4.2251	49.998
0.57500	4.7626	47.202
0.60000	5.3468	43.998
0.62500	5.9588	40.410
0.65000	6.5777	36.467
0.67500	7.1807	32.202
0.70000	7.7447	27.651
0.72500	8.2465	22.856
0.75000	8.6648	17.860
0.77500	8.9812	12.712
0.80000	9.1816	7.4633
0.82500	9.2569	2.1649
0.85000	9.2042	-3.1297
0.87500	9.0268	-8.3675
0.90000	8.7338	-13.496
0.92500	8.3395	-18.467
0.95000	7.8625	-23.231
0.97500	7.3242	-27.746
1.0000	6.7475	-31.971
1.0250	6.1554	-35.872
1.0500	5.5701	-39.418
1.0750	5.0122	-42.582
1.1000	4.4996	-45.341
1.1250	4.0476	-47.679
1.1500	3.6688	-49.580
1.1750	3.3727	-51.034
1.2000	3.1661	-52.035
1.2250	3.0533	-52.577
1.2500	3.0359	-52.661

Figure 6.2.4. A time history print-plot.

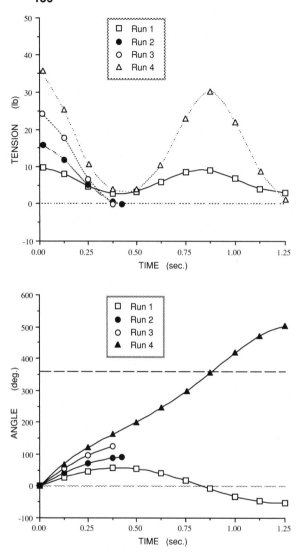

Figure 6.2.5.   Pendulum parameter study.

dropped to 9% of the initial value but is still positive. The damping reduces it more on later upward swings and the simulation terminates at 505°. If 12 rad/s is attempted as an initial angular velocity, the string immediately breaks. The first four cases are sketched in Figure 6.2.5.

6.2.2 Variable Cantilever

As another example consider the simulation of a thin tapered cantilever beam with an end load. The depth is not large enough to justify a two-dimensional FEA study, so we can begin with the well-known moment-curvature relation:

$$\frac{d^2u}{dx^2} = \frac{M(x)}{EI(x)}$$

where $M(x)$ is the moment distribution, $I(x)$ is the distribution of the second moment of the cross-sectional area, and u is the transverse deflection.

For a point load on the end, most designers know that M increases linearly from zero at the load end and reaches a maximum at the fixed end. Naturally they suspect that the maximum stress $\sigma = Mc/I$ will also be maximum at the fixed wall. For a constant EI, that would certainly be correct. But here it is not obvious how $I(x)$ will influence the results for stress and deflection. For a constant EI, we can either find the result in a handbook or directly integrate to obtain the solution.

When $I(x)$ is not constant we should resort to a numerical simulation or an FEA study. Here we will assume a Lagrangian cubic interpolation for the depth, $h(x)$, of the beam defined by four data points. For a rectangular section we know that

$$I(x) = \frac{1}{12} b(x) h^3(x) \tag{6.2.8}$$

where the width, b, will be assumed constant here. Figure 6.2.6 shows the beam of interest and the notation used. Figure 6.2.7 shows a simulation program employed to solve the problem for the assumptions made. A parameter called FACTOR is varied to show how increasing the minimum depth, while holding the shape constant, effects the stresses, weight, and deflection. A print-plot of the bending stress shows a result that may surprise some designers. Figure 6.2.8 shows that the maximum stress occurs near the load instead of at the fixed wall end. The maximum bending stress magnitude ranges up to a factor of three times the value expected for a constant EI. This behavior might have been missed if we simply relied on classical insight and calculated the stress at the wall. Items computed in the three simulations are as follows.

Item	Run:	1	2	3
Max stress (psi)		41,332	18,370	10,333
Volume (in.^{3})		14.3	21.5	28.7
Tip deflection (in.)		4.39	1.30	0.55

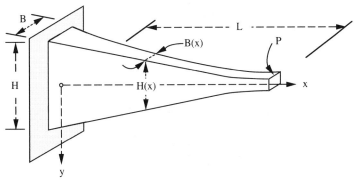

Figure 6.2.6   CSMP spring-mass simulation commands.

```
LABEL  CANTILEVER BEAM DESIGN
CONSTANT B = 1., L = 30., E = 10.E6, P = 60.
PARAMETER FACTOR = ( 1.0, 1.5, 2.0 )
* DEFINE DEPTH
 FUNCTION DEEP = (0.,0.9), (10.,0.6), (20.,0.3), (30.,0.2)
* FIND RANGES OF STRESS, VOL, DEFLECTION
   RENAME TIME = X
DYNAMIC
   M = P*(L - X)
   YDD = M/(E*I)
* GET CURRENT DEPTH BY NONLINEAR INTERPOLATION
   H = FACTOR*NLFGEN( DEEP, X)
   I = B*H*H*H/12.
   STRESS = 0.5*H*M/I
   AREA = B*H
* INTEGRATE
   VOL = INTGRL(0., AREA)
   YD = INTGRL(0., YDD)
   Y = INTGRL(0., YD)
RANGE STRESS, VOL
TERMINAL
 TIMER FINTIM=30., OUTDEL=0.75
 PAGE MERGE
 OUTPUT STRESS
 OUTPUT Y
END
STOP
ENDJOB
```

Figure 6.2.7 CSMP tapered cantilever simulation

The stresses drop from a level near the yield point of aluminum to a fourth of that value. The weight, which was neglected, is about 10% of the applied load.

The computed deflections suggest that the implied assumptions have been violated. The end deflection is greater than the "small deflection theory" limit of half the depth of the beam. Thus, our original differential equation for the curvature was not consistent with the results obtained. To correct this we would need to include the slope, du/dx, and express the curvature as

$$\frac{1}{\rho} = \frac{\frac{d^2u}{dx^2}}{\left[1 + \left(\frac{du}{dx}\right)^2\right]^{3/2}}. \tag{6.2.9}$$

Making this improvement gives us a nonlinear governing differential equation, and the need for an effective simulation system is increased.

There are several numerical algorithm libraries that allow the designer to integrate such equations. Most offer stiff integrators and accuracy control. The commercial

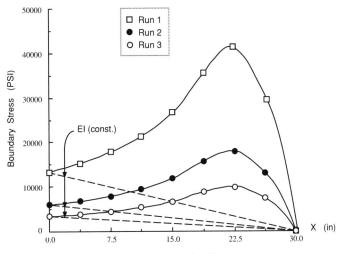

Figure 6.2.8   Exact bending stress.

simulation systems offer user-friendly descriptions, the most common feedback and control systems, Laplace transfer descriptions, block diagram formulations, and so on.

The preceding beam example was formulated as an initial value problem rather than as a boundary value problem. To solve boundary value problems with a simulator we must employ "shooting" methods to estimate the far-end boundary value and then iterate more toward a correct value. By comparison, an FEA system can solve boundary value problem directly.

6.2.3 Pilot Ejection

As another example of a nonlinear analysis that requires the use of a simulator, consider the problem of the ejection of a pilot from an aircraft or space shuttle. Obviously, we want the ejection trajectory to miss any exterior features such as a tail, wing, or engine. This requires the analysis of the motion of the center of mass subject to gravity and large aerodynamic drag forces. In this example we consider the ejection of a pilot from an aircraft in horizontal flight at a uniform speed. We assume that the motion takes place in a vertical plane and that the objective is to miss the tail structure that lies at a known location, relative to the point of exit from the aircraft. While we are interested in the relative motion, we must begin with the equations of motions described in terms of the absolute acceleration of the pilot. We evoke the usual relative kinematics, which states that the motion of the pilot equals the motion of the aircraft plus the motion of the pilot with respect to the aircraft. The aerodynamic drag force vector acts opposite to the velocity of the pilot. At the instant of exit, that velocity is

$$\mathbf{V}_P = \mathbf{V}_A + \mathbf{V}_{P/A} \qquad (6.2.10)$$

where $\mathbf{V}_A$ is the velocity of the aircraft, and we denote the velocity of the pilot with respect to the aircraft, $\mathbf{V}_{P/A}$, at that instant as $\mathbf{V}_E$, the exit velocity.

The sketch of the problem is shown in Figure 6.2.9, and the free- body diagram is shown in Figure 6.2.10. In the horizontal direction the equation of motion is

$$D_x = ma_x \tag{6.2.11}$$

while in the vertical direction

$$D_y - mg = ma_y \quad . \tag{6.2.12}$$

The drag force **D** is opposite to the velocity and has a magnitude given by

$$|D| = \frac{1}{2} \rho C_d S V^2 \tag{6.2.13}$$

where ρ is the mass density of the air, C_d is the drag coefficient, S is the surface area of the pilot and seat, and V is the magnitude of the velocity vector (the speed). The components of the drag force are found from geometry to be

$$D_x = -\frac{1}{2} C_d S V_x V \tag{6.2.14}$$

and similarly for D_y. Note that D_x depends on the sign of the horizontal velocity, V_x.

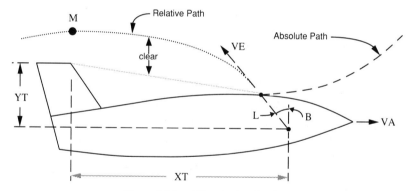

Figure 6.2.9   Pilot ejection sketch.

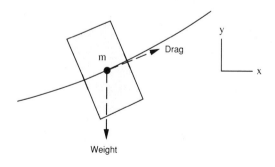

Figure 6.2.10   Free body diagram of ejection seat.

The density of air, ρ, varies greatly with the height, H, above sea level. Thus, the altitude, H, of ejection would be an important parameter to vary in a serious simulation.

To integrate these equations of motion, we must have the initial conditions on velocity and position. The ejection seat follows a rail of length L that is inclined backward from the vertical at an angle of B. We begin the ejection motion study at the instant the seat leaves the rail with a relative speed of V_E. Thus, the components of the initial position and velocity at exit are

$$X_E = -L \; \sin B, \qquad Y_E = L \; \cos B$$

and

$$V_{x_E} = V_A - V_E \sin B, \qquad V_{y_E} = V_E \cos B,$$

respectively. We denote the position of the corner of the tail relative to the original pilot position by X_T and Y_T.

During the simulation there are several auxiliary items that may be important to us. There are physiological limits to the acceleration that a human can withstand. Thus, we will compute the resultant acceleration and express it as a ratio to the gravitational constant, g. We can also imagine "an impact envelope" that the pilot must not enter. This runs from the point where the pilot exits to the corner of the tail surface and back to the end of the tail. We are interested in the vertical distance of those lines and the ejection trajectory. As long as it is positive, there will be no impact.

Figure 6.2.11 shows a typical CSMP implementation of this simulation. The results of the simulation are shown in Figure 6.2.12 for air densities corresponding to three different ejection altitudes, H.

```
LABEL  PILOT EJECTION MODEL
*   UNITS: SLUGS, FT, SEC
CONSTANT  M=7., S=10., CD=1., G=32.2, D2R=57.3
CONSTANT  XTI=-55., YT=12., YMAX=15.
CONSTANT  VE=40., VA=900., BDEG=15., XE=-0.93378, YE=3.8895
PARAMETER RHO = (0.00238, 0.00157, 0.00104)
FUNCTION TAILR = (-60., 12.), (-54.066, 12.), (0., 3.7)
INITIAL
  B = BDEG/57.3
  VEX = -VE*SIN(B) + VA
  VEY =   VE*COS(B)
  RCS = 0.5*RHO*CD*S
DYNAMIC
  V  = SQRT(VX*VX + VY*VY)
  DX = -RCS*VX*V
  DY = -RCS*VY*V
  AX = DX/M
  AY = -G + DY/M
  GS = 1./G*SQRT(AX*AX+AY*AY)
  VX = INTGRL(VEX,AX)
  VY = INTGRL(VEY,AY)
  X  = INTGRL(XE,VX)
  XREL = X - VA*TIME
  Y  = INTGRL(YE,VY)
  CLEAR = Y - AFGEN(TAILR, XREL)
TERMINAL
   TIMER  FINTIM=0.5 , PRDEL=0.1
   FINISH XREL=-60., Y=YMAX
PAGE MERGE
   OUTPUT CLEAR
END
STOP
ENDJOB
```

Figure 6.2.11   CSMP ejection simulation commands.

PILOT EJECTION MODEL
MERGED OUTPUT PRESENTATION FOR CLEAR

PARAMETER	RUN 1	RUN 2	RUN 3
RHO	0.23800E-02	0.15700E-02	0.10400E-02
	0.00000E+00	0.00000E+00	0.00000E+00
	6.000	6.000	6.000

'X'= RUN 3
'*'= RUN 2
'+'= RUN 1

TIME	RUN 1	RUN 2	RUN 3
0.00000E+00	4.61502E-02	4.61502E-02	4.61502E-02
1.00000E-02	0.40189	0.40633	0.40925
2.00000E-02	0.72872	0.74617	0.75771
3.00000E-02	1.0274	1.0660	1.0917
4.00000E-02	1.2988	1.3663	1.4114
5.00000E-02	1.5435	1.6472	1.7169
6.00000E-02	1.7623	1.9092	2.0085
7.00000E-02	1.9559	2.1526	2.2863
8.00000E-02	2.1248	2.3777	2.5504
9.00000E-02	2.2698	2.5849	2.8009
0.10000	2.3913	2.7743	3.0381
0.11000	2.4900	2.9463	3.2621
0.12000	2.5665	3.1012	3.4730
0.13000	2.6211	3.2392	3.6710
0.14000	2.6545	3.3607	3.8561
0.15000	2.6672	3.4658	4.0286
0.16000	2.6596	3.5549	4.1886
0.17000	2.6321	3.6282	4.3361
0.18000	2.5852	3.6859	4.4714
0.19000	2.5193	3.7282	4.5945
0.20000	2.4349	3.7555	4.7056
0.21000	2.3323	3.7679	4.8048
0.22000	2.2118	3.7656	4.8923
0.23000	2.0740	3.7488	4.9680
0.24000	1.9190	3.7179	5.0322
0.25000	1.7473	3.6728	5.0850
0.26000	1.5592	3.6140	5.1264
0.27000	1.3550	3.5414	5.1566
0.28000	1.1350	3.4555	5.1757
0.29000	0.89956	3.3563	5.1838
0.30000	0.64889	3.2439	5.1810
0.31000	0.38331	3.1186	5.1674
0.32000	0.51948	2.9806	5.1431
0.33000	0.69107	2.8300	5.1082
0.34000	0.85773	2.6670	5.0628
0.35000		2.4916	5.0070
0.36000		2.3043	4.9408
0.37000		2.1049	4.8644
0.38000		2.2414	4.7779
0.39000		2.4138	4.6814
0.40000		2.5817	

Figure 6.2.12   Trajectory histories.

6.3 UTILIZING BLOCK DIAGRAMS

Block diagrams were required to construct the original circuits employed to do continuous system simulations on analog computers. Since the development of digital computers, block diagrams are not required for continuous system simulation. However, several analysts feel that block diagrams are a good communication tool, especially when engineers from various disciplines are working on common projects, such as electromechanical systems and automatic control systems. Thus, there are some digital simulation systems that require the problem formulation to be expressed in terms of block diagrams. Several others, like CSMP and ACSL, will accept FORTRAN-like calls to functions that represent the most common block diagram components.

A block diagram can aid in the visualization of some problems and make them easier to explain to others. In the following sections we define some of the more common notations for block diagrams and illustrate their application to a few simple mechanical problems. Usually a typical component in the diagram is a block with a symbol to indicate its function. The input to the component enters from one side, is operated on by the component, and exits on the opposite side. We almost always need an integrator box, denoted by $\int$, an adder or summer box, denoted by $\sum$, a multiplier box, X, and a divider box, $\div$. Associated constants, such as initial conditions for the integrator or the multiplier coefficient, are shown as input quantities on another side of the block. These notations are sketched in Figure 6.3.1.

To illustrate these concepts recall the equation of motion of a single degree of freedom oscillator with viscous damping. Equating the product of the mass times the acceleration to the sum of the forces gives

$$m\ddot{x} = f - c\dot{x} - kx \tag{6.3.1}$$

where x is the displacement from the equilibrium position, m is the mass, f is the externally applied force, k is the stiffness, and c is the damping coefficient. Of course, $\dot{x}$ and $\ddot{x}$ represent the velocity and acceleration, respectively. To determine the displacement history, $x(t)$, we must integrate this equation subject to initial conditions on the position, x_o, and velocity, v_o. This will clearly require the equation

$$\ddot{x} = \frac{1}{m}(f - c\dot{x} - kx)$$

to be integrated twice. This clearly also involves a summation, two multipliers, a function evaluation, and one division. The external force, f, could be any kind of function. We will assume that it is a series of square pulses. The block diagram representation of this system is sketched in Figure 6.3.2, where v_0 and x_0 represent the initial velocity and displacement, respectively.

The Laplace transform is extremely useful in the analysis and design of linear systems. It is a form of operational mathematics. A designer can become adept at relating changes in the Laplace domain, s, to changes of the system in the time domain, t. A constant coefficient ODE in t transforms into algebraic equations in the s domain. For example, consider an equation of motion with constant coefficients A, B, and C:

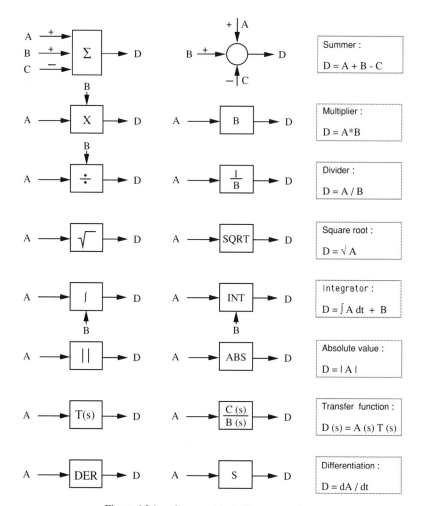

Figure 6.3.1   Common block diagram notations.

$$\frac{d^2x}{dt^2} + A\,\frac{dx}{dt} + Bx = Cu(t) \qquad (6.3.2)$$

where $u(t)$ represents the input forcing term and $x(t)$ is the corresponding response, or output. Let $X(s)$ and $U(s)$ denote the Laplace transform of those two variables. For zero initial conditions, recall that the Laplace transform of the preceding ODE is

$$s^2X + AsX + BX = CU \quad . \qquad (6.3.3)$$

The relationship between the input and output in the Laplace domain of a linear system is called the **transfer function,** $T(s)$. Specifically, it is the ratio of the transformed output to the transformed input:

$$T(s) = \frac{X(s)}{U(s)} \quad .$$

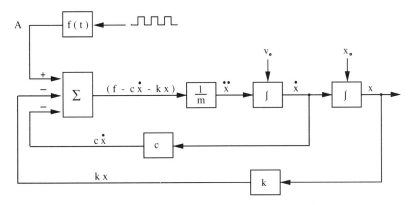

Figure 6.3.2   Block diagram for a forced, damped oscillator.

For the preceding example we see that

$$(s^2 + As + B) X(s) = CU(s)$$

so that its transfer function is

$$T(s) = \frac{X(s)}{U(s)} = \frac{C}{s^2 + As + B} \quad . \tag{6.3.4}$$

Thus, this linear second order ordinary differential equation can be represented in a block diagram as

$$U(s) \rightarrow \frac{C}{s^2 + As + B} \rightarrow X(s) \quad .$$

This example illustrates the fact that physical systems often have a transfer function that can be expressed as the ratio of two polynomials in s, $T(s) = N(s)/D(s)$. Since $D(s)$ is associated with the output, it effects the stability and general transient response to an input. The denominator, $D(s)$, is called the characteristic function of the system. By setting $D(s)$ equal to zero, we obtain the **characteristic equation**. Its roots can be real and/or complex. The numerator, $N(s)$, will be of lower order than $D(s)$ for physical systems.

Block diagrams and transfer functions are concepts that are often employed in control systems. Mechanical engineers are usually more interested in closed-loop, or feedback, systems than open-loop systems. These two concepts are shown in Figure 6.3.3. Block diagram representations can be applied to nonlinear systems as well. Continuous simulation programs are often used to model processes and their associated control systems.

From Equation (6.3.3) we recall that a derivative with respect to t is denoted by s. Likewise, the inverse, $1/s$, denotes the integration with respect to t from an initial

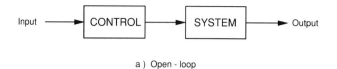

a) Open - loop

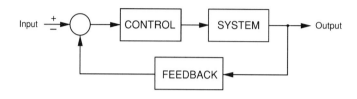

b) Closed - loop

Figure 6.3.3   Typical control loops.

condition. These two simple blocks, s and $1/s$, appear often in block diagram representations of mechanical systems. Other common transfer functions are included in simulation languages and are accessed by a single statement. These statements are similar to a subroutine call. A first-order lag is written as

$$A \ \frac{dx}{dt} + x \ = \ u \qquad (6.3.5)$$

and has a transfer function (called REALPL in CSMP) of

$$T(s) \ = \ \frac{1}{As \ + \ 1} \qquad . \qquad (6.3.6)$$

The general transformation is written for $m \leq n$ as

$$\frac{a_m \ s^m + a_{m-1} \ s^{m-1} \ + \ \cdots \ + \ a_1 s + a_{m+1}}{b_n \ s^n \ + \ b_{n-1} \ s^{n-1} \ + \ \cdots \ + \ b_1 \ s \ + \ b_{n+1}} \qquad . \qquad (6.3.7)$$

The coefficients can be placed in arrays, say **A** and **B**, to be passed to a general Laplace transforms evaluation function. If U is the input and X is the output, then commands in CSMP, ACSL, and PCESP are, respectively,

$$X = TRANSF \ (N, \textbf{B}, M, \textbf{A}, U)$$
$$X = TRAN \ (M, N, \textbf{A}, \textbf{B}, U),$$

and

$$X = TRNFR \ (N, M, IC, \textbf{A}, \textbf{B}, U).$$

To illustrate how a simulator can model a simple position-control system, consider the system shown in Figure 6.3.4. It is converted to an alternate form that matches the format of the blocks available in the simulation language (see part b) and then converted to command statements for simulation (in part c).

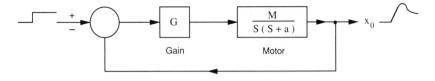

a) Original Control Diagram

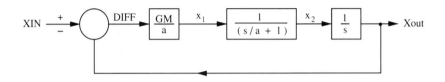

b) Equivalent Simulator Components

```
CONSTANT    G = 1.5,   M = 4,   A = 2,   XINI = 0.

XIN = STEP ( 0.0 )

DIFF = XIN - Xout

X₁  = DIFF * G * M / A

X₂  = REALPL ( XINI, 1. / A, X1 )

Xout = INTGRL ( XINI, X₂ )

PRTPLT    Xout
```

c) CSMP Simulator Commands

Figure 6.3.4   Model for position control.

As an illustration of these concepts consider the problem of designing a controller for a cable-reel system. As the cable is unwound from the reel, we want to maintain a constant linear cable velocity. We need to devise a controller for the motor that drives the reel rotation. A tachometer or other device will measure the velocity of the exiting cable. This value is compared to the desired value and the error is used to generate the motor control signal.

The mechanics of the system are governed by the moment of the inertia of the reel system, which consists of the cable and the reel shell. The moment of inertia decreases as the cable unwinds. Thus, we have a nonlinear equation for the angular motion of the reel system. Recall that the relation between the resultant torque, T, and the angular acceleration, α, is

$$T = I(R)\alpha = I\ddot{\theta} \tag{6.3.8}$$

where R denotes the effective outer radius of the cable portion of the reel system. The moment of inertia, I, has a constant portion for the shell I_s and a contribution for the cable that is proportional to R^4, where R is the radius at which the cable is being removed.

$$I = I_s + I_c$$

$$I_c = \frac{2\pi\rho W}{4} [R^4 - R_{min}^4]$$

where W is the width of the reel, $R_{min} = 2$ ft is the minimum radius, and the cable mass density is ρ. For the current problem this reduces to

$$I = (18.5R^4 - 221) \text{ slug} \sim \text{ft}^2$$

when R is in feet. Here R starts with a maximum value of $R_0 = 4$ ft.

From kinematics the speed of the cable being removed is

$$V = R\omega = R\dot{\theta} \tag{6.3.9}$$

but here R is a function of θ, since material is being removed. To find the relation between R and θ, we note that the number of cables in a layer on the reel is $N = W/D$, where D is the cable diameter. As the cable is removed the effective rate of change of radius is

$$\dot{R} = \frac{D}{\Delta t} \tag{6.3.10}$$

where Δt is the time to remove a complete layer:

$$\Delta t = \frac{\text{length of layer}}{\text{average speed at } R}$$

$$= \frac{2\pi R N}{V} = \frac{2\pi R N}{R\omega} .$$

Thus, we have an additional equation that

$$\frac{dR}{dt} = -\frac{D\dot{\theta}}{2\pi N} = -\frac{D^2\dot{\theta}}{2\pi W} \tag{6.3.11}$$

subject to the initial condition that $R = R_0$ at $t=0$. We solve the real dynamics with the nonlinear equation

$$\ddot{\theta} = \frac{T(\theta)}{I(\theta)}$$

with the initial conditions that $\theta_0 = 0$ and $\dot{\theta}_0 = 0$.

To establish the input torque, we need information on the instrumentation and controls. The preliminary motor output to input ratio is represented by a simple first-order transfer function:

$$\frac{\text{Torque (ft lb)}}{\text{Signal (V)}} = T_M(s) = \frac{500}{s+1} = 500 \left[\frac{1}{s+1} \right] . \tag{6.3.12}$$

This neglects the moment of inertia of the motor, which may need to be included in a final design. A tachometer on a constant-radius idler pulley gives us the cable velocity. It is accurately described by another first-order transfer function:

$$\frac{\text{Signal (V)}}{\text{Speed (ft / s)}} = T_T(s) = \frac{2}{s+2} = \frac{1}{0.5s+1} \ . \qquad (6.3.13)$$

The controller will multiply the error signal by some gain constant. The physical system and the associated block diagram are shown in Figure 6.3.5. The CSMP simulation commands are shown in Figure 6.3.6, and the output speed is shown in Figure 6.3.7 for different control gains. All approach the desired value, 50 pfs, but the gain of 0.5 appears to be the best. It avoids oscillations that may cause the cable to be jerked and possibly damaged.

6.4 REFERENCES

1. *Advanced Continuous Simulation Language,* Concord, Mass.: Mitchell & Gauthier, Assoc., 1981.

2. Beltrami, E. *Mathematics for Dynamic Modeling.* New York: Academic Press, 1987.

3. Crosheck, J., and Ford, M. "Simulation Takes Three-Wheeler for a Spin." *Mechanical Engineering,* 110, no. 11, (November 1988): 48-51.

4. Gould, H., and Tobochnik, J. *An Introduction to Computer Simulation: Application to Physical Systems.* Reading, Mass.: Addison-Wesley, 1986.

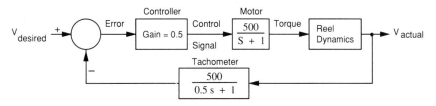

a) Closed - loop block diagram

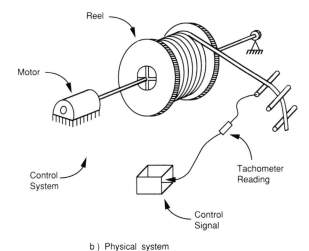

b) Physical system

Figure 6.3.5   Cable-reel control system model.

```
*  CABLE-REEL CONTROL DESIGN
*    UNITS: SLUGS, FT, SEC, FT-LB
CONSTANT RFULL = 4.0, REMPTY = 2.0, WIDTH = 2.0
CONSTANT D = 0.1, TWOPI = 6.2831853, VDESIR = 50., MOTOR = 500.
PARAMETER GAIN = ( 0.5, 1.0, 1.5 )
INITIAL
    CONST = -(D**2) / (TWOPI * WIDTH)
DYNAMIC
*  MECHANICAL SYSTEM
    I = 18.5 * (R**4) - 221.
    TH2DOT = TORQUE / I
    TH1DOT = INTGRL( 0.0, TH2DOT )
    R      = INTGRL( RFULL, (CONST * TH1DOT) )
    VACT   = R * TH1DOT
* CONTROL SYSTEM
    ERROR  = VDESIR - VMEAS
    CONTRL = GAIN * ERROR
    TEMP   = REALPL(0.0, 1.0, CONTRL)
    TORQUE = MOTOR * TEMP
    VMEAS  = REALPL(0.0, 0.5, VACT)
FINISH    R = REMPTY
TIMER     DELT=0.05, FINTIM=18., PRDEL=0.5, OUTDEL=0.5
PAGE MERGE
PRTPLT    VACT
END
STOP
ENDJOB
```

Figure 6.3.6 CSMP cable-reel simulation commands

5. Korn, G. A., and Wait, J. V. *Digital Continuous System Simulation.* Englewood Cliffs, N.J.: Prentice Hall, 1978.

6. Shah, M. *Engineering Simulation.* Englewood Cliffs, N.J.: Prentice Hall, 1988.

7. Speckhart, F. H., and Green W. L. *A Guide to Using CSMP — The Continuous System Modeling Program.* Englewood Cliffs, N.J.: Prentice Hall, 1976.

6.5 EXERCISES

1. Convert the string-mass example to a rod-mass system. Include mass (rotary inertia) of the rod. Note that the axial force in the rod varies with the radius. Unlike the string, the rod will support compression. Include a parameter that varies the rod-mass from 1/10 to 1 to 10 times that of the end-mass. Run the simulation for 2 s.

2. Extend the small deflection beam model to include a width that varies linearly from b at the load to $2b$ at the wall.

3. Modify the beam deflection model to utilize the exact curvature definition in Equation (6.2.9).

4. Extend the beam deflection model to include the weight of the member.

5. Prepare a block diagram description of (a) the pendulum model, (b) the beam model, and (c) the ejector simulation.

6. Extend the pilot ejection model to include variable air density of

CABLE-REEL CONTROL MODEL

PARAMETER	RUN 1	RUN 2	RUN 3
GAIN	0.50000	1.0000	1.5000

0.0000E+00
0.0000E+00
0.0000E+00

80.00
80.00
80.00

'X' = RUN 3
'*' = RUN 2
'+' = RUN 1

TIME	RUN 1	RUN 2	RUN 3
0.00000E+00	0.00000E+00	0.00000E+00	0.00000E+00
0.50000	1.1788	2.3558	3.5310
1.0000	4.0524	8.0616	12.028
1.5000	7.8854	15.527	22.927
2.0000	12.180	23.586	34.236
2.5000	16.598	31.402	44.488
3.0000	20.913	38.411	52.730
3.5000	24.980	44.282	58.493
4.0000	28.714	48.872	61.719
4.5000	32.072	52.182	62.667
5.0000	35.040	54.315	61.799
5.5000	37.626	55.439	59.680
6.0000	39.850	55.754	56.884
6.5000	41.740	55.469	53.926
7.0000	43.328	54.782	51.209
7.5000	44.648	53.866	49.009
8.0000	45.735	52.864	47.470
8.5000	46.620	51.886	46.616
9.0000	47.332	51.007	46.383
9.5000	47.900	50.273	46.645
10.000	48.346	49.705	47.245
10.500	48.692	49.304	48.022
11.000	48.957	49.057	48.835
11.500	49.156	48.940	49.570
12.000	49.302	48.927	50.154
12.500	49.407	48.988	50.549
13.000	49.479	49.098	50.750
13.500	49.527	49.233	50.780
14.000	49.556	49.373	50.676
14.500	49.571	49.506	50.486
15.000	49.577	49.621	50.255
15.500	49.576	49.713	50.023
16.000	49.570	49.781	49.822
16.500	49.562	49.825	49.671
17.000	49.552	49.849	49.577
17.500	49.542	49.855	49.540
18.000	49.532	49.849	49.550

Figure 6.3.7 Effect of gain on actual velocity.

$$\rho = 0.00238 \, e^{-H/24000}$$

in slugs per cubic feet when H is the altitude, in feet, at the point of ejection. Find the necessary exit velocity for (a) $H = 0$, (b) $H = 5{,}000$, and (c) $H = 10{,}000$.

7. The planar motion of a small satellite subject to the gravitational pull of a planet is described in radial and transverse coordinates by

$$\frac{d^2 R}{dt^2} = \frac{-K}{R^2} + R\left(\frac{d\theta}{dt}\right)^2$$

$$\frac{d^2 \theta}{dt^2} = \frac{-2}{R}\frac{dR}{dt}\frac{d\theta}{dt}$$

where K is a gravitational constant. For earth $K = 3.983 \times 10^{14}$ m^3/s^2. The initial conditions are the location, (R, θ), of the insertion into orbit and the initial velocity components. Develop the block diagram representation of this motion.

8. The cable-reel control design can be made more realistic by including the inertia, J, and dumping, μ, of the motor and the electrical transients. Include a second-order system given by

$$J\ddot{\theta} + \mu\dot{\theta} + kI = 0$$

$$L\dot{I} + RI + C\dot{\theta} = V$$

where I, V, L, and R represent the current, input voltage, inductance, and resistance of the motor. Revise the block diagram model.

9. A single-stage rocket is launched vertically, at sea level ($H = 0$). The equation of motion of this variable mass system is

$$m\dot{V} = \dot{m}v_e - mg - F_d$$

where m is the mass, $\dot{m}$ is the propellant mass flow rate, v_e is the propellant relative exit velocity, F_d is the aerodynamic drag force, mg is the weight of the rocket, and $\dot{V}$ is the velocity of the rocket. The earth's gravitational field varies as

$$g = 32.17 \left[\frac{r_e}{r_e + H}\right]^2 \, ft/s^2$$

where r_e is the radius of the earth and H is the altitude. The drag force is

$$F_d = \frac{1}{2}\rho C_d A V^2$$

and the mass density of the air is

$$\rho = 0.00238 \, e^{-H/24000} \quad slug/ft^3 \quad .$$

From kinematics we know that the altitude is the area under the velocity-time curve:

$$H = \int V \, dt \quad ,$$

Assume a drag area of $A = 410$ ft^2, and a mass flow rate of $\dot{m} = 75.5$ slugs/s at an exit velocity of $v_e = 14222$ ft/s. The structure has a mass of $m_s = 3781$ slugs. The maximum fuel capacity is $m_f = 30{,}200$ slugs. The minimum payload is $m_p = 832$ slugs. Determine the fuel load that will yield the maximum height, H, at the moment of burnout. Note $r_e = 6.373 \times 10^6$ m.

7

CASE SELECTION AND EXPERT SYSTEMS

7.1 INTRODUCTION

Numerical analysts and design engineers must often decide when a rule or equation can be satisfied. For decades we have done that by inspection. Today there is increasing pressure to interface numerical algorithms or applications software to expert systems (XS). Sometimes it is easier to modify large design applications software to make it act more like an XS. This chapter is intended to clarify some of the simpler numerical procedures that can be employed in several of these areas. It presents a useful procedure for the Boolean assessment of rules and equations (BARE).

For many engineers the need for equation assessment begins with elementary static equilibrium. It is easy to find a rigid body system that can require three or four free-body diagrams (FBD) with three equations of equilibrium each. Students often can master that phase of the task, but they do not know "how to get started" with the solution of the systems of equations. They watch the instructor solve an equation in one FBD, jump to another FBD to solve a new pair of equations, and so on until all variables have been evaluated. In effect, the instructor is attempting to teach BARE by example.

Most of us have dealt with special types of XSs. For example, procedural languages, such as FORTRAN, have special rules for relating the left-hand side (LHS) and right-hand side (RHS) of an expression. IF all of the variables on the RHS are known numerically (or logically), THEN invoke the standard hierarchy for expression evaluation to assign a numerical (or logical) value to the single unknown on the LHS, or ELSE the program fails. Today it is common to encounter equation writers, such as TK Solver and Eureka, that allow multiple unknowns on the LHS, RHS, or both. Such a system can be thought of as an XS where the rules are given as nonlinear algebraic equations. These equation evaluators often have a BARE procedure as the very foundation of the algorithm. Although these concepts have been in use for several years, this more formal statement of BARE should help design engineers and analysts better understand what the XS is really doing in the automatic assessment or selection of paths through the knowledge data base.

7.2 BOOLEAN INFERENCE ARRAY

The basic automation of an assessment procedure is probably easiest to understand when presented via a Boolean inference array. Here we will present an integer array that contains only 0s or 1s. These coefficients indicate whether or not two entities are related. A 0 indicates no relation between the corresponding row and column. In the future the reader should consider the merit of allowing the nonzero integer to take on a scaled value that in addition to signaling a relation gives some measure of the reliability of an associated value.

The information in an inference array, **N**, can sometimes be more efficiently utilized if stored in a topological form. However, educational utility is better served here in the current binary form. This is analogous to teaching Boolean assembly in finite element analysis while actually employing a direct assembly algorithm based on element topology.

For the selection and solution of simultaneous equations we need only one inference array, **N**. Its columns are associated with the variable numbers, and each row is associated with an equation number. For expert systems we typically need at least three inference arrays. One gives the "backward chaining" information about the goals, **B**, and is usually the smallest array. Another, **F**, describes the forward chaining of conditions to reach the goals. The largest is usually the one, **A**, that provides the assessment of current value of all of the attributes. It shows if an attribute is known or still unknown. These terms are defined in more detail later. For each of these three arrays the row number corresponds to a rule number, equations number, or case number.

To form the inference array we begin with a null matrix. For an equation evaluation we proceed to each equation in sequence. If a variable appears in the equation, then we set its column coefficient to unity:

$$N_{ij} = \begin{cases} 1 & \text{if variable } j \text{ is in equation } i \\ 0 & \text{if variable } j \text{ is not in equation } i \end{cases} \qquad (7.2.1)$$

Having completed that process we can evaluate the sum of each row, $\text{JSUM}(i)$, and the sum of each column, $\text{ISUM}(j)$. Any time a variable is input, or determined, its column in **N** is set to zero (or negated) and the row sums (of the unity terms) are updated. If a row sum is unity, then the corresponding equation has only one unknown, and it could be selected for solution.

7.3 EQUATION AND RULE SELECTORS

If we are dealing with an equation system, we wish to find the smallest number of simultaneous linear or nonlinear equations to solve at any point in the solution process. Having found such a list from an equation selector, the system could automatically invoke a Newton-Raphson or linear equation solver. A number of "equation selectors" are in use in the public domain in executable form. Perhaps the best known are the TK Solver system and the Eureka system. An equation selector can be viewed as an expert system where all the rules are supplied in equation form. Based on the input data it selects which rules can be evaluated, which cannot be evaluated, and which ones are overspecified.

As an example of how an equation selector works we use some rules of basic electricity. Our example is a reduced version of an example discussed by Konopasek for the TK Solver system. Here we will supplement the discussion with numerical examples of the actual inference arrays. The rules and variables are as follows:

i	i-th rule	j	j-th variable	
1	$I*r=V$	i	I	current
2	$I^2 = P/r$	2	V	voltage
3	$P=V*I$	3	r	resistance
4	$r/\rho = L/a$	4	P	power
		5	L	length
		6	ρ	resistivity
		7	a	area .

With these lists we can assign a topology array that defines the connectivity of a variable to a rule:

Rule	Variable Incidence
1	1, 3, 2
2	1, 4, 3
3	4, 2, 1
4	3, 6, 5, 7 .

These topological data are illustrated in the relation-graph in Figure 7.3.1. The inference array form for these data is

$$
\begin{array}{c}
\quad\quad\quad I \;\; V \;\; r \;\; P \;\; L \;\; \rho \;\; a \\[4pt]
\quad\quad\quad 1 \;\; 2 \;\; 3 \;\; 4 \;\; 5 \;\; 6 \;\; 7 \quad Sum \\
\mathbf{N} = \begin{array}{c} 1 \\ 2 \\ 3 \\ 4 \end{array}
\begin{array}{ccccccc}
1 & 1 & 1 & 0 & 0 & 0 & 0 \\
1 & 0 & 1 & 1 & 0 & 0 & 0 \\
1 & 1 & 0 & 1 & 0 & 0 & 0 \\
0 & 0 & 1 & 0 & 1 & 1 & 1
\end{array}
\begin{array}{c}
3 \\ 3 \\ 3 \\ 4
\end{array} \\[10pt]
Sum \;\; 3 \;\; 2 \;\; 3 \;\; 2 \;\; 1 \;\; 1 \;\; 1 \;\; A = 7
\end{array}
$$

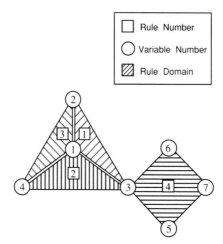

Figure 7.3.1 Example relation-graph between rules and variables.

Define the number of active variables, A, to be the number of nonzero column sums; here $A = 7$. The row sum indicates the number of active (unknown) variables in an equation. With no data this example represents four nonlinear equations for seven variables.

If we consider a subset of R rows, then we may get a reduced number of active variables, A. Clearly, to be a candidate for such a simultaneous solution subset, an equation must have a row sum that is less than or equal to R. If we find such a combination of rows such that $R = A$, then we can attempt to solve the set simultaneously. If we provided an input value to the length, L, and zeroed its (5th) column, we would still have more active variables ($A = 6$) than equations ($R = 4$). Instead of that, if we input the current, I, then the updated inference array would be

$$
\begin{array}{c}
\quad\quad I\ \ V\ \ r\ \ P\ \ L\ \ \rho\ \ a\ \ \ Sum \\[4pt]
\mathbf{N} = \begin{array}{ccccccc|c}
0 & 1 & 1 & 0 & 0 & 0 & 0 & 2 \\
0 & 0 & 1 & 1 & 0 & 0 & 0 & 2 \\
0 & 1 & 0 & 1 & 0 & 0 & 0 & 2 \\
0 & 0 & 1 & 0 & 1 & 1 & 1 & 4 \\
\end{array}
\end{array}
$$

$$Sum\ \ 0\ \ 2\ \ 3\ \ 2\ \ 1\ \ 1\ \ 1\ \ A = 6$$

There are still four equations with six unknowns. But now there is a subset (one of four combinations) that can be solved for three unknowns. The reduced partition for the first three rows is

$$
\begin{array}{c}
\quad\quad I\ \ V\ \ r\ \ P\ \ L\ \ \rho\ \ a\ \ \ Sum \\[4pt]
\mathbf{NR} = \begin{array}{ccccccc|c}
0 & 1 & 1 & 0 & 0 & 0 & 0 & 2 \\
0 & 0 & 1 & 1 & 0 & 0 & 0 & 2 \\
0 & 1 & 0 & 1 & 0 & 0 & 0 & 2 \\
\end{array}
\end{array}
$$

$$Sum\ \ 0\ \ 2\ \ 2\ \ 2\ \ 0\ \ 0\ \ 0\ \ A = 3$$

Thus with the current, I, as data we can solve simultaneously the three nonlinear equations for the voltage, resistance, and power (V, r, and P). After that solution we zero those three columns and discover that rule 4 is the only remaining rule, but it has three active unknowns. Thus, we must stop or accept two additional items of input. As a final observation for this example, note that if we originally input variables V and r (2 and 3), then rule 1 would be solved for I. Then rule 2 could be solved for P and rule 3 coud be used as a check.

7.4 EXPERT SYSTEMS

Expert systems (XS) have a great potential for assisting in mechanical design. For example, there are systems to guide a designer in the selection of materials to be used depending on the environment, required endurance limits, and so on. Most of the expert systems require the use of an extensive set of rules that are obtained from an expert or team of experts. Many design tasks involve the use of **design code**, such as the ASME Pressure Vessel Code, which contains analytical and empirical rules that have evolved from basic theoretical studies and lengthy committee studies of experimental and numerical models. Some design codes are so large that they have not yet been converted into a form usable in an XS. However, more design aids will appear as time goes on.

In the design of specialized products it is more common to find a relatively small number of rules to govern the design process. Thus, it should be possible for many design groups to utilize expert system software on a personal computer or engineering workstation. To take proper advantage of this new design aid, the engineer needs to understand the basic concepts of how it works and what its limitations might be. The following sections give an elementary introduction to the concepts of expert systems. They do not address the concepts of learning systems or neural networks that are being developed as other artificial intelligence tools.

The main segments of an XS that would be used by a designer are shown in Figure 7.4.1. For an engineer wishing to develop an XS design aid, the first problem is how to get the design rules into the **knowledge base**. This involves the expert and a **knowledge acquisition system**. Some large commercial systems sell the expensive services of an alleged "knowledge engineer" to build the knowledge base. This person goes through the process of obtaining knowledge from the experts, organizing it into a usable form, and inserting it into the knowledge base. Other systems, like Rulemaster, provide software for rule induction. They automatically generate rules by processing case examples and rules from the expert. This saves time in building the design aid, but the machine-generated rules may be difficult to debug. Some systems allow the knowledge base to be translated into a high-level computer language, like FORTRAN or C, so it can run faster or be embedded within other programs.

Of course, the main part of the architecture seen by the user is the user interface. It relies on the **inference engine**, **working memory**, or **blackboard** and the knowledge base to prompt the user for the goal to be reached and the information needed to reach that goal. The user, in turn may wish to ask why some conclusion was or was not

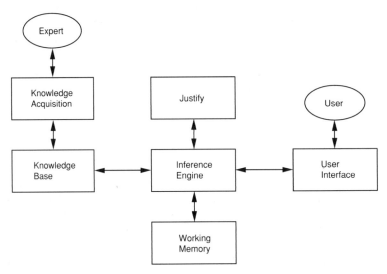

Figure 7.4.1   Expert system architecture.

reached. An **explanation module** is included to justify or explain the process that led to the conclusion being queried by the user.

Expert systems, or knowledge-based systems (KBS), are emerging from an experimental tool in computer science into a practical engineering and design aid. When a human expert is not available, a user can consult an XS for conclusions or recommendations and explanations on how they were reached. This is done by employing a previously stored knowledge base. This knowledge is typically represented as a set of rules. Each rule has at least two basic parts: a premise and a conclusion. If the conditions described by the rule's premises are determined to be true, then the actions or recommendations specified in its conclusions are deemed to be valid. The obvious problem with a KBS is that the rule base must be built and tested before it can be utilized.

The main part of an XS is called the **inference engine**. It supports a user interface that allows the problem to be posed. When the user requests a result, the inference engine uses the rules to try to reach a conclusion or recommendation that solves the problem. The engine may prompt the user to provide additional information or explain why it wants the information or how it reached previous intermediate conclusions. Most engines use some variant of a forward-chaining or a backward-chaining approach in selecting the rules to be evaluated. In **forward chaining** the premises of the selected rule are evaluated. If any are false, then the rule is discarded forever. If they are all true, then the conclusion is taken as true and its information is stored in a **working memory**, or **blackboard** area. If a premise is unknown, the rule is skipped for possible later evaluation.

In **backward chaining** the inference engine considers only those rules whose conclusions answer the current goal. The premises of a selected rule are tested. If all are true, then a solution or subsolution has been obtained. If any premise is false, then another rule in the backward-chaining list is tried. It is more likely that a premise will be unknown. Then it becomes necessary to make this item a subgoal to be evaluated before the true goal can be reached.

In a good forward-chaining application, there are many possible final states, and few initial states. Information is known about the initial states and the problem is to find an acceptable path from the initial state to the final state. Forward chaining reasons from given facts to the conclusions that follow from them. The known facts are the conditional elements that imply the conclusions, which are the actions of the rule. In a good backward-chaining case, there are relatively few final states and many initial states. The goal in backward chaining is to reason backward from conclusions to the facts that caused them. Since expert systems are expensive and time-consuming to develop, a number of commercial expert system **shells**, or user interfaces, have been developed that include an inference engine and a relatively friendly way to build the initial knowledge base. A common example is the **Rulemaster** system. It is based on a popular algorithm for transforming historical data into decision trees or rules. **CLIPS** is a public domain XS, based on forward chaining, that was developed for NASA.

Expert systems typically associated with engineering design or numerical analysis problem usually involve the use of IF-THEN rules. Before illustrating how BARE can be employed on these systems, some terminology will be introduced for completeness. We are interested in knowledge about goals and conditions that can be represented with object-attribute-value triplets. An object is a concept or physical entity that has one or more attributes that are defined in the expert system. An attribute is a property of an object that can be assigned a specific value. The value assigned may or may not have a confidence factor associated with it. The object may be a person having attributes such as surname, body part, and job. The attribute surname may have a single value, while the attribute "body part" could have many possible values such as foot, leg, hand, arm, ...

Instead of an equation, we typically have rules with a syntax such as:

IF   conditional clause
    AND   conditional clause
THEN   conclusion clause
    ELSE   conclusion clause.

A typical conclusion clause has the syntax:

Object or Attribute keyword IS Value assigned

Associated with each attribute keyword is a translation phrase that expands the keyword to make the rule clause readable by humans and a prompt phrase given to the user to request a value that can be provided only by a human. BARE provides one approach to an inference engine. Modern computer science provides several other approaches for implementing such engines. The inference engine is at the core of any expert system. It has access to the knowledge about which attributes (variables) are known. It includes an algorithm for selecting the next rule, evaluating the rule, acquiring more values, and propagating certainty factors.

The system works to satisfy a final goal. The inference engine also identifies any subgoals that must be satisfied in order to reach the final goal. Since the number of goals usually increases the backward inference array, **B** would increase in size by adding new rows that represent the current goals. To evaluate a rule we generally follow the procedure of comparing the attribute in the condition clause with the value in **A**. The possibilities for rule evaluation are as follows:

1. A condition clause is contradicted. Then we discard that rule forever (and zero its columns in **B**, **F**, and **A**).

2. One or more conditional clause is unknown. Make that unknown attribute the current goal. If that attribute goal is not in **B**, add a new row for it. Try to find a rule to evaluate the current goal.

3. Each conditional clause is correctly matched with the value associated with the attribute in **A**. Thus, the conclusion is true. Use the conclusion clause to update **A** and to associate a value with the attribute in the conclusion clause. If the conclusion attribute is a goal, then update **B**. If it is the final goal, then stop. Otherwise, select a previous goal, make it the current goal, and try to find a rule to evaluate it.

Sometimes the conditional attribute is marked as unknown in **A**, but it has a prompt phrase that can be issued to the user. The user may answer the prompt with a known value, or the answer may be that the value is unknown to the user.

Most XSs are goal-directed and employ a backward chaining strategy to evaluate the final goal. The inference engine must identify all the rules that have the final goal after the predicate "is" in their conclusion clause. That is how **B** is built. Of course, this clause is at the back of the rule. Attempting to evaluate the conditions of those rules will create other subgoals. Each of the subgoals are treated, in turn, as the current goal. They are also evaluated from rules selected by checking through their conclusion phrases. If the number of possible values of the goal attribute are reasonably small, then this backward-chaining procedure can be very efficient.

The number of candidate rules to be evaluated for the current goal is usually small. Thus, some XSs simply evaluate them in sequential order. The inference arrays described earlier provide additional data that allow the engine to make a more logical rule selection. Consider the current column sums for a candidate rule in **F** and **A**. These sums represent the remaining number of unknown conditions and attributes associated with the rule, respectively. Thus, in either array one can select from the candidates by picking the one with the smallest column sum. In the case of a tie we simply can evaluate the last one found.

Whenever a rule leads to a successful evaluation of an attribute or condition, then the corresponding rows of **A** or **F** would be set to zero and their column sums updated. If the updated column sum of any rule in **F** is zero, then it means that all the conditional clauses are known for it and, therefore, a conclusion can be reached from that rule. Clearly, that rule should be evaluated and the value from the conclusion clause inserted into working memory and **A**. This is called a data-driven, or forward-chaining, strategy. If there are multiple zero sum rules in **F**, then the engine can select which to evaluate first. For example, we may select the rule that has the unknown (conclusion) attribute that occurs most often in the list of rules activated by the previous subgoal tests.

To illustrate these concepts we employ an example botany XS considered in detail by Thompson and Thompson with another approach. Table 7.4.1 gives the condition and conclusion phrases of interest, while Table 7.4.2 lists the attributes and values. Note that to better correlate to Thompson's example, values of "unknown" or "why" have not been allowed as user responses to a prompt and the ELSE option has not been invoked to keep the rule numbers the same.

In the following inference arrays some of the names of the objects, attributes, and values are abbreviated by four letters. Since F and A are large and do not change size, they are listed only once. To denote the sequence in which their unity terms are set to zero (or negated), a series of overstrikes are employed. In sequential order they are: $/, \backslash, -, \wedge, /\text{-}, \wedge\text{-}$. The row sum values that change are also overstruck. When assigning a value we mention the source and the resulting value. The source includes a sequence number and other information denoted by: U=user, E=engine, F=forward chaining, and R#=Rule number in Table 7.4.2. Also, to aid in saving space here, all three inference arrays are listed in transposed form.

The procedures for working through the arrays are given in detail, but first note the F and A arrays are given in Tables 7.4.3 and 7.4.4. The reader should verify the initial unity entries by using the rules in Table 7.4.1. Array F notes the presence of an attribute occurring before the predicate, IS, in a condition clause. Array A notes an attribute that occurs after the predicate in a conclusion clause. The expert knows that the **final goal** is to determine the family. Thus, the initial backward-chaining goal inference array, B, is

Goal	Rule	1	2	3	4	5	6	7	8	9	10
family		1	1	1	1	0	0	0	0	0	0

since that object occurs in the conclusion clauses of the first four rules. The number of goals increase as we proceed through the XS.

Table 7.4.1   RULES FOR EXAMPLE BOTANY XS

Rule	Phrases
1	IF class IS gymnosperm AND leaf IS scalelike, THEN family IS cypress.
2	IF class IS gymnosperm AND leaf IS needlelike AND pattern IS random, THEN family IS pine.
3	IF class IS gymnosperm AND leaf IS needlelike AND pattern IS even AND silvery IS yes, THEN family IS pine.
4	IF class IS gymnosperm AND leaf is needlelike AND pattern IS even AND silvery IS no, THEN family IS bald.
5	IF type IS tree AND broad IS yes, THEN class IS angiosperm.
6	IF type IS tree AND broad IS no, THEN class IS gymnosperm.
7	IF stem IS green, THEN type IS herb.
8	IF stem IS woody AND upright IS no, THEN type IS vine.
9	IF stem IS woody AND upright IS yes AND trunk IS yes, THEN type IS tree.
10	IF stem IS woody AND upright IS yes AND trunk IS no, THEN type IS shrub.

Table 7.4.2 EXAMPLE VALUES AND TRANSLATIONS FOR ATTRIBUTES

Attribute	Translation	Prompt*	Value
stem	the stem of the plant	yes	woody
			green
upright	orientation of the stem	yes	yes
			no
trunk	a single trunk plant	yes	yes
			no
type	the type of the plant	no	herb
			shrub
			tree
			vine
broad	broad and flat leaf shape	yes	yes
			no
class	the class of the tree	no	angiosperm
			gymnosperm
leaf	the shape of the leaf	yes	needlelike
			scalelike
pattern	needle pattern along a branch	yes	even
			random
silver	does needle have a silver band	yes	yes
			no
family	the family of the plant	no	bald cypress
			cypress
			pine

*Is a phrase stored that can be issued to the user to prompt the user for additional information? If yes, then the value column gives the acceptable answer.

Table 7.4.3 FORWARD CONDITIONS ATTRIBUTE OPERATIONS, F

Cond.	Rule										Value	Source*
	1	2	3	4	5	6	7	8	9	10		
class	✶	✶	✶	✶	0	0	0	0	0	0	gymn	6, R6, E
leaf	1	1	1	1	0	0	0	0	0	0	scal	7, R1, U
pattern	0	1	1	1	0	0	0	0	0	0		
silvery	0	0	1	1	0	0	0	0	0	0		
type	0	0	0	0	X̸	X̸	0	0	0	0	tree	4, R9, F
broad	0	0	0	0	⊥̸	⊥̸	0	0	0	0	no	5, R6, U
stem	0	0	0	0	0	0	1̸	1̸	1̸	1̸	woody	1, R7, U
upright	0	0	0	0	0	0	0	⅄̸	⅄̸	⅄̸	yes	2, R8, U
trunk	0	0	0	0	0	0	0	0	⊥̸	⊥̸	yes	3, R10, U
Sums	2	3	4	4	2	2	1̸	2̸	3̸	3̸	**Steps:**	0
	2	3	4	4	2	2	0	⅄̸	2̸	2̸		1
	2	3	4	4	2	2		0	⊥̸	⊥̸		2
	2	3	4	4	X̸	X̸			0	0		3
	2	3	4	4	⊥̸	⊥̸						4
	✶	✶	✶	✶	0	0						5
	1	2	3	3								6
	0	1	2	2								7

*Source: Step found, rule used, source of value, U = User, E = Engine, F = Forward Chaining

Table 7.4.4 ATTRIBUTE VALUE FLAG OPERATIONS, A

Item					Rule						Value	Source
	1	2	3	4	5	6	7	8	9	10		
gymn	*	*	*	*	0	*	0	0	0	0	yes	6, R6, E
scale	1	0	0	0	0	0	0	0	0	0	yes	7, R1, U
cypress	1	0	0	0	0	0	0	0	0	0	yes	8, R1, E
needle	0	1	1	1	0	0	0	0	0	0		
random	0	1	0	0	0	0	0	0	0	0		
pine	0	1	1	0	0	0	0	0	0	0		
even	0	0	1	1	0	0	0	0	0	0		
silvery	0	0	1	1	0	0	0	0	0	0		
bald	0	0	0	1	0	0	0	0	0	0		
tree	0	0	0	0	X	X	0	0	X	0	yes	4, R9, F
broad	0	0	0	0	+	+	0	0	0	0	no	5, R6, U
angi	0	0	0	0	1	0	0	0	0	0		
green	0	0	0	0	0	0	1	0	0	0		
herb	0	0	0	0	0	0	1	0	0	0		
wood	0	0	0	0	0	0	0	1	1	1	yes	1, R7, U
vine	0	0	0	0	0	0	0	1	0	0		
upright	0	0	0	0	0	0	0	1	1	1	yes	2, R8, U
trunk	0	0	0	0	0	0	0	0	+	+	yes	3, R10, U
shrub	0	0	0	0	0	0	0	0	0	1		
Sums	3	4	5	5	3	3	2	3	4	4	**Steps:**	0
	3	4	5	5	3	3	2	2	3	3		1
	3	4	5	5	3	3	2	1	2	2		2
	3	4	5	5	3	3	2	0	X	1		3
	3	4	5	5	X	X	2		0	1		4
	X	X	X	X	1	X	2			1		5
	2	3	4	4	1	0	2			1		6
	1	3	4	4	1		2			1		7
	0	3	4	4	1		2			1		8

INFERENCE PROCEDURE

1. The final goal involves rules 1 through 4. Thus, the engine must select one of those. From the column sums for array **F**, we see that rule 1 has the minimum number of unknown conditions (2 versus maximum of 4). From **A** we see that rule 1 also has the minimum unknown values (3 versus maximum of 5). Thus, we select the rule with the minimum number of unknown values in **A**. Here that is rule 1.

2. Having selected rule 1 in **B**, we proceed to the rule 1 column in **F**. There we find that the attribute "class" is marked as the first unknown for that rule. From Table 7.4.2 we see that "class" does not have an input prompt for the user. Thus, that attribute must become our **current goal** and **B** must be expanded to include a second row:

Goal	Rule	1	2	3	4	5	6	7	8	9	10
family		-1	1	1	1	0	0	0	0	0	0
class		0	0	0	0	1	1	0	0	0	0.

A negative sign flags rule 1 as tried but not yet successful. That is, it is currently an **active rule**. From the updated **B** array we see that the new subgoal, "class," is associated with rules 5 and 6. One of them must be evaluated. From **A** we see that they both have three unknown values, so we take the last one, i.e., rule 6.

3. Leaving rule 6 in **B** and considering its column entries in **F** we find that the attribute "type" is the first marked as unknown. It also has no user input prompt. Thus, **B** is expanded to give

Goal	Rule	1	2	3	4	5	6	7	8	9	10
family		-1	1	1	1	0	0	0	0	0	0
class		0	0	0	0	1	-1	0	0	0	0
type		0	0	0	0	0	0	1	1	1	1

and we make "type" the new current goal. From the four new rules select number 7, since it has the smallest number of unknown values, 2, in **A**.

4. Going to rule 7 in **F** we find that its condition attribute, "stem," is the first marked unknown. But the current column sum shows it to be the only unknown, and Table 7.4.2 shows that there is a user input prompt for its value. The prompt is issued and the user returns an acceptable answer (stem = woody). The new data violate the rule and rule 7 is discarded forever.

Next we insert the value (woody) and source (user) in the stem row in **F**. We also zero out the condition row in **F** and update the column sums associated with it. These operations are denoted by the first overstrike, /, in Table 7.4.3. Likewise, the value flags and column sums in **A** are reset in the same manner. We are completely finished with rule 7, since its column sum in **F** is zero, so we set its flag to zero in **B**.

5. Our current goal is still to find the attribute, "type," and there are three remaining candidate rules remaining in **B**. From **A** we see that rule 8 has only two unknown values. Thus, we select rule 8 in **B** and then scan that column in **F**. The first conditional clause ("stem") is known from the first user input and that data satisfies the first condition. The second condition attribute ("upright") is marked as unknown, but Table 7.4.2 indicates that a user prompt is available. The prompt is issued and the user returns an acceptable answer (yes).

But that answer violates the second conditional clause, so the rule fails and must be discarded forever. First we insert the value in working memory of **A**, zero the row for that attribute, and update the column sum in **A**. The terms marked as now known are denoted by the second overstrike, \. We do the same for that condition attribution in **F**. Finally, we zero the current rule (8) for the current goal ("type") in **B**.

6. The current goal ("type") is still unknown, and **B** shows that two candidate rules (9 and 10) remain. The column sum of array **A** shows they have the same number of unknown values (2), so keep the last one (10). Issuing the user input prompt for the third condition clause attribute in rule 10 gives an acceptable answer (trunk = yes), but the condition clause is violated and the rule must be discarded. We store the value and source in **A** and **F** and zero rule 10 in **B**.

7. At this point a check of the column sum in **F** shows that there is a rule (9) for which all condition attributes are known. Thus, we evaluate that rule by forward chaining before proceeding with the backward chaining for the current goal. Evaluating rule 9, all conditions are satisfied and we have a new valid conclusion clause value (type = tree).

We use that new value to update **A**, **F**, their column sums, and **B**. These updates are marked with overstrike - . Note that this has satisfied the current goal ("type"), and we now return to the previous goal, since there are no additional zero column sums in **F**.

8. Now we return to rule 6 with the current goal ("class") reactivated. Proceeding to that column in **F**, we find the first condition clause is now satisfied (type = tree), but the second is unknown. We issue the prompt and get an acceptable user answer (broad = no). All conditions are satisfied and we reach a new conclusion (class = gymnosperm), which happens to be the current goal. The updates to **F**, **A**, and **B** are marked as /. The column sum of **F** shows that rule 5 can be evaluated by forward chaining. The second condition is violated and the rule is discarded forever (zeroed in **B**). Now we are back to **B** with the current goal equal to the original final goal ("family"). Rule 1 was active and still has the smallest number of unknowns (2), so we return to it. The first condition is now satisfied (class = gymn), but the second is unknown. The user input gives an acceptable value (leaf = scalelike). All conditions are satisfied and a new conclusion is reached (family = cypress).

We update all the working memory and then stop, since the final goal is now known. The final array **B** is

Goal						Rule					Value	Source
	1	2	3	4	5	6	7	8	9	10		
family	-1	1	1	1	0	0	0	0	0	0	cypr	8, R1, E
class	0	0	0	0	1	-1	0	0	0	0	gymn	6, R6, E
type	0	0	0	0	0	0	1	1	1	1	tree	4, R9, E

In a number of cases the user may wish to give a response of Why? to the input prompt for an attribute. Knowing the rule number that issued the prompt, the system can respond with:

"We wish to find a value for" (translation of) conclusion attribute.

"We know that" (translation of each) condition clause attribute that is correct.

"If we can show that" (translation of unknown) condition clause attribute, "is" (translation of acceptable) values.

"Then we will know that" (translation of) conclusion attribute "is" (translation of) conclusion value.

In doing this, some of the known items in step 2 will be generated by the inference engine and others will have come from the user. The user may also inquire: "How do you know that" condition clause "is" value? To answer that, the system checks the "working memory" for the value to determine the rule number and whether the user supplied the value or the engine determined it.

If the user decides to correct or fix an input value, then the system must reset itself. This can be done if we store a sequence number with each value determined and if we negate each unity term rather than set it to zero. Starting with the sequence number to be fixed, we loop through the working memory of **A**. If the source sequence number is greater than or equal to the fixed value, then the value and source are cleared, the negative unity terms in the value column are set back to unity, and the unity terms are added to the corresponding row sums to restore their previous values. Next we apply the same operations to **F** and **B**.

An elementary expert system, called XSimple, was developed at Rice by Peter Navratil and the author. This collection of simple interactive FORTRAN programs has been used to generate an expert system on various subjects in order to help the nonexpert arrive at some conclusion or to acquire some knowledge on that subject.

The rules constructed and stored in the knowledge acquisition phase on an automobile engine are

1.	IF cranks IS normal	THEN battery IS ok.
2.	IF cranks IS slow	THEN battery IS weak.
3.	IF cranks IS no AND lights IS dim/off	THEN battery IS dead.
4.	IF fires IS yes	THEN fuel IS present.
5.	IF carb-throt IS wet	THEN fuel IS flooded.
6.	IF carb-throt IS no-pump AND gauge IS some-left	THEN fuel IS plugged.
7.	IF cranks IS normal	THEN starter IS okay.
8.	IF cranks IS slow	THEN starter IS okay.
9.	IF jump IS yes AND cranks IS no	THEN starter IS bad.
10.	IF cranks IS normal	THEN solenoid IS okay.
11.	IF cranks IS slow	THEN solenoid IS okay.
12.	IF clicks IS yes	THEN solenoid IS okay.
13.	IF clicks IS no AND jump-start IS yes	THEN solenoid IS bad.
14.	IF fires IS yes	THEN spark IS okay.
15.	IF battery IS ok AND carb-throt IS normal AND fires IS bad	THEN spark IS bad.
16.	IF cranks IS no AND lights IS okay	THEN cables IS bad.
17.	IF battery IS dead AND jump-start IS no	THEN remedy IS get-jump.
18.	IF gauge IS empty	THEN remedy IS get-gas.
19.	IF fuel IS flooded	THEN remedy IS wait-&-try.
20.	IF spark IS bad	THEN remedy IS tune-up.
21.	IF cables IS bad	THEN remedy IS new-cables.
22.	IF fuel IS plugged	THEN remedy IS fuel-filter.
23.	IF starter IS bad	THEN remedy IS new-starter.
24.	IF solenoid IS bad	THEN remedy IS new-solenoid.

The attributes, prompt flag, and acceptable values are as follows:

ATTRIBUTE	P	VALUES
cranks	y	normal, slow, no, unknown
lights	y	ok, dim/off, unknown
gas-gauge	y	some left, empty, unknown
jump-start	n	yes, no
fires	y	yes, no, unknown
carb-throt	y	wet, normal, no-pump, unknown
clicks	y	yes, no, unknown
remedy	n	get-jump, get-gas, wait-&-try, fuel-filter, new-starter, new-solenoid, tune-up, new-cables.
battery	n	ok, weak, dead
fuel	n	flooded, present, plugged
starter	n	okay, bad
solenoid	n	okay, bad
spark	n	okay, bad
cables	n	okay, bad

XSimple utilizes the procedures illustrated earlier, but it selects the first candidate rule for evaluation rather than the last one. The following is a sample session with that system while utilizing the preceding knowledge base. Prompts to the user and the user response are shown indented to the right after the # symbol. The reader should follow the printed solution path through the rules and knowledge base and record how the working memory is being built. The latter can be checked against the summary printed at the end of XSimple.

```
                            XSimple

Subject: Remedies for an Automobile that Doesn't Start

Number of Rules in the System.........................  24
Maximum Number of Conditions per Rule........   3

Do you wish to select a specific goal? (y/n)
(If no, the program will select the default.)

< default goal of remedy selected >

Goal  1 :  Attribute  8 - remedy
To evaluate the current goal, remedy, the rule having
the least unknowns is  18   (prompt)

#   Which of the following values best describes the
```

```
#    attribute gauge? (Enter the number, or 0 if unknown.)
#    1:some-left    2:empty
#    1
```

Goal 1 : Attribute 8 - remedy
To evaluate the current goal, remedy, the rule having
the least unknowns is 19 (no prompt)

In order to find a value for the current unknown
attribute, a new goal is defined:

Goal 2 : Attribute 10 - fuel
To evaluate the current goal, fuel, the rule having
the least unknowns is   4 (prompt)

```
#    Which of the following values best describes the
#    attribute kicks? (Enter the number, or 0 if unknown.)
#    1:yes          2:no
#    1
```

Goal 1 : Attribute 8 - remedy
To evaluate the current goal, remedy, the rule having
the least unknowns is 19 (no prompt)

Goal 1 : Attribute 8 - remedy
To evaluate the current goal, remedy, the rule having
the least unknowns is 22 (no prompt)

Goal 1 : Attribute 8 - remedy
To evaluate the current goal, remedy, the rule having
the least unknowns is 20 (no prompt)

In order to find a value for the current unknown
attribute, a new goal is defined:

Goal 2 : Attribute 13 - spark
To evaluate the current goal, spark, the rule having
the least unknowns is 14 (rule true)

Goal 1 : Attribute 8 - remedy
To evaluate the current goal, remedy, the rule having
the least unknowns is 20 (rule false)

Goal 1 : Attribute 8 - remedy
To evaluate the current goal, remedy, the rule having
the least unknowns is 21 (no prompt)

In order to find a value for the current unknown
attribute, a new goal is defined:

```
Goal  2 :  Attribute 14 - cables/trm
To evaluate the current goal, cables/trm, the rule having
the least unknowns is  16  (no prompt)
```

```
In order to find a value for the current unknown
attribute, a new goal is defined:
```

```
Goal  3 :  Attribute  9 - battery
To evaluate the current goal, battery, the rule having
the least unknowns is   1 (prompt)
```

```
#   Which of the following values best describes the
#   attribute cranks? (Enter the number, or 0 if unknown.)
#   1:normal    2:slow       3:no
#   3
```

```
Goal  3 :  Attribute  9 - battery
To evaluate the current goal, battery, the rule having
the least unknowns is   2  (rule false)
```

```
Goal  3 :  Attribute  9 - battery
To evaluate the current goal, battery, the rule having
the least unknowns is   3  (prompt)
```

```
#   Which of the following values best describes the
#   attribute lights? (Enter the number, or 0 if unknown.)
#   1:okay       2:dim/no-lit
#   1
```

Goal 3 : Attribute 9 - battery
No more rules available to evaluate the attribute battery

Goal 2 : Attribute 14 - cables/trm
To evaluate the current goal, cables/trm, the rule having
the least unknowns is 16 (rule true)

Goal 1 : Attribute 8 - remedy
To evaluate the current goal, remedy, the rule having
the least unknowns is 21 (rule true, reached final goal)

************* CONCLUSIONS *************

The value of the current goal, remedy, is new-cables.

*** Intermediate Goals: ***

Attribute, cranks	, has the value, no	, from user.
Attribute, lights	, has the value, okay	, from user.
Attribute, gauge	, has the value, some-left	, from user.
Attribute, kicks	, has the value, yes	, from user.

Attribute, fuel	, has the value, present	, from R 4.
Attribute, spark	, has the value, okay	, from R 14.
Attribute, cables/trm	, has the value, bad	, from R 16.

Exiting XSimple.

This description of BARE shows that relatively simple numerical methods can be employed to build an expert system. Relatively small FORTRAN programs can be written to envoke the equation selector. The most difficult part is to generate the lists of possible solvable set combinations for a given simultaneous equation set size. The carry-over to expert systems is even simpler than the equation selector. There we have three arrays, and **B** is allowed to add rows as subgoals are created. We also associate a small "working memory" array with each of these three items. Today there are several commercial codes available for rule selection or for evaluating an expert system. This discussion should help an analyst to better understand how these tools work, even if the analyst does not wish to program such a system.

The reader is warned that the approach described here is elementary and that much more powerful approaches for artificial intelligence (AI) and XS are available. Most are built on the use of recursive languages such as the LISt Processor or Pascal. Numerous approaches to AI and XS are given in the survey by Wilson. The case selectors and equation solvers like TK! Solver and Eureka are user-friendly examples of other programming tools known as constraint programming languages. All the approaches will be of increasing importance in mechanical design. The goal here is simply to give some concepts on how they can work to the benefit of the engineer.

7.5 REFERENCES

1. Adeli, H. Expert Systems in Construction and Structural Engineering. Chapman and Hall, 1988.

2. Culbert, C. J. *CLIPS Reference Manual.* NASA, JSC 22552, 1987.

3. Kahn, P. *Eureka: The Solver.* Scotts Valley, Cal.: Borland International, 1987.

4. Konopasek, M., and Jayaraman, S. "Expert Systems for Personal Computers," *BYTE* (May 1984): 137-56.

5. Konopasek, M., and Jayaraman, S. *The TKSolver Book: A Guide to Problem Solving in Science, Engineering, Business and Education.* Osborne/McGraw-Hill, 1984.

6. Kumar, A., Kinzel, G. L., and Singh, R. "A Preliminary Expert System for Mechanical Design," *Computers in Engineering 1985*, ASME 2 (1985): 29-35.

7. Leler, W. *Constraint Programming Languages.* Reading, Mass.: Addison-Wesley, 1988.

8. Michie, D., Muggleton, S., Riese, C.E., and Zubrick, S.M. "RuleMaster: A Second Generation Knowledge Engineering Facility," *Proc. 1st Conf. on Artificial Intelligence Applications,* IEEE Comp. Soc., December 1984.

9. Navratil, P., and Akin, J.E. "XSimple: A Simple FORTRAN Expert System." Report 87-1, Rice University, MEMS Dept., Houston, Texas, 1987.

10. Michie, D. "Rulemaster: A Software Tool for Building Expert Systems." Radian Corp.,

Austin, Texas, 1986.

11. Pham, D.T. *Expert Systems in Engineering.* New York: Springer-Verlag, 1988.

12. Prasad, A. K., and Kinzel, G. L. "A Case Selection Routine for Interactive Design Pro-grams," *Computers in Engineering Conf. 1986,* ASME 1 (1986): 95-99.

13. Riese, C.E., and Stuart, J.D. "The RuleMaster Knowledge Engineering Facility," *Proceedings of the Symposium on Applications of Artificial Intelligence in Chemistry,* Amer. Chem. Soc., 1985.

14. Stuart, J.D., and Vinson, J.W. "Turbomac: An expert system to aid in the diagnosis of causes of vibration-production problems in large turbomachinery." *Proc. Conf. Computers in En-gineering,* Amer. Soc. Mech. Eng. II (1985): 319-25.

15. Thompson, B. A., and Thompson, W. A. "Inside an Expert System," *BYTE* (April 1985): 315-30.

16. Waterman, D.A. *A Guide to Expert Systems.* Reading, Mass.: Addison-Wesley, 1985.

17. Wilson, P. H. *Artificial Intelligence.* Reading, Mass.: Addison-Wesley, 1984.

18. Wilson, P. H., and Horn, B. K. *LISP.* Reading, Mass.: Addison-Wesley, 1981.

7.6 EXERCISES

1. For the car to run properly, it must have good gas, electrical system, oil, and properly inflated tires. The rules established by the expert are

   1. The gas is good if the fuel gauge reads not empty.

   2. The battery is good if the car lights are bright.

   3. The starter motor is good if the battery is good and the engine turns over when the ignition key is turned.

   4. The oil is good if the oil dipstick indicates between add and full.

   5. The tires are properly inflated if their pressure is between 28 and 32 lb/in.^{2}. Develop the arrays and prompts necessary to build an XS. Test at least two paths through the system.

2. A system of six equations with seven variables has a connection array of

$$\mathbf{N} = \begin{bmatrix} 1 & 1 & 1 & 1 & 0 & 0 & 1 \\ 1 & 1 & 0 & 0 & 0 & 0 & 0 \\ 0 & 0 & 1 & 1 & 0 & 1 & 0 \\ 0 & 1 & 1 & 0 & 0 & 0 & 0 \\ 1 & 0 & 1 & 0 & 0 & 0 & 0 \\ 0 & 1 & 1 & 1 & 1 & 0 & 0 \end{bmatrix}.$$

   Assume that the fifth variable is known. How many sets of one, two, and three equations will be needed to solve these six relations (instead of the standard six for this special case)? List the order of the solution sets.

3. Repeat the botany example but change the heuristics for selecting from the rules that have the minimum number of unknown values. Instead of picking the last rule in the event of a tie pick: (a) the first rule; (b) every rule.

4. Consider a rectangular block sitting on a rough horizontal surface. It is subjected to an in-clined force at a top corner. Develop the rules that describe whether the block is in stable equilibrium, impending to slide, and/or impending to tip.

5. An automobile expert has established the following rules:

1. If X is a car, then X has an engine.
2. If X is a sedan, then X has four doors.
3. If X is a coupe, then X has two doors.
4. If X is a sedan, then X is a car.
5. If X is a coupe, then X is a car.
   We are given the fact that X is a sedan.
   a. Repeatedly apply forward chaining to all the rules to determine all the facts about X.
   a. Develop the inference arrays for this system. Then use backward chaining to reach a final goal of determining if X has an engine. List any additional facts learned.

8

COMPUTER AIDED DRAFTING

8.1 INTRODUCTION

Probably the most common early use of computer-assisted techniques in design was associated with drafting. Computer-aided design (CAD) will continue to be widely used and is rapidly spreading to personal computers and most design offices. It can be a terrific time saver. This is especially true as an organization builds up a library of design drawings that are often changed slightly to produce a new design. If each design is significantly different from the other, then computer drafting may not result in increased productivity. Yet it is still important for the purpose of quality control, the generation of associated nongraphical data, and as a means of connecting to other processes such as finite element analysis.

The use of computer drafting is so simple, it can result in careless oversights. During a tour of a company, one of their "designers" offered to demonstrate their state-of-the-art finite element system. He connected his drawing data base to the FEA system and proudly displayed obviously wrong answers. When I inquired as to his background, I found he was a high school level drafter who was assigned to FEA because he was using the workstation when the company purchased the additional FEA system. That is not the proper way to improve the design process. That converts CAD to CAS: computer-aided stupidity.

8.2 IMPORTANT FEATURES AND TYPICAL CAPABILITIES

Computer-aided drafting (CAD) systems are two-dimensional, two-and-a-half-dimensional, or three-dimensional. The two-and-a-half-dimensional systems can look like a three-dimensional system in some cases but are really just two-dimensional systems that have associated thickness data for various regions of the two-dimensional system. Generally a three-dimensional system is much more expensive than a two-dimensional system.

Of course, two-dimensional systems have been in use the longest. They offer significant capabilities in supplying details such as text, notes, automatic dimensions, and so on. The U.S. government developed a standard, the Initial Graphics Exchange Standard (IGES), that allows two-dimensional systems to transfer data between different vendors. It is slowly being expanded to include three-dimensional feature exchange. Most systems have the same capabilities, yet the difference in user-friendliness between various products is still quite noticeable. Here we will mainly be interested in emphasizing the most significant features of CAD that are important to the design process. Then we will catalog the most common capabilities and time-saving features.

Probably the most useful feature is the ability to create **macro**, or variable processor, commands. This allows the user to replace several CAD commands with a single command. The best systems allow a user essentially to describe a part in a programminglike language. The macro language offers the user a means whereby routines may be written that string together any number of the standard CAD menu commands. Thus, the user can create customized menu commands, which are frequently needed in a specialized design process. Most parametric languages are similar to BASIC and support a similar range of mathematical and logical operations. They provide a link between design calculations and design checks and the graphic input and output.

Macro languages allow the creation of a library of **parametric parts**, which have dimensions that are parameterized. These parameters can have default values, and/or they may be requested from the user for digitized or alphanumeric input. This creates the concept of a family of parts originating from a single parametric part. A parametric routine can read from, and write to, external data files. Therefore, it can construct a drawing according to data generated by other programs and/or output data required by other software. Some of the macro languages employ the LISP language and thereby provide a powerful access to knowledge based systems and recursive calculations.

Another useful and important feature is the ability to associate nongraphical data with a graphical entity or part. This **associative data** allows the construction of a **bill of materials**, parts lists, material vendors, component schedules, cost estimates, and so on. Usually the CAD system will provide an editor to manipulate these data in much the same way as spreadsheets do. Typically, this allows the user to produce part lists automatically and place them on a drawing. It allows user defined **property tables** to be created and to be automatically updated by the CAD system. It can sort, compress or total the data in the tables. Output of the associative data is enhanced by selecting any columns and combining them to form new data or by searching them for particular types of data.

The nongraphical data should be tied to the graphical data by the concept of **connectivities**. When one graphical entity is selected, the system will automatically determine the adjacent entities to which it is connected. If a branch is encountered on the connectivity path, the system should prompt the user to indicate which branch to follow in establishing the connectivity path. For an endless, or very long, connectivity path the user may wish to indicate two end points that define the path. For example, consider a piping run in a processing plant. The user could select two points along the processing run and ask for the parts cost, weight, vendors, and bill of materials. The run would consist of different types or sizes of pipes and values. The associated data may describe the weight and cost of each value type and the weight and cost, per unit length, of the various parts. The connectivity of the line allows the CAD system to use the graphical display to **measure** the length of each constant pipe section. The system then takes the product of the sum of the appropriate lengths and the stored cost per unit length to compute and output the total cost of that particular class of pipe. Likewise, it would sum the number of values of a given type to generate the total value cost. This is very important in understanding and controlling costs during the design process. The **measure** option is important for reasons other than use in manipulating the nongraphical data. In two-dimensional systems the user can define the desired accuracy and have the system compute the area, perimeter, center of mass, and the moments of inertia of a part or subpart. This is speeded if the connectivity feature can detect when it has closed on itself to form a closed part. Interior holes can be detected in a similar manner to assure the correctness of the above calculations. These computations can be used to create new columns in the properties tables. For example, to lift a part safely we may wish to have the system compute and output the combined center of mass of an assembly.

The measure feature of a CAD system is essential to the use of **automatic dimensioning**. Here the system determines the distance between two points or the angle between two lines. It can find the radius or angle of an arc and the length and orientation of a line. These data are converted to the standard dimension format, selected by the user, and added to drawing. Dimensions can also be defined by parametric entities. Often they are automatically recalculated when their defining entities, such as the intersection of two lines, is changed. Connectivity capabilities can be coupled with dimensioning to provide the **chaining** of dimensions. For example, we could detect two points on a pipeline and request a chaining of all of the horizontal dimensions between its vertices so that the dimensions appear side by side continuously along the same line.

A user-friendly feature is to have memory stacks for recording the last measured values for lengths, angles, areas, grid coordinates, and so on. These are often needed to describe the input of some later entity. It is nice to be able to simply point to the memory stack on the menu rather than reentering a long string of numbers.

Once a part of a drawing has been completed, it may have many other uses. It may be useful to define it as a **symbol**, or **icon**, that is to be named and placed in a library and/or added to the menu as a selection option. A symbol may be considered as fixed, like a company logo, and not subject to editing or changes. Or, it may simply be a common shape that can be edited or distorted. For example, in an isometric drawing the shape may be scaled or distorted to be viewed from any of the possible angles required.

The number of drawings and symbols can rapidly grow beyond the size that should be kept stored on-line. Then an effective archive facility becomes essential. It provides a cataloguing system for management of the stored designs. It may record information such as the designer's name, the data produced, the modification dates, the title, or the client name. These data can be searched to locate a design in the drawing index, with the desired features or criteria. An archive system can also provide a system for merging different designs. The archive can tell the user which off-line storage was used to store the design. This encourages the designer to use auxiliary storage and thus free disk space to enhance system performance.

The usual features found on a CAD **menu** include:

Control Facilities

Select scale
Select units
Select paper size
Define tolerances
Select menu page
Define properties
Digitize menu
Edit symbols
Examine archive

View Selection

Redraw
Pick view numbers
Create view
Move view
Window
Zoom
Delete view
Text display switch
Fit active view

Line Format

Solid line
Dashed line
Centerline
Break line
User defined
Select width
Select color
Change type

Text Format

Roman
Italic
Upper case
Lower case
Height
Select color
Parallel to
Edit text

Line Generation

Continuous straight line
Continuous curve
Counterclockwise circle
Three-point circle
Parallel to
Continuous parallel
Fixed angle(s) line
Manual fillet
Perpendicular to

Separate straight line
B-spline curve
Clockwise circle
Three-point arc
Tangent to
Concentric arc
Automatic fillet
Semiauto fillet
Common tangent arc

Dimension Format	**Hatch Format**
Linear dimension	Standard list
Angular dimension	User defined
Radial dimension	Change spacing
Diameter dimension	Change color
Leader or note	Change width
Select decimal	Change angle

Measure	**Delete Item**
Cartesian coordinates	Area
Polar coordinates	Line
Relative position	Circle
Length	Text
Angle	Dimension
Radius	Hatch
Area	Window
Perimeter	Construction lines

Copying	**Dragging**
Window	Window
Entity	Entity
Mirror copy	Text
Rotate copy	Line
Number of copies	Circle
Include truncations	Include truncations
Ignore truncations	Ignore truncations

Construction Aids

Points	Snap grids
Project from point	Project from line
Project from circle	Project from window
Include truncation	Ignore truncation
Line intersections	Arc intersections

Most two-dimensional systems offer these above menu options. Usually the menu is available in a printed form that can be placed on a small digitizing pad for selection by a stylus or mouse. The menus may consist of several pages and allow the user to define one or more menu pages that are specific to their business. When utilized on a workstation or personal computer, it is increasingly common to see pull-down and pop-up menus to aid the designer. In addition to a menu or submenu space, the display area will often include a scratchpad area, where system prompts, help files, and user input are displayed.

To illustrate briefly how such systems can speed the construction of drawings, consider the sequence shown in Figure 8.2.1. We could begin with a view window that will contain one-sixteenth of the component, as shown in part (a). Four circular arcs are constructed through an angle of 22.5°. Then half of the trapezoidal hole and circular hole are added. The one-eighth segment model in part (b) is created by a mirror copy of the original window contents about the inclined edge. Next we could issue a single command to make seven rotational copies of the figure shown in part (b). By rotating about the bottom point and incrementing the copy angle by 45° after each copy is made, we obtain the component shown in part (c).

To build a section view we could input a section line like $A-A$ in part (c). The system can add horizontal construction lines at every line or arc that intersects the section line, $A-A$. Using these horizontal construction lines and the known thickness of the segments, we can quickly construct the section shown in part (d). The cross-

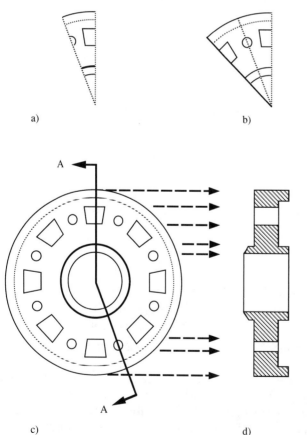

a)   b)

c)   d)

Figure 8.2.1   Typical labor-saving drafting procedures.

hatching of a typical polygon starts by simply touching a line or arc on the polygon. The system follows the connected segments around the path until it reaches the starting point. Then the hatch fills the polygon area. If a branch is encountered while traveling counterclockwise around the path the user is prompted to indicate which line at the junction is the one that limits the hatching area.

The automatic dimensions and text notes can be quickly added to produce a complete drawing. This can be assigned a name and stored on auxiliary storage for future use or modification. The user can provide nongraphical associated data, such as the material type, part number, cost, or supplier name and address. The associated data can be manipulated in a **spreadsheet** fashion to produce tables that can be printed and/or copied into other documents. Most systems also allow the macro language to access the associated graphical data.

Usually the computer-aided drafting results in a time savings even if the drawing is only to be utilized once. If that is not the case, there is still an important benefit in having the associated nongraphical data in the database. Indeed, this is a very important management tool since it allows quick revisions of cost estimates, materials inventories, and so on.

Commercial computer-aided drafting systems are important to mechanical design. As just mentioned, most of them offer the same features. However, they employ significantly different command syntax and have different data base structures. The references included in this chapter illustrate most of the features in detail. In the future the main importance of a CADD (computer-aided design and drafting) system will be the effectiveness of its two-way communication, or data exchange, with other design and manufacturing systems, such as numerically controlled machines, solid modeling systems, FEM generators, FEA systems, optimization system, report generators, and so on. When several firms cooperate on a large project, the differences in databases make it difficult to exchange technical data. The IGES was developed to help ease that problem. It was originally developed as a two-dimensional system. Lines, arcs, text, and similar terms transfer well. There continue to be problems in exchanging three-dimensional items. Some three-dimensional extensions have been incorporated and other true three-dimensional exchange standards have been proposed. Figure 8.2.2 shows an example standard for exchanging finite element model data. It defines the topology of the edges, forces, and total enclosed volume of the most common element types. It also includes material code numbers, and so on. The actual coordinates of the points are passed in other parts of the exchange package.

The reader is encouraged to become familiar with a mechanical drafting system and typical publications associated with it. It is best to invest the effort in a system that has a true three-dimensional capability and at least supports IGES.

8.3 REFERENCES

1. Barr, P. C., Krimper, R. L., Lazear, M. R., and Stammen, C. *CAD Principles and Applications.* Englewood Cliffs, N.J.: Prentice-Hall, 1985.

2. Goetsch, D.L. *Microcadd: Computer Aided Design and Drafting.* Englewood Cliffs, N.J.: Prentice-Hall, 1988.

BEAM

E1 = 1, 2

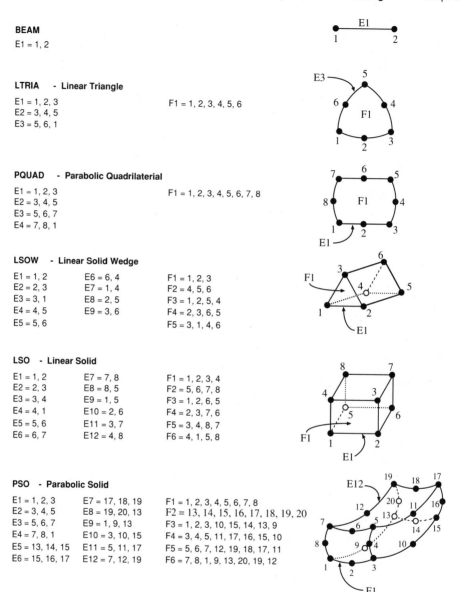

LTRIA   - Linear Triangle

E1 = 1, 2, 3   F1 = 1, 2, 3, 4, 5, 6
E2 = 3, 4, 5
E3 = 5, 6, 1

PQUAD   - Parabolic Quadrilaterial

E1 = 1, 2, 3   F1 = 1, 2, 3, 4, 5, 6, 7, 8
E2 = 3, 4, 5
E3 = 5, 6, 7
E4 = 7, 8, 1

LSOW   - Linear Solid Wedge

E1 = 1, 2   E6 = 6, 4   F1 = 1, 2, 3
E2 = 2, 3   E7 = 1, 4   F2 = 4, 5, 6
E3 = 3, 1   E8 = 2, 5   F3 = 1, 2, 5, 4
E4 = 4, 5   E9 = 3, 6   F4 = 2, 3, 6, 5
E5 = 5, 6   F5 = 3, 1, 4, 6

LSO   - Linear Solid

E1 = 1, 2   E7 = 7, 8   F1 = 1, 2, 3, 4
E2 = 2, 3   E8 = 8, 5   F2 = 5, 6, 7, 8
E3 = 3, 4   E9 = 1, 5   F3 = 1, 2, 6, 5
E4 = 4, 1   E10 = 2, 6   F4 = 2, 3, 7, 6
E5 = 5, 6   E11 = 3, 7   F5 = 3, 4, 8, 7
E6 = 6, 7   E12 = 4, 8   F6 = 4, 1, 5, 8

PSO   - Parabolic Solid

E1 = 1, 2, 3   E7 = 17, 18, 19   F1 = 1, 2, 3, 4, 5, 6, 7, 8
E2 = 3, 4, 5   E8 = 19, 20, 13   F2 = 13, 14, 15, 16, 17, 18, 19, 20
E3 = 5, 6, 7   E9 = 1, 9, 13   F3 = 1, 2, 3, 10, 15, 14, 13, 9
E4 = 7, 8, 1   E10 = 3, 10, 15   F4 = 3, 4, 5, 11, 17, 16, 15, 10
E5 = 13, 14, 15   E11 = 5, 11, 17   F5 = 5, 6, 7, 12, 19, 18, 17, 11
E6 = 15, 16, 17   E12 = 7, 12, 19   F6 = 7, 8, 1, 9, 13, 20, 19, 12

Figure 8.2.2   Typical IGES element standards.

3. Hordeski, M. F. *CAD/CAM Techniques.* Reston, Va.: Reston, 1986.

4. Lurie, P.M., and Weiss, B.D. "Computer Assisted Mistakes," Civil Engineering, 58, no. 12, (December 1988): 78–81.

5. Machover, C. and Blauth, R. E. (eds). *The CAD/CAM Handbook.* Bedford, Mass.: Computervision Corp., 1980.

6. McKissick, M.L. *Computer Aided Drafting and Design.* Englewood Cliffs, N.J.: Prentice-Hall, 1987.

7. Reichard, D.C. *Exploring CADKEY.* Englewood Cliffs, N.J.: Prentice-Hall, 1988.

Appendix I

CAME JOURNALS

Select two article references to review for reports on CAD-CAM literature of interest to you. Review the table of contents and index for typical keyword subjects. Be alert for source language programs that could be of value for future projects. The following is a list of periodicals that you may find most useful. Consider articles from 1975 to the present. Include a discussion of the references used in your review article.

Journal	Library of Congress
Advances in Engineering Software	TA345.A38
ACM Trans. on Graphics	T385.A18
Bull. Japan Soc. Mech. Eng.	TJ4.J15
Computer Aided Design	TA174.C58
Computer Aided Engineering	TA345.C638
Computer Aided Engineering J.	TA345.C639
Computer Graphics	T385.C56
Computer Methods in Applied Mech. & Eng.	TA345.C6425
Computer Vision Graphics & Image Processing	T385.C752
Computers and Fluids	QC150.C65
Computers in Mechanical Engineering	TJ153.C632
Computers and Structures	TA641.C65
Engineering Computations	TA345.E54
Engineering with Computers	TA345.E55

Finite Elements in Analysis and Design	TA347.F5
IEEE Computer Graphics and Applications	T385.I15
IEEE J. of Robotics and Automation	TJ212.I35
Inter. J. for Modelling and Simulation	TA342.I57
Inter. J. for Numerical Methods in Eng.	TA329.I57
Machine Design	TJ1.M15
Mechanism and Machine Theory	TJ175.J62
Robotics Age	TJ211.R56
Robotics Research	TJ211.I485
Soma: Eng. for Human Body	TA164.S65
Visual Computer	T385.V55

Appendix II

ACRONYMS/GLOSSARY FOR COMPUTER AIDED MECHANICAL ENGINEERING

access time: Interval between the instant a computer instruction requests that data be placed on a storage device and the instant at which the data actually begins moving to the device.

achromatic color: One that is found on the gray scale from white to black.

ACM: Association for Computing Machinery.

acoustic coupler: A low-speed device to convert digital signal to audible tones.

ACSL: Advanced Continuous Simulation Language.™

activation: A rule is activated if all its conditions are satisfied and it is ready to fire. An activated rule is placed on the agenda in front of all the rules that have priority values less than or equal to its own.

adaptive control: Automatically adjusting NC speeds to an optimum by sensing cutting conditions.

AEC: Architecture, Engineering, and Construction.

agenda: The agenda is a list of all the rules that are presently ready to fire. It is sorted by priority values.

AGV: Automatically Guided Vehicle.

AI: Artificial Intelligence.

AIX: Advanced Interactive eXecutive system.™

algorithm: A set of well-defined procedures for the solution of a problem in a limited number of steps.

aliasing: The occurrence of jagged lines on a raster-scan display image when the detail of a design exceeds the resolution of the display.

alphanumeric character: An upper- or lowercase letter (A to Z, a to z), a dollar sign ($), an underscore (_), or a decimal digit (0 to 9).

alphanumeric display: Device consisting of a keyboard and a display (CRT) screen on which text is viewed.

analog: Continuous-value representation of a physical quantity.

annotation: Process of inserting text on a drawing.

anisotropic: Dependent on direction.

ANSI: American National Standards Institute.

ANSYS: ANalysis SYStem for finite elements.™

anti-aliasing: A filtering technique to give the appearance of smooth lines and edges in a raster image.

AP: Array Processor.

APL: A high-level computer language used for algorithmic interactive programming (A Programming Language).

APT: A program language used to prepare numerical control tapes (Automatically Programmed Tools).

architecture: Physical and logical arrangement of a computer that determines how the computer operates.

ASCE: American Society of Civil Engineers.

ASCII: Standard data in specific groupings for computer applications (American Standard Code for Information Interchange).

ASM: American Society for Metals.

ASM: The form of solid modeling that uses hyperpatches as its basic building block (Analytic Solid Modeling).

ASME: American Society of Mechanical Engineers.

assembler: Program that converts user-written symbolic instructions into equivalent machine-executable instructions.

assembly drawing: A drawing of a group of parts constituting a major subdivision of the final product.

associativity: A nongraphical entity that defines a link between different entities.

asynchronous transmission: The transmission of information by individual characters having start and stop signals. Data are transmitted in irregular spurts, where the time interval varies between successive transmitted characters.

attribute: Any description property that applies to an output primitive, including aspects that affect appearance, a modeling transformation, view definition or name set; a property of an object that can be assigned a specific value.

attributes: Data associated with an entity that defines its appearance.

automatic dimensioning: Capability that automatically measures distances and places extension lines, dimension lines, and arrowheads required to draw a dimension.

BARE: Boolean Assessment of Rules and Equation.

BASIC: An interactive programming language (Beginners' All-purpose Symbolic Instruction Code).

backward chaining: Working backward in a rule from a goal in the conclusion phrase to evaluate the condition in the rule to make them current goals.

batch: Group of jobs to be run on a computer in succession, without intervention.

baud rate: A measure of serial data flow between communication devices.

benchmark: A set of standards used in testing a software or hardware product, or system. Benchmarks are often run on a system to verify that they perform according to specifications.

beta test: A site selected to test a new release of hardware or software.

Bezier curve: Smooth, continuous parametric lines passing through end points and controlled by interior points as if they had gravity.

bicubic patch: A bounded surface defined by a parametric cubic equation of two variables.

binary code: Representing numbers, using the characters 0 and 1 to represent any number (base of two).

bit: Smallest unit of information in binary notation. It has two possible values, 0 or 1.

bitree: Hierarchical data structure in that each node has two children.

bit-mapped graphics: Control of individual pixels on a display screen to produce graphics of superior resolution.

blackboard: Storage containing current attribute values and how obtained by XS.

blending: Joining two or more surfaces or lines so that they form a single continuous surface.

block diagram: Representation of the interconnection of functional blocks constituting a simulation model.

BOM: A listing of the parts, materials, and quantities required to make one assembled product (Bill Of Materials).

Boolean operation: A solid modeling construction operation that combines two parts. Boolean operators include union, difference, and intersection.

boundary file: List of edges and faces that describe the periphery of a solid model.

bpi: Number of bits of binary data that can be stored on 1 in. of magnetic tape (bits per inch).

Brep: Boundary representation, a method of modeling solids using their bounding faces or edges.

B-spline: A parametric mathematical representation of a smooth curve.

B-spline surface: The mathematical description of a surface that passes through a set of B-splines.

buffer: A storage device used to compensate for a difference rate of data flow when transmitting data from one device to another.

bug: Mistake in a program.

bus: A channel along that data can be sent; often refers to physical connections.

byte: The number of bits used to represent a character.

C: A high-level programming language commonly used on UNIX based systems.

CAD: Use of a computer to assist in the creation or modification of a design (Computer Aided Design).

CADD: Computer Aided Design and Drafting.

CAE: Computer Aided Engineering.

CAEDM: Computer Aided Engineering, Design, and Manufacturing.

CAI: Computer Aided Instruction.

CAK: Computer Assisted Kinematics.

CAM: Use of computer technology to manage and control the operations of a manufacturing facility (Computer Aided Manufacturing).

CAME: Computer Assisted Mechanical Engineering.

cartesian robot: A robot with mutually perpendicular motion directions plus rotations.

cartography: Mapping data for a geographic area.

CAS: Computer Aided Stupidity; garbage in, garbage out.

cassette: Small cartridge containing two spools of magnetic tape for the electronic storage of data.

CAT: Computer Aided Testing.

CATIA: Computer Aided Three-dimensional Interactive Application.™

CDC: Control Data Corporation.™

certainty factor: Number representing degree of confidence in value assigned to an attribute in XS.

CFD: Computational Fluid Dynamics.

character: An alphabetic, numeric, or special graphic symbol.

chip: A piece of semiconductor material containing microscopic integrated circuits.

choice: Provides a nonnegative integer choice number. Zero means no choice.

CIE diagram: A diagram developed to show the entire gamut of perceivable colors.

CIEDS: Computer Integration Engineering Design System ™ for circuits.

CIM: Computer Integrated Manufacturing.

CL File: Output of an APT or graphics system that provides coordinates and NC information for target machine tool processing (Cutter Location File).

clipping: Removing parts of display elements that lie inside or outside defined bounds.

CLIPS: C Language Intelligent Production System. A public domain forward chaining XS.

closed loop: Loop controlled by an active feedback.

CMS: Conversational Monitor System.™

CNC: A technique in that a machine-tool control uses a computer to store NC instructions generated earlier by CAD/CAM for controlling the machine (Computer Numerical Control).

color map: A table storing the definitions of the red, green, and blue components of colors to be displayed.

color space: The type of three-dimensional coordinate system that defines colors organized in space by attributes such as hue, lightness and saturation.

COBOL: COmmon Business Oriented Language.

COM: Computer Output to Microfiche

COMPACT II: A common language used to program NC machine tools for CAM.™

compatible: A characteristic of a software or hardware to be used on more than one computer.

compiler: Program that translates user-written FORTRAN instructions into binary, machine-level code.

component: A symbol that has a physical meaning.

computer graphics: A term encompassing any discipline or activity that uses computers to generate, process, and display graphic images.

concave polygon: Closed straight-sided polygon with at least one interior angle exceeding 180°.

conditions: A set of patterns of a rule, that must all be satisfied before a rule can fire.

configuration: Combination of computer and peripheral devices.

continuous system: A system that can be modeled by a set of differential equations in terms of an independent variable.

controller: Circuit board that interfaces a peripheral device to the computer.

convex polygon: Closed straight polygon with interior angles less than 180°.

core: Main memory resident in the computer.

CPM: Critical Path Method.

CP/M: Controlling Program/Monitor, an operating system used by many personal computers.

cps: Measure of the speed with which data is input or output (characters per second).

CPU: Unit of the processor that includes the circuits controlling the interpretation and execution of instructions (Central Processing Unit).

crash: System becomes inoperative due to a hardware or software malfunction.

cross hairs: A horizontal line intersected by a vertical line to indicate a point on the display.

cross-hatching: Process of filling in an outline with hatching marks.

CSG: Constructive Solid Geometry, a method for solids modeling using primitive shapes and Boolean operations.

CRT: Device that presents data in visual form by means of controlled electron beams (Cathode Ray Tube).

CSMP: Continuous Systems Modeling Program.™

cursor: A manually movable marker used to indicate the location of a point on the display.

cut plane: Intersection on a plane with a solid object in order to derive a sectional view.

cutter path: Path the cutting tool follows as it moves around the workpiece.

CV: ComputerVision.™

DAC: Digital-to-Analog Converter.

DADS: Dynamic Analysis and Design System.™

daisy chain: A method of propagating signals along a bus whereby devices not requesting service respond by passing the signal on. The first device requesting the signal responds by performing an action and breaks the signal continuity.

database: Comprehensive collection of information having structure and organization suitable for communication, interpretation, or processing.

DBMS: Data Base Management System.

DC: Device Coordinates.

DEC: Digital Equipment Corporation.™

default: Predetermined value of a parameter used when another value is not input.

detectability: Controls whether an application can select a visible entity from the display screen.

developable surface: One that can be unrolled onto a plane without distortion.

device driver: Generates device dependent graphics output and interacts with the host computer.

device: A piece of hardware that performs some specific function.

DG: Data General Corporation.™

DIF: Document Interchange Format.

digital: A discrete representation of a physical quantity.

digitize: Convert graphical information into digital form.

digitizer: A device that converts coordinates into numeric form readable by a digital computer.

directory: Table of contents of a file system.

discrete system: A system that can be modeled by a sequence of events at discrete points in time.

disk: Device on which information is stored. Usually a flat circular plate with a magnetizable surface layer.

display: Representation of a view of data on an output device.

distributed processing: Data processing tasks performed simultaneously in several interconnected processors of a network.

DMA: High-speed data transfers between a peripheral and the main memory (Direct Memory Access).

DNC: Direct Numerical Control.

DOF: Degrees of Freedom.

DOGS: Design Oriented Graphics System.™

DOS: Desk Operating System.

DP: Data Processing.

DPI: Dots Per Inch.

dragging: Moving a user-selected item on the display along a path defined by a graphic input device.

dot matrix printer: A printer that forms characters from a two-dimensional array of dots.

DRC: Check of design data for user-selected types of errors and manufacturing tolerance violations (Design Rules Checking).

drum plotter: Plotter that draws an image on a medium mounted on a drum.

DVST: Direct View Storage Tube.

DXF: Data eXchange Format.

EBCDIC: Extended Binary-Coded Decimal Information Code used to represent characters on most IBM machines.

ECM: Error-Correcting Memory.

edge curve: The lines added to the faces of a solid as a result of a Boolean operation.

EDP: Electronic Data Processing.

element: Lowest-level design entity having an identifiable function.

elementary diagram: Electrical schematic diagram containing components, elements, miscellaneous graphic and nongraphic information, and text annotation.

end effector: A robot's "hand" or device for doing work.

Email: A feature that allows memos or messages to be sent to another computer (Electronic mail).

entity: Fundamental building blocks used to represent a product, e.g., arc, circle, line, text, point.

ES: Diagram of detailed arrangement of hardware, using component symbols (Electrical Schematic). Also used to denote an Expert System.

ESC: Nonprinted character that causes the terminal or host or both to interpret subsequent characters differently (ESCape).

ethernet: A network protocol for connecting different computers.

Eureka: An equation solver and optimization system.™

FEA: Finite Element Analysis used for stress analysis, heat transfer, and vibrations using an FEM.

FEM: Finite Element Model or Mesh used to define the geometry, supports, and loads of a component.

fiber optics: Technology based upon lightweight, smooth hairlike strands of transparent material used for transmission of data at high rates of speed.

file: A collection of logically related records or data treated as a single item.

fill area: Single polygonal interior area filled with lines on patterns.

fillet surface: A surface connecting two other surfaces in a smooth transition.

fire: A rule is said to have fired if all its conditions are satisfied and the actions are then executed.

firmware: Sets of instructions cast into user-modifiable hardware.

flatbed plotter: Plotter that draws an image on a medium mounted on a flat table.

flat-pattern generation: A capability for automatically unfolding a three-dimensional design of a sheet metal part into its corresponding flat-pattern design.

floating point: A method of representing a numeric value that contains a decimal point.

floppy: A soft disk for storing data. Usually $5\frac{1}{4}$-in. or 8-in. diameter.

flowchart: Symbolic representation of a program sequence.

FOF: Factory of the Future.

fonts, line: Repetitive pattern used to give meaning to a line, e.g., solid, dashed, dotted, etc.

fonts, text: A complete set of one character type.

FORTRAN: FORmula TRANslation, a common programming language.

frame buffer: Memory device that stores the contents of an image pixel by pixel. Frame buffers are used to refresh a raster image.

free-form surface: A surface exhibiting compound curvature that cannot be described in terms of any set of simple geometric shapes.

function key: Specific key that causes a predefined function to be requested of the system. Often user-defined.

full-duplex transmission: A data communications channel that allows data to be sent in both directions at the same time.

gamut: Total range of colors that can be displayed on a monitor (see pallet).

giga: Metric term used to represent the number 10^9, though in the computer industry it is often used to mean 2^{30}, that is about 7.4% larger.

GINO: Graphics INput and OUTput via FORTRAN.

GKS: Graphic Kernal System international standard.

graphic tablet: A surface through which coordinates can be transmitted with a cursor or stylus (digitizer).

graPHIGS: The IBM implementation of PHIGS.™

GRASP: General Robot Arm Simulation Program.™

grid: Network of uniformly spaced points or lines on an input device used for locating position. Sometimes a single geometric point.

GU: Graphical Unit.

hard copy: Printed copy of output, e.g., drawings, reports, listings.

hardware: The physical components of a computer system.

hidden lines: Line segments that would be obscured from view in the display of an opaque three-dimensional object.

hierarchy: A tree structure consisting of a root and several branches.

highlight: Ability to distinguish one group of entities by adjusting brightness or blinking.

high-level language: Programming language that allows a user to operate a computer at a more convenient and efficient level than machine language.

high resolution: Quality of graphics display systems or printers capable of reproducing images in great detail to a high degree of accuracy.

homogeneous coordinates: A system where n-space is replaced by $n + 1$ coordinates. New coordinate is a scaling weight. Allows all motions to be computed via matrix product.

HP: Hewlett Packard Corporation.™

HSV: The Hue, Saturation, and Value system for color definition.

Hz: A unit of frequency equal to 1 cycle per second (Hertz).

IBM: International Business Machines, Inc.™

IC: Complex of electronic components and their connections produced on a slice of material such as silicon (Integrated Circuit).

icon: A small graphical symbol to visualize a command meaning.

I-DEAS: Integrated-Design Engineering Analysis Software.™

IGES: Initial Graphical Exchange Specification. The ANSI standard for transfer of data for CAD/CAM and FEM systems.

impact printer: Mechanical printing device that forms characters by striking ribbon onto paper.

IMSL: International Mathematical Subroutine Library.™

inference engine: The user interface to an XS that examines values, selects the rules, and evaluates rules to acquire more values and to propagate certainty factors.

ink-jet printer: Device that prints characters by electrostatically aiming a jet of ink onto the paper.

instancing: A method of defining an object once in a database and replicating it (without copying) multiple times with different positions, sizes, orientations, and other attributes.

instantiated: The pattern or variable has matched successfully against a fact or field in the current factlist.

instantiation: Process of determining values for attributes stored in a static knowledge base.

intelligent terminal: A terminal with local processing power whose characteristics can be changed under program control.

interactive graphics: Capability to perform graphics operations directly with immediate feedback.

interlace: The process of scanning or displaying an image by alternating between two sets of scan lines to reduce flicker in the display.

interrupt: To stop a process so that it cannot proceed.

I/O device: Input/output equipment used to communicate with a system.

ips: Measure of the speed of a magnetic tape device (inches per second).

IR: Industrial Robot.

ISO: International Standards Organization.

IVP: Initial Value Problem.

joystick: A data entry device to manually move a cursor.

JIRA: Japanese Industrial Robot Association.

JSME: Japanese Society of Mechanical Engineers.

KB: KiloByte, 2^{10} = 1024 bytes.

KBS: Knowledge-Based System.

KE: Knowledge Engineer.

keyboard: A set of alphanumeric keys with a layout similar to a standard typewriter. It allows the user to enter information in a typed form when necessary.

keypunch: A keyboard-actuated device that punches holes in cards.

kinematic analysis: A display of the geometric motion of mechanical devices.

LAN: Local Area Network for data communications; e.g., ETHERNET, ProNet.

layer: Logical concept used to distinguish subdivided group(s) of data within a given drawing. May be thought of as a series of transparancies (overlayed) having no depth.

layout: A display of a complete physical entity, usually to scale.

leaf node: Last node on a tree structure, e.g., bitree, quadtree.

letter-quality printer: The printer used to produce final copies comparable in quality to those of a typewriter.

library: Collection of often-used parts, symbols, or programs.

LISP: LISt Processing language, used for symbolic computation.

locator: Provides a position in world coordinates and a view index.

logic element: Symbol that has logical meaning, e.g., gates, flip-flops, etc.

lookup table: Data relating numbers to output color.

loop: Sequence of instructions that are executed repeatedly until a terminating condition is satisfied.

LSI: Large-Scale Integration.

LQ: Letter-Quality printer.

LUT: LookUp Table, memory that sets output values of colors.

machine instruction: Instructions that are machine-recognizable and executable.

machine language: The language used by the computer when it performs operations, usually binary code.

macro: Combination of commands that are executed as a single command.

mainframe: A central processing unit of a large scale computer configuration.

main storage: The general-purpose addressable storage of a computer from which data can be loaded directly into registers (also memory).

mantissa: Significant digits of a number in scientific notation.

mass properties: Calculation of physical and geometric properties of part, e.g., perimeter, area, volume, weight, and moments of inertia.

mass storage: Auxiliary bulk memory that can store large amounts of data, e.g., a disk or magnetic tape.

MB: MegaByte, 10^6.

MCD: Machine Control Data.

memory: The main high-speed storage area in a computer where instructions for a program being run are temporarily kept.

menu: Input device consisting of command regions on a digitizing surface or display.

menu-driven: A system that primarily uses menus for its user interface rather than a command language.

mesh generator: Automatic mesh generation automatically creates grid points and elements for specific regions of a model allowing creation of data necessary for FEM programs.

microcomputer: A computer with a single integrated circuit, which has a limited basic instruction set.

minicomputer: A 16-bit (or smaller) computer with limited memory addressability, and based on LSI circuits.

mirroring: Ability to create a mirror image of a graphic entity.

MIS: Management Information System.

model: A geometrically accurate and complete representation of a real object stored in a CAD/CAM database.

MODEM: A communication device often connected to a telephone line (MOdulator, DEModulator).

mouse: A manually operated directional control device used to input coordinate data.

MRP: Materials Requirements Planning.

MTBF: Mean Time Between Failures.

multibutton cursor: A special type of digitizer cursor with, typically, 13 buttons. This may be used for selection of menu options and retrieval of symbols by using the 12 numbered buttons. The thirteenth button is the large master button used to define input.

multiprocessor: A computer architecture that can execute one or more computer programs using two or more processing units simultaneously.

NAPLPS: North American Presentation Level Protocol System for connecting text and graphics.

NASTRAN: NASA STRuctural ANalysis System.™

NBS: National Bureau of Standards.

NC: Prerecorded information providing instructions for the automatic computer control of machine tools and other operations (Numerical Control).

NCGA: National Computer Graphics Association.

NDC: Normalized Device Coordinates.

nesting: Fitting individual flat parts into an area to minimize waste.

network: Two or more central processing facilities interconnected.

NFS: Network File Server.™

NLQ: Near-Letter-Quality printer.

NPC: Normalized Projection Coordinates.

node: A point located in space. Also the endpoint of a branch.

nonhomogeneous: Dependent on location.

NSF: National Science Foundation.

NTSC: National Television Systems Committee for color transmission.

numerical integration: Replacing an integral with a summation.

OAV: Object-Attribute-Value triplets used to represent factual information for XS.

object: A concept or physical entity that has one or more attributes in XS.

OCR: Optical Character Recognition.

octree: Hierarchical data structure in that each branch node has eight children.

ODE: Ordinary Differential Equation.

OEM: Original Equipment Manufacturer.

off-line: Equipment in a system that is not under the direct control of the computer.

on-line: Equipment in a system that is directly connected to the computer.

open loop: Loop without feedback control.

operating system: Software that controls the execution of computer programs and the peripheral devices.

OPTDES: OPTimal DESign system.™

order: To place in sequence according to some rules or standards.

orthographic: A type of layout, drawing, or map in that the projecting lines are perpendicular to the plane of the drawing.

overlay: A superimposed view. Also, a menu card placed on a graphics tablet.

PAFEC: Programs for Automatic Finite Element Calculations.™

PAL: Phase-Alternating Line, European color transmission standard.

palette: The number of displayable colors selected from the full gamut.

paradigm: A problem solving scenario.

parallel processing: Simultaneous execution on two or more processes on processing
units.

parametric symbol: Part created with user defined (parametric) dimensions or text.

patch: A surface defined by two parameters that blend together three or more boundary curves.

PATRAN: Commercial solid and surface modeling system.

PC: Personal Computer, microcomputer.

PCB: Insulated substrate upon which interconnection wiring is applied by photogra-
phic techniques (Printed Circuit Board).

PDE: Partial Differential Equation.

PDES: Proposed Data Exchange System.

PDMS: Plant Design Management System.™

peripheral device: Any device that can provide input to and/or accept output from
the computer.

photoplotter: Device used to generate graphical output photographically.

PHIGS: Programmer's Hierarchical Interactive Graphics Standard.

PIGS: PAFEC Interactive Graphics Suite.™

pixel: A picture element on a display.

plasma panel: A touch panel for input consisting of two transparent electrode panels
with a gas or plasma between them. When touched together, an electrical
discharge locates the touch point.

plotter: A device used to make a permanent copy of a display image.

plug-compatible: Devices or components that may be interchanged without requiring
any modifications to the rest of the system.

polyline: Set of connected lines defined by a sequence of points.

polymarker: Symbols of one type centered at given positions.

postprocessor: Software program or procedure that processes computed results into alternate forms.

preprocessor: A procedure for generating concerting data into computer usable form for processing and output.

primary colors: A set of colors from which all other colors can be derived but which cannot be produced from each other. The additive primaries (light) are red, green, and blue. The subtractive primaries (colorant) are yellow, magenta (a deep pink), and cyan (a greenish blue).

primitive: Any general collection of faces that form the boundary of a valid solid part.

primitive tree: The treelike structure of simple shapes that are combined by Boolean operators to formulate the final model.

procedural program: A program in which the order of the statements determines the order of their execution.

program: Set of machine instructions or symbolic statements combined to perform a task.

PROM: Memory that may be initially programmed with a desired set of patterns. Once programmed, the patterns are permanently stored as in a standard ROM device (Programmable Read-Only Memory).

prompt: Symbol or message from the computer system informing the user of possible actions or operations.

protocol: Set of rules governing the format of message exchange between two communication processes.

puck: A manually operated directional control device used to input coordinate data (mouse).

PUMA: Programmable Universal Machine for Assembly.™

QC: Quality Control.

quadtree: Hierarchical data structure in which each branch has four children.

queue: A priority-ranked collection of tasks waiting to be performed on the system.

RAM: Memory from which data can be retrieved regardless of input sequence (Random Access Memory).

raster display: A display in which the entire display surface is scanned at a constant refresh rate.

raster scan: Line-by-line sweep across the entire display surface to generate elements of a display image.

RBS: Rule-Based System.

record: A collection of related data items.

reflectance model: Function that describes light on a surface by making assumptions concerning light sources, angles, surface texture, etc.

refresh: CRT display requiring continuous restroking of the display image.

repaint: Redraw a display image on a CRT to reflect its updated status.

replay: The process of displaying one or more graphics files that have been previously stored.

request: Prompt the user for data and wait for a response.

resolution: The smallest spacing between points on a graphic device at which the points can be detected as distinct.

response time: The elapsed time from initiation of an operation at a work station to the receipt of the results.

RGB: Red, Green, Blue color code at a raster point.

RJE: Entering jobs in a batch processing system at a location remote from the central computer site (Remote Job Entry).

robotics: The use of computer-controlled manipulators or arms to automate a variety of processes.

RO: Receive Only, Read Only.

ROI: Return On Investment.

ROM: Memory generally used for control programs, the content of which is not alterable (Read-Only Memory).

router: Program that automatically determines the routing path for the component or node connections.

RS 2 -232:   Serial interface to link host and peripherals over long distances.

rubber banding: Displaying a straight line that has one end fixed and the other end following a cursor.

rule: A collection of conditions and actions. When all patterns are satisfied, the actions will be taken.

ruled surface: One generated by a family of straight lines.

SAE: Society of Automotive Engineers

sample: Read a current without waiting for user action.

SAP: Structural Analysis Program

saturation: A subjective term that usually refers to the difference of a hue from a gray of the same value.

SCAD: Super Computer-Aided Design.

scale: Ratio of the current displayed image with respect to the database.

scanning: Process of reading data in regular horizontal sweeps to cover the entire image or screen.

scratchpad: An area along the bottom edge of the graphics display screen used for printing messages and typed input text.

scrolling: A capability in video display systems that allows the user to move the text past the "window."

SCSI: Small Computer System Interface, called scuzzy.

sculptured surface: A surface consisting of connected parametric surface patches.

secondary colors: Yellow = red + green, cyan = green + blue, magenta = blue + red.

serial: Handling of data in a sequential fashion.

shading: Darken a surface color with its orientation relative to the light source.

shape fill: The solid painting-in within the boundaries of a shape. A solid hatching.

SIGGRAPH: Special Interest Group on computer GRAPHics of ACM.

simplex: An n-dimensional space bounded by $n + 1$ vertices.

SME: Society of Manufacturing Engineers.

snap: The action taken by a graphics program when it interprets a user-specified location as the nearest of a set of reference locations.

snapping: Automatically pulling input data to the nearest grid point or geometric entity.

software: Set of programs, procedures, rules, and associated documentation that directs the operation of a computer.

solid of revolution: Rotation of an area about a curve through a specified angle.

solids modeler: Software for constructing three-dimensional solids.

source: Instruction statements prior to translation by the computer into machine-executable form.

SPE: Society of Petroleum Engineers.

SPICE: Simulation Program for Integrated Circuits Engineering.

spline: A piecewise smooth curve with certain continuity conditions at the node points.

SSA: Simplex Search Algorithm

storage tube: A CRT that retains an image for a considerable period of time without redrawing. DVST.

stroke: Provides a sequence of positions in world coordinates.

stylus: A hand-held object that provides coordinate input to the display device.

SUMT: Series of Unconstrained Minimization Techniques.

surface of revolution: Rotation of a plane curve around an axis through a specified angle.

surface machining: The ability to output NC toolpaths using three-dimensional surface definition capabilities, e.g., ruled surfaces, tabulated cylinders, and surfaces of revolutions.

sweeping: To form a solid by moving a two-dimensional section normal to its plane.

synchronous: Fixed rate transmission of bits of data, synchronized for both the sender and the receiver.

syntax: Structure of expressions in a language or macro command.

tablet: An input device that digitizes coordinate and/or other data indicated by stylus position.

TCP/IP: Transmission Control Protocol/Internet Protocol for communication.

TCS: Terminal Control System graphics code characters.

terminal: Data entry or exit point in a communication network.

timesharing: The use of the same computer memory for two or more simultaneous tasks.

toolpath: Center line of an NC cutting or drilling tool in motion of a specific cutting operation, e.g., milling, boring.

topology: The collection of entities that bound a model: vertices, edges, and faces — and the connective relations between these entities.

trace: Scanning path of the beam in a raster display.

track ball: Graphics input device in the form of a mounted ball for controlling cursor coordinates.

transform: Performance of mathematical calculations such as matrix algebra to rotate, scale, or otherwise manipulate a graphic image whose coordinates are stored in the computer.

transformations: Changing a display by rotation, translation, sealing, etc.

tree: A hierarchical data structure. Root at the top, branch points called nodes.

turnkey: A computer system sold in a ready-to-use state.

two-and-a-half D: Adding thickness to a two-dimensional drawing to display a solid.

UDK: User-Defined Key, a key that causes a computer to perform a specific function, such as clearing the screen, or to execute a program.

ULSI: Ultra Large Scale Integration.

UNIX: Mini- and microcomputer operating system (developed by Bell Labs) that features multiprogramming, a hierarchical file structure, and numerous useful utilities.™

valuator: Provides a real number to a variable.

value: Quality or quantity that can be assigned to an attribute in XS.

VAX: Virtual Address eXtension.™

VDI: A common device level graphics interface (Virtual Device Interface).

VDU: Visual Display Unit.

view up vector: A vector in world coordinates relative to the view reference point, which would appear upright on the display surface.

virtual memory: Concept where user appears to have vast storage circuit access from disk at a rapid rate. In fact, the system is paging.

virtual storage: Storage method in that portions of a program are stored on auxiliary storage until needed, giving the illusion of unlimited memory.

visibility: An attribute that indicates whether output primitives are actually visible on the display surface.

VLSI: Very Large Scale Integration.

VRP: View Reference Point.

warping: Mapping an image on even surface onto another surface.

Winchester disk: A mass storage hard disk permanently sealed in a drive unit to prevent contaminants from affecting the read/write head.

window: An area on the display screen selected by the operator.

wire list: List containing the connections or topology of each wire.

wireframe: Displaying only the edges of a surface or solid, WF.

wiring diagram: Diagram containing components, wire runs, wires, and miscellaneous information.

word: Greatest number of bits a computer is capable of handling in any one operation.

work cell: A manufacturing unit consisting of one or more robot work areas.

working memory: Output from XS, see blackboard.

workspace: The area of the screen on which a drawing is being produced.

workstation: An interactive terminal and other associated equipment. The workstation always incorporates a graphics display screen, a keyboard, and some form of graphics input device (e.g. thumbwheels). In addition, it may contain a digitizer, tablet, joystick, or instant hard-copy unit.

world coordinates: Device-independent Cartesian coordinates used by the application program to organize objects for display (WC).

wraparound: Extending a display entity so it appears on the opposite side of the screen.

WYSIWYG: What You See Is What You Get.

XS: eXpert System.

yaw: Rotation of a body around an axis perpendicular to the front line and top line.

z-clipping: To specify depth parameters for a three-dimensional drawing such that all elements that are above or below the specified depth(s) become invisible.

zoom: To proportionately change the size of the display entities by rescaling.

Appendix III

ALGORITHM FOR SIMPLEX SEARCH PROCEDURE

This appendix includes a short help file explaining the input order, the files utilized, and the purpose of the subroutines. The help file is followed by a listing of the FORTRAN source of the program called SIMPLX.

III.1 SIMPLX HELP FILE

The interactive (or batch) data items are:

1. A title with no blanks or commas. (Periods are okay.)
2. Initial Control consisting of:
   a) The maximum number of trials, (say 999).
   b) The number of terms in the trial vector, N.
   c) The desired accuracy in the penalized merit function (say 1d-12).
3. Starting Values and Names
   a) The N starting values of the Design Variables
   b) The N initial step sizes for the Design Variables
   c) The names of each of the Design Variables
   d) The name of the Merit Function
4. Stopping or Restarting Options
   a) Number of trials, and desired accuracy.
       To stop enter 0 0 .
   b) The N starting values.
   c) The N step sizes. Loop to 4a) as many times as desired.

The above input stream can be read from a file on most computer systems. The input and output are stored in a history file named SIMPLEX.OUT.

III.2 SUBROUTINES

The following user supplied subroutines are required:

1. MAIN a dummy program that calls SIMPLX as well as anything else of interest to the user.
2. The Double Precision Function FN must be supplied to evaluate the user defined merit function. It has two arguments; N the size of the trial vector, and X the entering trial vector. The value of FN is returned. The trial vector is not changed. The user also has the option of providing a subroutine called SUMARY that will execute user defined calculations after a search has stopped. It has two arguments; N the size of the trial vector and X the best value of the trial vector found in the search.

The provided subroutines include:
1. SIMPLX: Define array sizes and control the solution.
2. CONTRL: Read application dependent data.
3. VERTIX Build the initial simplex from start point and step sizes.
4. SEARCH The Nelder-Mead simplex search algorithm.
5. OPTOUT Output the results for the two best trial vectors.

III.2.1 The Simplex Search Algorithm

This section gives the FORTRAN source for the full algorithm. That is followed by a dummy MAIN and sample application source.

```
      SUBROUTINE  SIMPLX
C     ----------------------------------------------------------
C              SIMPLEX ALGORITHM FOR OPTIMIZATION
C     ----------------------------------------------------------
C     COPYRIGHT J. E. AKIN 1987
      IMPLICIT REAL*8 (A-H,O-Z)
      CHARACTER  FNAME*12, RNAMES*12, TITLE*60
      PARAMETER (NMAX=30, NMP1=31)
      DIMENSION  START(NMAX), STEP(NMAX), XMIN(NMAX), XSEC(NMAX),
     1           PT(NMAX,NMP1), TEST(NMAX), EXTEND(NMAX),
     2           CENTER(NMAX), Y(NMP1), RNAMES(NMAX)
      DATA  KALL / 1 /
C     FN IS THE NAME OF USER INPUT PROBLEM FUNCTION
C     SUMARY IS AN AUXILARY USER OUTPUT SUBROUTINE
C     I/O UNITS:5 - STANDARD INPUT, 6 - STANDARD OUTPUT (TERMINAL)
C              8 - HISTORY FILE COPY OF TERMINAL I/O
```

```
C
C  ***  USER INPUT REQUIRED  ***
C
    5 CALL  CONTRL ( TITLE, KALL, ICOUNT, N, NMAX, REQMIN )
      NPLUS1 = N + 1
C
C  ***    READ STARTING VERTIX AND STEPS    ***
C
      CALL  VERTIX  ( N, START, STEP, KALL, RNAMES, FNAME )
      DO 30 I = 1,N
       XMIN(I) = 0.D0
   30 XSEC(I) = 0.D0
      YNEWLO = 0.D0
      YSEC = 0.D0
C
C  ***  RUN NELDER - MEAD SUBROUTINE  (CALLS FUNCTION FN)  ***
C
      CALL  SEARCH ( N, NPLUS1, START, XMIN, XSEC, YNEWLO,
     1               YSEC, REQMIN, STEP, ICOUNT, PT, TEST,
     2               EXTEND, CENTER, Y )
C
C  ***  OUTPUT FROM PROGRAM  ***
C
      CALL  OPTOUT ( TITLE, ICOUNT, N, RNAMES, XSEC, XMIN,
     1               FNAME, YSEC, YNEWLO )
      BEST = FN ( N, XMIN)
      CALL  SUMARY ( N, XMIN )
C         ALLOW RESTART
      GO TO 5
      END
      SUBROUTINE  SEARCH ( N, NPLUS1, START, XMIN, XSEC, YNEWLO,
     1               YSEC, REQMIN, STEP, ICOUNT, PT, TEST,
     2               EXTEND, CENTER, Y )
C     ----------------------------------------------------------
C        ***  NELDER - MEAD SIMPLEX SEARCH SUBROUTINE ***
C     ----------------------------------------------------------
C-->  REFERENCE: D. M. OLSSON  " A SEQUENTIAL SIMPLEX PROGRAM FOR
C     SOLVING MINIMIZATION PROBLEMS", J QUALITY TECH., 6, 1, JAN74
      IMPLICIT REAL*8 (A-H,O-Z)
      DIMENSION  START(N), STEP(N), XMIN(N), XSEC(N),
     1           PT(N,NPLUS1), TEST(N), EXTEND(N), CENTER(N),
     2           Y(NPLUS1)
C     START(N)     - STARTING VERTIX OF SIMPLEX
C     STEP(N)      - STEP SIZES TO FORM P FROM START
C     PT(N,NPLUS1) - N SIMPLEX COORDINATES AT N + 1 VERTICES
C     CENTER(N)    - CENTROID OF FIXED FACE
C     TEST(N)      - TEST POINT
C     EXTEND(N)    - EXTENSION OR CONTRACTION OF TEST
C     Y(NPLUS1)    - MERIT FUNCTION AT ALL VERTICES
```

```
C     XMIN(N)        - BEST VERTEX FOUND SO FAR
C     XSEC(N)        - NEXT BEST VERTIX FOUND
C     FN             - FUNCTION SUPPLIED TO EVALUATE MERIT FUNCTION
      DATA  ZERO,  HALF,  ONE,  TWO,  RCOEFF,  ECOEFF,  CCOEFF
     1   / 0.D0, 0.5D0, 1.D0, 2.D0,    1.D0,    2.D0,    0.5D0 /
      DATA  BIGNUM,       DABIT,  MAXLOP
     1   /   1.D38, 2.04607D-35,     5 /
      KCOUNT = ICOUNT
      ICOUNT = 0
      IF ( REQMIN .LE. ZERO ) REQMIN = DABIT + DABIT
      KONVGE = MAXLOP
      DN = DFLOAT(N)
C
C  ***  CONSTRUCTION OF THE INITIAL SIMPLEX  ***
C
    5 DO 10 I = 1,N
   10 PT(I,NPLUS1) = START(I)
      Y(NPLUS1) = FN(N, START)
      ICOUNT = ICOUNT + 1
      DO 20 J = 1,N
       DCHK = START(J)
       START(J) = DCHK + STEP(J)
       DO 15 I = 1,N
   15   PT(I,J) = START(I)
       Y(J) = FN(N, START)
       ICOUNT = ICOUNT + 1
   20  START(J) = DCHK
C
C  ***  SIMPLEX CONSTRUCTION COMPLETE  ***
C
C     FIND HIGHEST AND LOWEST Y VALUES
C     YNEWLO (Y(IHI)) INDICATES THE VERTEX OF
C        THE SIMPLEX TO BE REPLACED
C
   25 YLO = Y(1)
      YNEWLO = YLO
      ILO = 1
      IHI = 1
      DO 35 I = 2,NPLUS1
       IF ( Y(I) .GE. YLO )  GO TO 30
       YLO = Y(I)
       ILO = I
   30  IF ( Y(I) .LE. YNEWLO )  GO TO 35
       YNEWLO = Y(I)
       IHI = I
   35 CONTINUE
C
C  ***  PERFORM CONVERGENCE CHECKS ON FUNCTION  ***
C
```

```
      DCHK = (YNEWLO + DABIT)/(YLO + DABIT) - ONE
      IF ( DABS(DCHK) .LT. REQMIN )  GO TO 135
C
      KONVGE = KONVGE - 1
      IF ( KONVGE .NE. 0 )  GO TO 55
      KONVGE = MAXLOP
C
C  ***  CHECK CONVERGENCE OF COORDINATES ONLY ***
C       EVERY FIVE SIMPLEXES
C
      DO 50 I = 1,N
       COORD1 = PT(I,1)
       COORD2 = COORD1
       DO 45 J = 2,NPLUS1
         IF ( PT(I,J) .GE. COORD1 )  GO TO 40
         COORD1 = PT(I,J)
   40    IF ( PT(I,J) .LE. COORD2 )  GO TO 45
         COORD2 = PT(I,J)
   45  CONTINUE
       DCHK = (COORD2 + DABIT)/(COORD1 + DABIT) - ONE
       IF ( DABS(DCHK) .GT. REQMIN )  GO TO 55
   50 CONTINUE
      GO TO 135
   55 IF ( ICOUNT .GE. KCOUNT )  GO TO 135
C
C  ***  CALCULATE CENTER, THE CENTROID OF THE SIMPLEX VERTICES  ***
C       EXCEPTING THAT WITH Y VALUE YNEWLO
C
      DO 65 I = 1,N
       Z = ZERO
       DO 60 J = 1,NPLUS1
   60    Z = Z + PT(I,J)
       Z = Z - PT(I,IHI)
   65  CENTER(I) = Z/DN
C
C  ***  REFLECTION THROUGH THE CENTROID  ***
C
      DO 70 I = 1,N
   70 TEST(I) = (ONE + RCOEFF)*CENTER(I) - RCOEFF*PT(I,IHI)
      YTEST = FN(N, TEST)
      ICOUNT = ICOUNT + 1
      IF ( YTEST .GE. YLO )  GO TO 90
      IF ( ICOUNT .GE. KCOUNT )  GO TO 125
C
C  ***  SUCESSFUL REFLECTION, SO TRY EXTENSION  ***
C
      DO 75 I = 1,N
   75 EXTEND(I) = ECOEFF*TEST(I) + (ONE - ECOEFF)*CENTER(I)
      Y2STAR = FN(N, EXTEND)
```

```
      ICOUNT = ICOUNT + 1
C
C  ***  RETAIN EXTENSION OR CONTRACTION  ***
C
      IF ( Y2STAR .GE. YTEST )  GO TO 125
   80 DO 85 I = 1,N
   85 PT(I,IHI) = EXTEND(I)
      Y(IHI) = Y2STAR
      GO TO 25
C
C  ***  NO EXTENSION  ***
C
   90 L = 0
      DO 95 I = 1,NPLUS1
       IF ( Y(I) .GT. YTEST )  L = L + 1
   95 CONTINUE
      IF ( L .GT. 1 )  GO TO 125
      IF ( L .EQ. 0 )  GO TO 105
C
C  ***  CONTRACTION ON THE REFLECTION SIDE OF THE CENTROID  ***
C
      DO 100 I = 1,N
  100 PT(I,IHI) = TEST(I)
      Y(IHI) = YTEST
C
C  ***  CONTRACTION ON THE Y(IHI) SIDE OF THE CENTROID  ***
C
  105 IF ( ICOUNT .GE. KCOUNT )  GO TO 135
      DO 110 I = 1,N
  110 EXTEND(I) = CCOEFF*PT(I,IHI) + (ONE - CCOEFF)*CENTER(I)
      Y2STAR = FN(N, EXTEND)
      ICOUNT = ICOUNT + 1
      IF ( Y2STAR .LT. Y(IHI) )  GO TO 80
C
C  ***  CONTRACT THE WHOLE SIMPLEX  ***
C
      DO 120 J = 1,NPLUS1
       DO 115 I = 1,N
       PT(I,J) = (PT(I,J) + PT(I,ILO))*HALF
  115  XMIN(I) = PT(I,J)
  120 Y(J) = FN(N, XMIN)
      ICOUNT = ICOUNT + NPLUS1
      IF ( ICOUNT .LT. KCOUNT )  GO TO 25
      GO TO 135
C
C  ***  RETAIN REFLECTION  ***
C
  125 DO 130 I = 1,N
  130 PT(I,IHI) = TEST(I)
```

```
      Y(IHI) = YTEST
      GO TO 25
C
C  ***  SELECT THE TWO BEST FUNCTION VALUES (YNEWLO AND YSEC)  ***
C       AND THEIR COORDINATES (XMIN AND XSEC)
C
  135 DO 145 J = 1,NPLUS1
       DO 140 I = 1,N
  140   XMIN(I) = PT(I,J)
  145  Y(J) = FN(N, XMIN)
      YNEWLO = BIGNUM
      DO 150 J = 1,NPLUS1
       IF ( Y(J) .GE. YNEWLO )  GO TO 150
       YNEWLO = Y(J)
       IBEST = J
  150 CONTINUE
      Y(IBEST) = BIGNUM
      YSEC = BIGNUM
      DO 155 J = 1,NPLUS1
       IF ( Y(J) .GE. YSEC )  GO TO 155
       YSEC = Y(J)
       ISEC = J
  155 CONTINUE
      DO 160 I = 1,N
       XMIN(I) = PT(I,IBEST)
  160  XSEC(I) = PT(I,ISEC)
      RETURN
      END
      SUBROUTINE  CONTRL ( TITLE, KALL, ICOUNT, N, NMAX, REQMIN )
C     ------------------------------------------------------------
C           ***  READ THE STARTING VERTIX DATA ***
C     ------------------------------------------------------------
      IMPLICIT REAL*8 (A-H,O-Z)
      CHARACTER  TITLE*60
      PARAMETER (MCOUNT=999, RMIN=1.D-8)
      IF  ( KALL .EQ. 0 )  GO TO 10
      WRITE (6, * ) ' INPUT A LINE OF DESCRIPTIVE TEXT'
      WRITE (8, * ) ' INPUT A LINE OF DESCRIPTIVE TEXT'
      READ  (5, * ) TITLE
      WRITE (8, * ) TITLE
      WRITE (6, 1010)
      WRITE (8, 1010)
 1010 FORMAT (/,' ALL NUMERIC DATA REQUESTED ARE TO BE INPUT IN', /,
     1         ' FREE FORMAT, PIECES OF DATA MUST BE SEPERATED', /,
     2         ' BY A COMMA OR A SINGLE SPACE')
      WRITE (6, 1015)
      WRITE (8, 1015)
 1015 FORMAT (/,' INPUT ON ONE LINE THE FOLLOWING DATA:', /,
     1         ' 1. ICOUNT = MAXIMUM NUMBER OF ITERATIONS', /,
```

```
      2              ' 2. N = NUMBER OF VARIABLES', /
      3              ' 3. REQMIN = CONVERGENCE CRITERION')
      READ  (5, * )    ICOUNT, N, REQMIN
      WRITE (8, 1016 ) ICOUNT, N, REQMIN
 1016 FORMAT ( 2I6, 1PD12.5 )
      IF ( N .GT. NMAX )  GO TO 45
      GO TO 15
   10 WRITE (6, 1020)
      WRITE (8, 1020)
 1020 FORMAT (/,' INPUT ON ONE LINE THE FOLLOWING DATA:', /,
      1              ' 1. ICOUNT = MAXIMUM NUMBER OF ITERATIONS', /,
      2              ' 2. REQMIN = CONVERGENCE CRITERION', /,
      3              '     (ENTER 0 0 TO STOP)' )
      READ  (5, * )    ICOUNT, REQMIN
      WRITE (8, 1021 ) ICOUNT, REQMIN
 1021 FORMAT ( I6, 1PD12.5 )
   15 IF ( ICOUNT .LT. 0 )  ICOUNT = MCOUNT
      IF ( ICOUNT .EQ. 0 )  CALL EXIT
      IF ( RLEMIN .LE. ZERO )  REQMIN = RMIN
      RETURN
   45 WRITE (6, * ) ' N TOO LARGE, CHANGE NMAX IN PARAMETER'
      WRITE (8, * ) ' N TOO LARGE, CHANGE NMAX IN PARAMETER'
      STOP
      END
      SUBROUTINE  VERTIX  ( N, START, STEP, KALL, RNAMES, FNAME )
C     ------------------------------------------------------------
C          ***  INPUT NAMES AND STARTING VALUES ***
C     ------------------------------------------------------------
      IMPLICIT REAL*8 (A-H,O-Z)
      CHARACTER  RNAMES*12, FNAME*12
      DIMENSION  START(N), STEP(N), RNAMES(N)
      WRITE (6, 1025) N
      WRITE (8, 1025) N
 1025 FORMAT (/,' INPUT THE STARTING VALUES OF THE', I3,' VARIABLES')
      READ  (5, * )    ( START(I), I = 1,N)
      WRITE (8, 1026 ) ( START(I), I = 1,N)
 1026 FORMAT ( 5(1PD12.4), ( /, 5(1PD12.4) ) )
      WRITE (6, 1030) N
      WRITE (8, 1030) N
 1030 FORMAT (/,' INPUT INITIAL STEP SIZES OF THE', I3,' VARIABLES')
      READ  (5, * )    ( STEP(I), I = 1,N)
      WRITE (8, 1026 ) ( STEP(I), I = 1,N)
      IF ( KALL .EQ. 0 )  RETURN
      DO 20 J = 1,N
       WRITE (6, * ) ' INPUT NAME OF DESIGN VARIABLE ', J
       WRITE (8, * ) ' INPUT NAME OF DESIGN VARIABLE ', J
       READ  (5, * )    RNAMES(J)
   20  WRITE (8, * )    RNAMES(J)
      WRITE (6, * ) ' INPUT NAME OF MERIT FUNCTION'
```

```
      WRITE (8, * ) ' INPUT NAME OF MERIT FUNCTION'
      READ  (5, * )  FNAME
      WRITE (8, * )  FNAME
C     FLAG N AND ALL NAMES AS KNOWN
      KALL = 0
      RETURN
      END
      SUBROUTINE  OPTOUT ( TITLE, ICOUNT, N, RNAMES, XSEC, XMIN,
     1                     FNAME, YSEC, YNEWLO )
C     ------------------------------------------------------------
C        ***  OUTPUT BEST AND SECOND BEST TRIAL VECTORS ***
C     ------------------------------------------------------------
      IMPLICIT REAL*8 (A-H,O-Z)
      CHARACTER  RNAMES*12, FNAME*12, TITLE*60
      DIMENSION  XSEC(N), XMIN(N), RNAMES(N)
      WRITE (6, 1060 ) TITLE
      WRITE (8, 1060 ) TITLE
 1060 FORMAT ( 60A )
      WRITE (6, * ) ICOUNT, ' TRIALS USED, RESULTS ARE:'
      WRITE (8, * ) ICOUNT, ' TRIALS USED, RESULTS ARE:'
      WRITE (6, * ) ' DESIGN VARIABLE    NEXT TO BEST      BEST'
      WRITE (8, * ) ' DESIGN VARIABLE    NEXT TO BEST      BEST'
      DO 35 I = 1,N
       WRITE (8, 1070) RNAMES(I), XSEC(I), XMIN(I)
   35  WRITE (6, 1070) RNAMES(I), XSEC(I), XMIN(I)
 1070 FORMAT ( 2X, A12, 1PD20.6, 1PD17.6 )
      WRITE (6, * ) ' MERIT FUNCTION    NEXT TO BEST      BEST'
      WRITE (8, * ) ' MERIT FUNCTION    NEXT TO BEST      BEST'
      WRITE (6, 1070) FNAME, YSEC, YNEWLO
      WRITE (8, 1070) FNAME, YSEC, YNEWLO
      RETURN
      END
```

Sample application source: Gear Train Inertia Minimization

```
C     DUMMY MAIN PROGRAM TO CALL SIMPLEX ALGORITHM
C     PASS USER DATA THROUGH COMMON /USER/
      OPEN (UNIT=8, FILE='GEAR.OUT',STATUS='UNKNOWN)
      CALL  SIMPLX
      STOP
      END
      DOUBLE PRECISION FUNCTION FN(N, X)
C==>>  GEAR TRAIN INERTIA OPTIMIZATION EXAMPLE
C-->  DEFINE EVERYTHING AS DOUBLE PRECISION
      IMPLICIT REAL*8 (A-H, O-Z)
      COMMON /USER/  R, TRAIN, RSQ, RMID, BIG, ONE
      DIMENSION X(2)
      DATA  KALL /1/
C     FIRST CALL CALCULATIONS
```

```
      IF ( KALL .EQ. 0 )   GO TO 10
      KALL = 0
      R = 10.D0
      RSQ = R*R
      RMID = ( 1.D0 + R )*0.5D0
      BIG = 1.D5
      ONE = 1.D0
  10  CONTINUE
C     CALCULATIONS FOR EACH CALL
      PNLTY1 = 0.D0
      PNLTY2 = 0.D0
      A = X(1)**2
      B = X(2)**2
      IF ( A.GT.RSQ .OR. A.LT.ONE ) PNLTY1 = BIG*(X(1)-RMID)**2
      IF ( B.GT.RSQ .OR. B.LT.ONE ) PNLTY2 = BIG*(X(2)-RMID)**2
      TRAIN = ONE + A + ONE/A + B/A + ONE/A/B + RSQ/(A*A*B*B)
      FN = TRAIN + PNLTY1 + PNLTY2
      RETURN
      END
      SUBROUTINE SUMARY (N, X)
C->   PROBLEM DEPENDENT OUTPUT
      IMPLICIT REAL*8 (A-H,O-Z)
C     GEAR REDUCTION PROBLEM
      COMMON /USER/  R, TRAIN, RSQ, RMID, BIG, ONE
      DIMENSION X(2)
C     TI IS TORSIONAL INERTIA
      TIM = 10.D0
      TIP = 1.D0
      TIL = 15.D0
      THIRD = R/X(1)/X(2)
      TOTAL = TIM + TIP*TRAIN + TIL/R/R
      WRITE (6,10) X(1), X(2), THIRD
      WRITE (8,10) X(1), X(2), THIRD
  10  FORMAT (' GEAR REDUCTION RATIOS ARE', 3F10.3)
      WRITE (6,20) TOTAL
      WRITE (8,20) TOTAL
  20  FORMAT (' TOTAL INERTIA = ', F10.3, / )
      RETURN
      END
```

Appendix IV

BEGIN.FEA A FORTRAN CODE FOR FINITE ELEMENT ANALYSIS

This appendix presents a typical FORTRAN program to solve for the primary variables in a finite element analysis. It does not provide for post-processing to recover other data. That is left as an exercise for the user. Suggested procedures are included in the references cited below. The program help file is listed, followed by the source files, and selected application codes.

BEGIN.HLP

A help file describing input data for the finite element code BEGIN.FEA. This file describes input options and certain applications of BEGIN.FEA. The reference for most of the tabulated examples is:

J. E. Akin, "Finite Element Analysis for Undergraduates" Academic Press, London, 1986.

Most of the algorithms employed in BEGIN are similar to those explained in reference:

J. E. Akin, "Application and Implementation of Finite Element Methods," Academic Press, London, 1982.

```
     ++++ ++++ ++++  SECTION 1  ++++ ++++ ++++

        **** INPUT DATA ****

C     --- READ AND ECHO TITLE AND CONTROL ITEMS ---

     Enter a 40 character TITLE.
```

```
      READ   (5, *)  M, NE, NG, N, NSPACE, NPROP, NMAT, NFORCE
      NUMBER OF NODES IN SYSTEM...................
      NUMBER OF ELEMENTS IN SYSTEM...............
      NUMBER OF DEGREES OF FREEDOM PER NODE.......
      NUMBER OF NODES PER ELEMENT................
      DIMENSION OF SPACE.........................
      NUMBER OF PROPERTIES PER MATERIAL..........
      NUMBER OF DIFFERENT MATERIALS..............
      NUMBER OF NODAL FORCE COMPONENT INPUTS......


C     --- READ  NODAL POINT DATA ---
C     NODAL POINT DATA:
C         J--------NODE NUMBER
C         IBC------BOUNDARY CONDITION FLAG, ONE DIGIT PER DOF
C               =0   --IF NO B.C. AT THAT DOF
C         X(J,K)---K SPATIAL COORDINATES
C         BC(J,L)--B. C. VALUES TO BE USED IF IBC DIGIT L NOT ZERO
      READ (5, 1001) J, IBC(J), (X(J,K),K=1,NSPACE), (BC(J,L),L=1,NG)
 1001 FORMAT (2 I5, (7 F10.0) )

C     --- READ  ELEMENT DATA ---
C     ELEMENT DATA:
C         J------ELEMENT NUMBER
C         MAT----MATERIAL NUMBER OF ELEMENT
C         NODES--ELEMENT CONNECTIVITY
      READ  (5, 1002) J,  MAT(J), ( NODES(J,K), K=1,N )
 1002 FORMAT ( 2 I5, (10 I5) )

C     --- READ  PROPERTY DATA ---
C     PROPERTY DATA:
C         J---------MATERIAL NUMBER
C         PROP(I,J)--I TH PROPERTY FOR THE MATERIAL,1<I<NPROP
      READ  (5, 1003) J, ( PROP(K,J), K=1,NPROP )
 1003 FORMAT ( I5, ( 8 F10.0 ) )

C     READ FORCE DATA, IF NFORCE .GT. 0
      READ ( 5, 1006 )  NODE, IDIR, VALUE
 1006 FORMAT ( 2 I5, F10.0 )
```

+++++ SECTION 2, USER PROGRAMS +++++

The user must supply at least subroutine LSQCOL which calculates the eLement SQuare matrix and the COLumn matrix (if any) for the specific application of interest.

The arguments for LSQCOL are:

```
      SUBROUTINE  LSQCOL (N,NSPACE,NPROP,LEMFRE,COORD,PROP,C,S)
C     ***********************************************************
```

```
C                    GENERATE ELEMENT SQUARE MATRIX
C      *************************************************************
       DIMENSION  COORD(N, NSPACE), C(LEMFRE), PROP(NPROP),
     1            S(LEMFRE, LEMFRE)
C   N = NUMBER OF NODES PER ELEMENT
C   LEMFRE = NUMBER OF DEGREES OF FREEDOM PER ELEMENT
C   NSPACE = DIMENSION OF SPACE
C   NPROP = NUMBER OF PROPERTIES FOR ELEMENT MATERIAL
C   PROP = PROPERTIES OF CURRENT MATERIAL
C   COORD = SPATIAL COORDINATES OF ELEMENT'S NODES
C   S  = ELEMENT SQUARE (STIFFNESS) MATRIX
C   C  = ELEMENT COLUMN (FORCING) MATRIX
```

This section would be followed with a set of application dependent statements. For example, for an axially loaded quadratic Lagrangian bar with body forces (gravity) the statements would be:

```
C      .................................................
C      *** PROBLEM DEPENDENT STATEMENTS FOLLOW ***
C      .................................................
C==>>  1-D QUADRATIC BAR, PROB 6.5-3, FIG 4.7, AXIAL LOADS
C        TOPOLOGY:  1 *-----*3----*2 ==> R
C      DEFINE PROPERTIES: E-MODULUS, A-AREA, X-BODY FORCE
       E  = PROP(1)
       A  = PROP(2)
       X  = PROP(3)
C      MEMBER LENGTH
       DX = COORD(2,1) - COORD(1,1)
C      STIFFNESS
       EABYL = E*A/DX/3.
       S(1,1) = 7.*EABYL
       S(2,1) = EABYL
       S(3,1) = -8.*EABYL
       S(1,2) = S(2,1)
       S(2,2) = 7.*EABYL
       S(3,2) = -8.*EABYL
       S(1,3) = S(3,1)
       S(2,3) = S(3,2)
       S(3,3) = 16.*EABYL
C      BODY FORCE
       AXLBY6 = A*X*DX/6.
       C(1) = AXLBY6
       C(2) = AXLBY6
       C(3) = AXLBY6*4.
       RETURN
       END
```

   ++++ SECTION 3, OTHER FILES ++++

begin.f - has all but lsqcol.f
lsqcol.f - has the current application code
lsqcol.lib - has library of sample applications
begin.dat - has library of sample data to go with lsqcol.lib

The above files are listed in the following sections. A sample output appears at the end

File begin.f

```
C-->                          ***BEGIN.FEA***
C                A BEGINNER'S PROGRAM FOR FINITE ELEMENT ANALYSIS
C                          COPYRIGHT 1985
C                            DR. J.E. AKIN
C       ********************************************************
        COMMON  R(1000), I(500)
        DATA  LIMITR, LIMITI  / 4000, 1000 /
C       --- READ AND ECHO TITLE AND CONTROL ITEMS ---
        READ  ( 5, 10) ( R(K), K=1, 10 )
     10 FORMAT (10 A4)
        WRITE (6, 20) ( R(K), K=1, 10 )
     20 FORMAT (' TITLE: ', 10 A4)
        CALL  ZERO   (R, I, LIMITR, LIMITI)
        READ (5, *)  M, NE, NG, N, NSPACE, NPROP, NMAT, NFORCE
        WRITE (6, 30) M, NE, NG, N, NSPACE, NPROP, NMAT, NFORCE
     30 FORMAT (
     1  ' NUMBER OF NODES IN SYSTEM...................=',I4,/,
     2  ' NUMBER OF ELEMENTS IN SYSTEM...............=',I4,/,
     3  ' NUMBER OF DEGREES OF FREEDOM PER NODE.......=',I4,/,
     4  ' NUMBER OF NODES PER ELEMENT................=',I4,/,
     5  ' DIMENSION OF SPACE.........................=',I4,/,
     6  ' NUMBER OF PROPERTIES PER MATERIAL..........=',I4,/,
     7  ' NUMBER OF DIFFERENT MATERIALS..............=',I4,/,
     8  ' NUMBER OF NODAL FORCE COMPONENT INPUTS......=' ,I4)
C       ----- REAL ARRAY STORAGE POINTERS, K1 TO K10 -------
C       K1-X, K2-COORD, K3-BC, K4-C, K5-CC, K6-D, K7-DD, K8-S,
C       K9-PROP, K10-SS
        K1 = 1
        K2 = K1 + M*NSPACE
        K3 = K2 + N*NSPACE
        K4 = K3 + M*NG
        K5 = K4 + N*NG
        K6 = K5 + M*NG
        K7 = K6 + N*NG
        K8 = K7 + M*NG
        K9 = K8 + (N*NG)**2
        K10= K9 + NPROP*NMAT
        LEFTR = LIMITR - K10
        LIMITB = LEFTR/(M*NG)
C       ---- INTEGER ARRAY STORAGE POINTERS, L1 TO L5 -----
```

```
C     L1-IBC, L2-NODES, L3-MAT, L4-LNODES, L5-INDEX, L6=KODES
      L1 = 1
      L2 = L1 + M
      L3 = L2 + NE*N
      L4 = L3 + NE
      L5 = L4 + N
      L6 = L5 + N*NG
      LEFTI = LIMITI - NG
C     ----- CHECK STORAGE -----
      IF ( LEFTR .GT. 0 .AND.
     1      LEFTI .GT. 0 .AND.
     2      LIMITB .GT. 1)  GO TO 40
      WRITE (6,*) ' STORAGE EXCEEDED, STOP'
      STOP
C     -----  CALL REAL MAIN PROGRAM  -----
C     CALL  BEGIN  (M, NE, NG, N, NSPACE, NPROP, NMAT, LIMITB,
C    1             X, COORD, BC, C, CC, D, DD, S, PROP, SS, IBC,
C    2             NODES, MAT, LNODES, INDEX, KODES, NFORCE )
   40 CALL  BEGIN  (M, NE, NG, N, NSPACE, NPROP, NMAT, LIMITB,
     1             R(K1), R(K2), R(K3), R(K4), R(K5),
     2             R(K6), R(K7), R(K8), R(K9), R(K10),
     3             I(L1), I(L2), I(L3), I(L4), I(L5), I(L6), NFORCE)
      WRITE (6,*) ' NORMAL ENDING OF BEGIN.FEM'
      STOP
      END
      SUBROUTINE  AT (N)
C     ****************************************************************
C     A DEBUGGING AID
C     ****************************************************************
      WRITE (6,5) N
    5 FORMAT (' ======>>> AT ',I9)
      RETURN
      END
      SUBROUTINE  BEGIN (M, NE, NG, N, NSPACE, NPROP, NMAT, MAXBAN, X,
     1             COORD, BC, C, CC, D, DD, S, PROP, SS, IBC,
     2             NODES, MAT, LNODES, INDEX, KODES, NFORCE )
C     ****************************************************************
C         THE REAL MAIN PROGRAM
C     ****************************************************************
C     M = NUMBER OF NODES OF SYSTEM
C     N = NUMBER OF NODES PER ELEMENT
C     NELFRE = NUMBER OF DEGREES OF FREEDOM PER ELEMENT
C     NSPACE = DIMENSION OF SPACE
C     COORD = SPATIAL COORDINATES OF ELEMENT'S NODES
C     S = ELEMENT SQUARE (STIFFNESS) MATRIX
C     C = ELEMENT COLUMN (FORCING) MATRIX
      DIMENSION X(M, NSPACE), COORD(N, NSPACE), BC(M, NG), C(N*NG),
     1           CC(M*NG), D(N*NG), DD(M*NG), S(N*NG, N*NG),
     2           PROP(NPROP, NMAT), SS(M*NG, MAXBAN), IBC(M),
```

```
     3             NODES(NE, N), MAT(NE), LNODES(N), INDEX(N*NG),
     4             KODES(NG)
       NGPLUS = NG + 1
       NDFREE = NG*M
       LEMFRE = NG*N
C    --- READ  NODAL POINT DATA ---
C    NODAL POINT DATA:
C        J--------NODE NUMBER
C        IBC------BOUNDARY CONDITION FLAG, ONE DIGIT PER DOF
C              =0   --IF NO B.C. AT THAT DOF
C        X(J,K)---K SPATIAL COORDINATES
C        BC(J,L)--B. C. VALUES TO BE USED IF IBC DIGIT L NOT ZERO
       DO 1 I = 1, M
   1   READ  (5,900) J, IBC(J), (X(J,K), K=1,NSPACE), (BC(J,L), L=1,NG)
  900  FORMAT ( 2 I5, (7 F10.0) )
       WRITE (6, 901)
  901  FORMAT ( 15X, '* ECHO OF NODAL DATA *' ,/, ' B. C. CODES' )
       WRITE (6, 902)  IBC
  902  FORMAT ( 5 I12, (/, 5 I12 ) )
       WRITE (6, 903)
  903  FORMAT ( ' X - COORDINATES' )
       WRITE (6, 904) ( X(J,1),  J = 1,M )
  904  FORMAT ( 5( 1PE12.4 ), (/, 5 ( 1PE12.5 ) ) )
       IF ( NSPACE .LT. 2 )  GO TO 950
       WRITE (6, 905)
  905  FORMAT ( ' Y - COORDINATES' )
       WRITE (6, 904) ( X(J,2),  J=1,M )
       IF ( NSPACE .LT. 3 )  GO TO 950
       WRITE (6, 906)
  906  FORMAT ( ' Z - COORDINATES ')
       WRITE (6, 904) ( X(J,3),  J=1,M )
  950  WRITE (6, 907)
  907  FORMAT ( ' B. C. VALUES' )
       DO  909  IG = 1,NG
       WRITE (6, 908)  IG
  908  FORMAT ( ' FOR D.O.F. NUMBER', I2 )
  909  WRITE (6, 904) ( BC(J,IG), J=1,M )
C    --- READ  ELEMENT DATA ---
C    ELEMENT DATA:
C        J------ELEMENT NUMBER
C        MAT----MATERIAL NUMBER OF ELEMENT
C        NODES--ELEMENT CONNECTIVITY
       WRITE (6,910)
  910  FORMAT ( 15X, '* ECHO OF ELEMENTS *', /,
      1 ' ELEM  MAT  NODAL LIST' )
       DO 2  I = 1, NE
       READ  (5, 1002) J,  MAT(J), ( NODES(J,K), K=1,N )
   2   WRITE (6, 1002) J,  MAT(J), ( NODES(J,K), K=1,N )
 1002  FORMAT ( 2 I5, (10 I5) )
```

```
C      --- READ  PROPERTY DATA ---
C      PROPERTY DATA:
C          J----------MATERIAL NUMBER
C          PROP(I,J)--I TH PROPERTY FOR THE MATERIAL,1<I<NPROP
       WRITE (6, 911)
 911   FORMAT ( 15X, '* ECHO OF PROPERTY DATA *' , /,
      1 ' MAT  PROPERTY LISTS' )
       DO 7 I = 1, NMAT
       READ  (5, 1003) J, ( PROP(K,J), K=1,NPROP )
     7 WRITE (6, 912)  J, ( PROP(K,J), K=1,NPROP )
 1003  FORMAT ( I5, ( 8 F10.0 ) )
 912   FORMAT ( I5,  5 ( 1PE12.4 ), (/, 5X, 5 (1PE12.4) ) )
C      READ FORCE DATA
       IF ( NFORCE .LT. 1 )  GO TO 10
       WRITE (6, 913)
 913   FORMAT ( 15X, '* ECHO NODAL FORCE DATA *', /,
      1 ' NODE  DIR  VALUE' )
       DO 8  I = 1, NFORCE
       READ ( 5, 1006 )  NODE, IDIR, VALUE
       WRITE (6, 914)    NODE, IDIR, VALUE
 1006  FORMAT ( 2 I5, F10.0 )
 914   FORMAT ( 2 I5, 1PE12.4 )
       IDOF = NG*(NODE - 1) + IDIR
 8     CC(IDOF) = VALUE
 10    CONTINUE
C      DETERMINE SYSTEM HALF-BANDWIDTH
       CALL  SYSBAN ( NE, N, NG, IBW, NODES, LNODES)
       IF ( IBW .GT. MAXBAN )  WRITE (6,1004)
 1004  FORMAT ('0BANDWIDTH EXCEEDED')
C      CALCULATE AND ASSEMBLE ELEMENT MATRICES
       DO 3  IE = 1, NE
       DO 9  IG = 1, N
       LNODES(IG) = NODES(IE,IG)
       DO 9  K = 1, NSPACE
 9     COORD(IG,K) = X(LNODES(IG),K)
       LMAT = MAT(IE)
       CALL  LSQCOL (N, NSPACE, NPROP, LEMFRE, COORD, PROP(1,LMAT),
      1            C, S )
       CALL  INDXEL (N, NG, LEMFRE, LNODES, INDEX)
       CALL  STORSQ (INDEX, S, SS, NDFREE, LEMFRE, IBW)
       CALL  STORCL (INDEX, C, CC, NDFREE, LEMFRE)
 3     CONTINUE
C      ASSEMBLY COMPLETED
C      APPLY BOUNDARY CONDITIONS ON NODAL POINT VALUES
       DO 4  J = 1, M
       IF ( IBC(J) .EQ. 0 )  GO TO 4
       CALL  PTCODE (J, NG, IBC(J), KODES )
       CALL  INDXPT (J, NG, INDEX)
       DO 5  IG = 1, NG
```

```
          IF ( KODES(IG) .EQ. 0 )   GO TO 5
          INDX = INDEX(IG)
          CALL  MODIFY (SS, NDFREE, IBW, INDX, BC(J,IG), CC)
   5      CONTINUE
   4      CONTINUE
C     SOLVE FOR UNKNOWNS,    DD
          CALL  FACTOR (NDFREE, IBW, SS)
          CALL  SOLVE  (NDFREE, IBW, SS, CC, DD)
C     ------- SOLUTION COMPLETED --------
C     PRINT RESULTS
          WRITE (6,1005) NSPACE, NG
  1005 FORMAT ( '  ** COMPUTED RESULTS **', /,
      1 ' NODE,', I2, 'COORDINATES,', I2, ' DEGREES OF FREEDOM')
          CALL  WRTPT  (M, NG, NDFREE, NSPACE, X, DD, INDEX)
          WRITE (6, *) ' NORMAL ENDING OF BEGIN.FEA'
          STOP
          END
          SUBROUTINE  ELBAND (NUMNOD, NDF, IBW, LNODES)
C     **********************************************************************
C     FIND ELEMENT BANDWIDTH
C     **********************************************************************
          DIMENSION  LNODES(NUMNOD)
          NLESS = NUMNOD - 1
          DO 1  I = 1, NLESS
          II = I + 1
          DO 1  J = II, NUMNOD
          NEW = NDF * (IABS(LNODES(J) - LNODES(I)) + 1)
          IF ( NEW .GT. IBW ) IBW = NEW
     1    CONTINUE
          RETURN
          END
          SUBROUTINE  FACTOR (N, IBW, S)
C     **********************************************************************
C     FACTORING OF A BANDED SYMMETRIC MATRIX
C     **********************************************************************
          DIMENSION  S(N,IBW)
          TEMP = S(1,1)
          DO 10  J = 2, IBW
    10 S(1,J) = S(1,J) / TEMP
          DO 100  I = 2, N
          LL = I - 1
          NN = N - LL
    20 IF ( NN  .GT.  IBW ) NN = IBW
          DO 100  J = 1, NN
          L = IBW - J
          SUM = 0.
          IF ( L .EQ. 0 ) GO TO 75
          IF ( LL .LT. L ) L = LL
    30 DO 50  K = 1, L
```

```
      K1 = I - K
      K2 = 1 + K
      K3 = J + K
  50 SUM = SUM + S (K1,K2) * S(K1,K3) * S(K1,1)
  75 S(I,J) = S(I,J) - SUM
     IF ( J .EQ. 1 ) GO TO 100
     S(I,J) = S(I,J) / S(I,1)
 100 CONTINUE
     RETURN
     END
     SUBROUTINE  INDXEL (N, NG, LEMFRE, LNODES, INDEX)
C    ******************************************************************
C       COMPUTE DEGREES OF FREEDOM ON AN ELEMENT
C    ******************************************************************
     DIMENSION  INDEX(LEMFRE), LNODES(N)
     DO 5  K = 1, N
     DO 5  IG = 1, NG
     IELM = NG * (K - 1) + IG
  5  INDEX(IELM) = NG * (LNODES(K) - 1) + IG
     RETURN
     END
     SUBROUTINE  INDXPT (IPT, NG, INDEX)
C    ******************************************************************
C       COMPUTE DEGREES OF FREEDOM NUMBERS AT A POINT
C    ******************************************************************
     DIMENSION   INDEX(NG)
     DO 1  J = 1, NG
  1  INDEX(J) = NG * (IPT - 1) + J
     RETURN
C    THIS ROUTINE WILL BE FOLLOWED WITH LSQCOL
     END
     SUBROUTINE  MADD (A, B, C, M, N)
C    ******************************************************************
C    ADD TWO MATRICES:  C = A + B
C    ******************************************************************
     DIMENSION  A(1), B(1), C(1)
     MN = M*N
     DO 10  I = 1,MN
  10  C(I) = A(I) + B(I)
     RETURN
     END
     SUBROUTINE  MMULT  (A, B, C, N)
C    ******************************************************************
C     MULTIPLY TWO SQUARE MATRICES:  C = A * B
C    ******************************************************************
     DIMENSION  A(N,N), B(N,N), C(N,N)
     DO 1  I = 1, N
     DO 1  J = 1, N
     C(I,J) = 0.0
```

```
         DO 1   K = 1, N
    1    C(I,J) = C(I,J) + A(I,K) * B(K,J)
         RETURN
         END
         SUBROUTINE  MODIFY (SS, NE, IBW, I, U, F)
C        ****************************************************************
C        MODIFY COMPACTED SQ MATRIX FOR ESSENTIAL BOUNDARY CONDITIONS
C        ****************************************************************
         DIMENSION  SS(NE,IBW), F(NE)
C           AND SYSTEM COLUMN MATRIX
         IL = I - IBW + 1
         IF ( IL .LE. 0)  IL = 1
         DO 2   J = IL, I
         JJ = I - J + 1
         F(J) = F(J) - SS(J,JJ) * U
    2 SS(J,JJ) = 0.0
         DO 3   JJ = 2, IBW
         J = I + JJ - 1
         F(J) = F(J) - SS(I,JJ) * U
    3 SS(I,JJ) = 0.0
         SS(I,1) = 1.0
         F(I) = U
         RETURN
         END
         SUBROUTINE  MTMULT (A, B, C, N)
C        ****************************************************************
C        (N*N) TRANPOSE MULTIPLICATION.   C=AT*B
C              WHERE AT = A TRANPOSE
C        ****************************************************************
         DIMENSION  A(N,N), B(N,N), C(N,N)
         DO 1   I = 1, N
         DO 1   J = 1, N
         C(I,J) = 0.0
         DO 1   K = 1, N
    1    C(I,J) = C(I,J) + A(K,I) * B(K,J)
         RETURN
         END
         SUBROUTINE  PTCODE (JPT, NG, KODE, KODES)
C        ****************************************************************
C        EXTRACT LIST OF BOUNDARY CONDITION CODES AT A POINT
C        ****************************************************************
         DIMENSION  KODES(NG)
         NGPLUS = NG + 1
         IOLD = KODE
         ISUM = 0
         DO 10   I = 1,NG
         II = NGPLUS - I
         INEW = IOLD / 10
         IK = IOLD - INEW * 10
```

```
        ISUM = ISUM + IK * 10**(I-1)
        IOLD = INEW
  10    KODES(II) = IK
        IF ( KODE .GT. ISUM )  WRITE (6,5000) JPT
5000    FORMAT ('0BC NOT RIGHT JUSTIFIED AT NODE',I5)
        RETURN
        END
        SUBROUTINE  SOLVE (N, IBW, S, P, D)
C       *********************************************************************
C       PART TWO OF CHOLESKY-GAUSSIAN SOLUTION
C       FOLLOWS FACTOR OF SYMMETRIC EQUATIONS
C       *********************************************************************
        DIMENSION  S(N,IBW), P(N), D(N)
        D(1) = P(1) / S(1,1)
        DO 50  I = 2, N
        II = I + 1
        J = II - IBW
        IF ( II .LE. IBW ) J = 1
        IK = I - 1
        SUM = 0.
        DO 25  K = J, IK
        KK = II - K
  25    SUM = SUM + S(K,KK) * S(K,1) * D(K)
  50    D(I) = ( P(I) - SUM ) / S(I,1)
        DO 100  NN = 2, N
        I = N + 1 - NN
        LL = I - 1
        J = LL + IBW
        IF ( J .GT. N ) J = N
        L = I + 1
        SUM = 0.
        DO 75  K = L, J
        KK = K - LL
  75    SUM = SUM + S(I,KK) * D(K)
 100    D(I) = D(I) - SUM
        RETURN
        END
        SUBROUTINE  STORCL (N, C, CC, NE, NDF)
C       *********************************************************************
C       STORE ELEMENT COLUMN MATRIX IN SYSTEM COLUMN MATRIX
C       *********************************************************************
        DIMENSION  C(NDF), CC(NE), N(NDF)
        DO 1  I = 1, NDF
        J = N(I)
  1     CC(J) = C(I) + CC(J)
        RETURN
        END
        SUBROUTINE  STORSQ (INDEX, S, SS, NE, NDF, IBW)
C       *********************************************************************
```

```
C       STORE ELEM SQ MATRIX IN UPPER HALF BAND OF COMPACT SYS SQ MATRIX
C       ****************************************************************
        DIMENSION  INDEX(NDF), S(NDF,NDF), SS(NE,IBW)
C       I AND J ARE THE ROW AND COLUMN POSITIONS IN THE
C          UNPACKED SYSTEM MATRIX
C       JJ IS THE COLUMN POSITION IN THE PACKED SYSTEM MATRIX
        DO 1  L = 1, NDF
        I = INDEX(L)
        DO 1  K = 1, NDF
        J = INDEX(K)
        IF ( I .GT. J) GO TO 1
        JJ = J - I + 1
        SS(I,JJ) = SS(I,JJ) + S(L,K)
      1 CONTINUE
        RETURN
        END
        SUBROUTINE  SYSBAN ( NE, N, NG, IBW, NODES, LNODES)
C       ****************************************************************
C       FIND SYSTEM HALF BANDWIDTH FROM ELEMENT DATA
C       ****************************************************************
        DIMENSION  NODES(NE,N), LNODES(N)
        IBW = 1
        DO 1  I = 1, NE
        DO 2  J = 1, N
      2 LNODES(J) = NODES(I,J)
        CALL  ELBAND (N, NG, IBW, LNODES)
      1 CONTINUE
        RETURN
        END
        SUBROUTINE  WRTPT (M, NG, NDF, NSPACE, X, DD, INDEX)
C       ****************************************************************
C       PRINT SOLUTION D AT A SPECIFIED POINT
C       ****************************************************************
        DIMENSION  X(M,NSPACE), DD(NDF), INDEX(NG)
        DO 6  I = 1, M
        CALL  INDXPT (I, NG, INDEX)
        WRITE (6,1004) I,(X(I,L), L=1,NSPACE), (DD(INDEX(K)), K=1,NG)
   1004 FORMAT ( I5, (7 ( 1X, 1PE12.5 )) )
      6 CONTINUE
        RETURN
        END
        SUBROUTINE  ZERO (R, I, NR, NI)
C       ****************************************************************
C       ZERO A REAL AND INTEGER ARRAY
C       ****************************************************************
        DIMENSION  R(NR), I(NI)
        DO 5  N = 1, NR
      5 R(N) = 0.0
        DO 10 N = 1, NI
```

```
10    I(N) = 0
      RETURN
      END
```

File lsqcol.f

```
      SUBROUTINE  LSQCOL (N,NSPACE,NPROP,LEMFRE,COORD,PROP,C,S)
C     ************************************************************
C                 GENERATE ELEMENT SQUARE MATRIX
C     ************************************************************
      DIMENSION  COORD(N, NSPACE), C(LEMFRE), PROP(NPROP),
     1             S(LEMFRE, LEMFRE)
C     ..........................................................
C     *** PROBLEM DEPENDENT STATEMENTS FOLLOW ***
C     ..........................................................
C==>>   SIMPLE SPRING, AXIAL LOADS
      EK = PROP(1)
      S(1,1) = EK
      S(2,1) = -EK
      S(1,2) = S(2,1)
      S(2,2) = EK
      RETURN
      END
      SUBROUTINE  LSQCOL (N,NSPACE,NPROP,LEMFRE,COORD,PROP,C,S)
C     ************************************************************
C                 GENERATE ELEMENT SQUARE MATRIX
C     ************************************************************
      DIMENSION  COORD(N, NSPACE), C(LEMFRE), PROP(NPROP),
     1             S(LEMFRE, LEMFRE)
C     ..........................................................
C     *** PROBLEM DEPENDENT STATEMENTS FOLLOW ***
C     ..........................................................
C==>>  BAR WITH HEAT CONDUCTION ONLY
      DIST = COORD(2,1) - COORD(1,1)
      A = PROP(2)
      IF ( A .LE. 0.0 )  A = 1.0
      EK = PROP(1)*A/DIST
      S(1,1) = EK
      S(2,1) = -EK
      S(1,2) = S(2,1)
      S(2,2) = EK
      RETURN
      END
      SUBROUTINE  LSQCOL (N,NSPACE,NPROP,LEMFRE,COORD,PROP,C,S)
C     ************************************************************
C                 GENERATE ELEMENT SQUARE MATRIX
C     ************************************************************
      DIMENSION  COORD(N, NSPACE), C(LEMFRE), PROP(NPROP),
     1             S(LEMFRE, LEMFRE)
```

```
C      .....................................................
C      *** PROBLEM DEPENDENT STATEMENTS FOLLOW ***
C      .....................................................
C==>>  HEAT CONDUCTION BAR WITH SOURCE
       DIST = COORD(2,1) - COORD(1,1)
       A = PROP(2)
       IF ( A .LE. 0.0 )  A = 1.0
       EK = PROP(1)*A/DIST
       S(1,1) = EK
       S(2,1) = -EK
       S(1,2) = S(2,1)
       S(2,2) = EK
C-->   SOURCE TERM
       Q = PROP(3)
       C(1) = 0.5*Q*DIST
       C(2) = C(1)
       RETURN
       END
       SUBROUTINE  LSQCOL (N,NSPACE,NPROP,LEMFRE,COORD,PROP,C,S)
C      ************************************************************
C                GENERATE ELEMENT SQUARE MATRIX
C      ************************************************************
       DIMENSION  COORD(N, NSPACE), C(LEMFRE), PROP(NPROP),
      1           S(LEMFRE, LEMFRE)
C      .....................................................
C      *** PROBLEM DEPENDENT STATEMENTS FOLLOW ***
C      .....................................................
C==>>  1-D QUADRATIC BAR, FEAUG PROB 6.5-3, AXIAL LOADS
C      DEFINE PROPERTIES: E-MODULUS, A-AREA, X-BODY FORCE
       E  = PROP(1)
       A  = PROP(2)
       X  = PROP(3)
C      MEMBER LENGTH
       DX = COORD(2,1) - COORD(1,1)
C      STIFFNESS
       EABYL = E*A/DX/3.
       S(1,1) = 7.*EABYL
       S(2,1) = EABYL
       S(3,1) = -8.*EABYL
       S(1,2) = S(2,1)
       S(2,2) = 7.*EABYL
       S(3,2) = -8.*EABYL
       S(1,3) = S(3,1)
       S(2,3) = S(3,2)
       S(3,3) = 16.*EABYL
C      BODY FORCE
       AXLBY6 = A*X*DX/6.
       C(1) = AXLBY6
       C(2) = AXLBY6
```

```
      C(3) = AXLBY6*4.
      RETURN
      END
      SUBROUTINE  LSQCOL (N,NSPACE,NPROP,LEMFRE,COORD,PROP,C,S)
C     **************************************************************
C               GENERATE ELEMENT SQUARE MATRIX
C     **************************************************************
      DIMENSION  COORD(N, NSPACE), C(LEMFRE), PROP(NPROP),
     1           S(LEMFRE, LEMFRE)
C     ....................................................
C     *** PROBLEM DEPENDENT STATEMENTS FOLLOW ***
C     ....................................................
C==>>  BEAM BENDING, FEAUG FIG 8.3
      DIST = COORD(2,1) - COORD(1,1)
C     PROPERTIES: 1-MODULUS 2-MOMENT OF INERTIA
      EIBYL3 = PROP(1)*PROP(2)/DIST**3
      S(1,1) = 12. * EIBYL3
      S(2,1) = 6. * DIST * EIBYL3
      S(3,1) = -12. * EIBYL3
      S(4,1) = 6. * DIST * EIBYL3
      S(1,2) = S(2,1)
      S(2,2) = 4. * DIST * DIST * EIBYL3
      S(3,2) = -6. * DIST * EIBYL3
      S(4,2) = 2. * DIST * DIST * EIBYL3
      S(1,3) = S(3,1)
      S(2,3) = S(3,2)
      S(3,3) = S(1,1)
      S(4,3) = S(3,2)
      S(1,4) = S(4,1)
      S(2,4) = S(4,2)
      S(3,4) = S(4,3)
      S(4,4) = S(2,2)
C-->   LINEAR LOADING: 4,5 LINE LOAD NODE 1,2
      P1 = PROP(3)
      P2 = PROP(4)
      DBY20 = DIST/20.
      C(1) = DBY20 * ( 7.*P1 + 3.*P2 )
      C(2) = DBY20 * ( DIST*P1 + 2.*DIST*P2/3. )
      C(3) = DBY20 * ( 3.*P1 + 7.*P2 )
      C(4) = DBY20 * ( -2.*DIST*P1/3. - DIST*P2 )
      RETURN
      END
      SUBROUTINE  LSQCOL (N,NSPACE,NPROP,LEMFRE,COORD,PROP,C,S)
C     **************************************************************
C               GENERATE ELEMENT SQUARE MATRIX
C     **************************************************************
      DIMENSION  COORD(N, NSPACE), C(LEMFRE), PROP(NPROP),
     1           S(LEMFRE, LEMFRE)
C     ....................................................
```

```
C     *** PROBLEM DEPENDENT STATEMENTS FOLLOW ***
C     ....................................................
C==>>  CYLINDER WITH PRESSURE, FEAUG  SEC. 14.5
      DATA TWOPI, T / 6.28318531, 1.0 /
C     PROPERTIES: 1-MODULUS, 2-POISSON RATIO, 3&4 PRESSURES
      E = PROP(1)
      V = PROP(2)
      P1 = PROP(3)
      P2 = PROP(4)
      D11 = E * ( 1.-V )/(1. + V)/(1. - 2.*V)
      D12 = V * E/(1. + V)/(1. - 2.*V)
      D22 = D11
      R1 = COORD(1,1)
      R2 = COORD(2,1)
      RMID = 0.5 * (R1 + R2)
      DIST = R2 - R1
      C1 = 0.5 * TWOPI * D11 * T * ( R2 + R1 )/DIST
      C2 = TWOPI * D12
      C3 = TWOPI * D22 * DIST / ( 4. * RMID )
      S(1,1) = C1 - C2 + C3
      S(2,1) = C3 - C1
      S(1,2) = C3 - C1
      S(2,2) = C1 + C2 + C3
C     PRESSURE
      C(1) = TWOPI * T * R1 * P1
      C(2) = TWOPI * T * R2 * P2
      RETURN
      END
```

File begin.dat

```
AXIAL BAR, L3 ELEM, FEAUG PROB 6.5-3
    5    2    1    3    1    3    2    1
    1    1 0.
    2    0 210.
    3    0 420.
    4    0 540.
    5    0 660.
    1    1    1    3    2
    2    2    3    5    4
    1 30000000. 10.              .283
    2 13000000. 8.            .3
    5    1 10000.
CYLINDER WITH PRESSURE, SINGLE ELEM, FEAUG SEC. 14.6
    2    1    1    2    1    3    1    0
    1    0 10.
    2    0 11.
    1    1    1    2
    1 10000.   0.3       1.
```

```
CYLINDER WITH PRESSURE, FOUR ELEMENTS, FEAUG SEC. 14.6
    5    4    1    2    1    3    2    0
    1     0 10.
    2     0 10.25
    3     0 10.50
    4     0 10.75
    5     0 11.
    1    1    1    2
    2    2    2    3
    3    2    3    4
    4    2    4    5
    1 10000.    0.3        1.
    2 10000.    0.3        0.
CANTILEVER BEAM, FEAUG FIG. 8.3
    2    1    2    2    1    4    1    0
    1     0 0.
    2    11 10.        0.          0.
    1    1    1    2
    1 10.        2.          0.          30.
 SIMPLE CONDUCTION, FEAUG FIG. 3.7
    4    3    1    2    1    3    3    0
    1    1 0.          1500.
    2    0 0.75
    3    0 1.166667
    4    1 1.791667 150.
    1    1    1    2
    2    2    2    3
    3    3    3    4
    1 0.72        1.
    2 0.08        1.
    3 0.50        1.
 SIMPLE CONDUCTION WITH SOURCE, FEAUG FIG. 4.4
    4    3    1    2    1    3    1    0
    1     0 0.
    2     0 1.
    3     0 2.
    4    1 3.          0.
    1    1    1    2
    2    1    2    3
    3    1    3    4
    1 4.          1.          3.
 SIMPLE SPRINGS, FEAUG FIG. 3.6
    3    2    1    2    1    1    2    1
    1    1 0.          0.1
    2     0 1.
    3    1 2.          0.
    1    1    1    2
    2    2    2    3
    1 200.
```

```
2 400.
2   1  20.
SIMPLE SPRINGS, FEAUG FIG. 3.5
3   2   1   2   1   1   2   2
1   0 0.
2   0 1.
3   1 2.          0.
1   1   1   2
2   2   2   3
1 200.
2 400.
1   1 -30.
2   1  20.
```

File begin.out

```
TITLE:   AXIAL BAR, L3 ELEM, FEAUG PROB 6.5-3

NUMBER OF NODES IN SYSTEM...................= 5
NUMBER OF ELEMENTS IN SYSTEM................= 2
NUMBER OF DEGREES OF FREEDOM PER NODE.......= 1
NUMBER OF NODES PER ELEMENT.................= 3
DIMENSION OF SPACE..........................= 1
NUMBER OF PROPERTIES PER MATERIAL...........= 3
NUMBER OF DIFFERENT MATERIALS...............= 2
NUMBER OF NODAL FORCE COMPONENT INPUTS......= 1

              * ECHO OF NODAL DATA *
B. C. CODES
          1         0         0         0         0

X - COORDINATES
 0.0000E+00  2.1000E+02  4.2000E+02  5.4000E+02  6.6000E+02

B. C. VALUES
FOR D.O.F. NUMBER 1
 0.0000E+00  0.0000E+00  0.0000E+00  0.0000E+00  0.0000E+00

              * ECHO OF ELEMENTS *
ELEM  MAT  NODAL LIST
   1    1    1    3    2
   2    2    3    5    4

              * ECHO OF PROPERTY DATA *
MAT  PROPERTY LISTS
   1  3.0000E+07  1.0000E+01  2.8300E-01
   2  1.3000E+07  8.0000E+00  3.0000E-01

              * ECHO NODAL FORCE DATA *
NODE  DIR  VALUE
   5    1  1.0000E+04
```

```
** COMPUTED RESULTS **
NODE, 1COORDINATES, 1 DEGREES OF FREEDOM
    1  0.00000E+00   0.00000E+00
    2  2.10000E+02   8.02721E-03
    3  4.20000E+02   1.56384E-02
    4  5.40000E+02   2.76753E-02
    5  6.60000E+02   3.93799E-02

 NORMAL ENDING OF BEGIN.FEA


   TITLE:   SIMPLE CONDUCTION, FEAUG FIG. 3.7

   NUMBER OF NODES IN SYSTEM....................=    4
   NUMBER OF ELEMENTS IN SYSTEM................=    3
   NUMBER OF DEGREES OF FREEDOM PER NODE.......=    1
   NUMBER OF NODES PER ELEMENT.................=    2
   DIMENSION OF SPACE..........................=    1
   NUMBER OF PROPERTIES PER MATERIAL...........=    2
   NUMBER OF DIFFERENT MATERIALS...............=    3
   NUMBER OF NODAL FORCE COMPONENT INPUTS......=    0

               * ECHO OF NODAL DATA *
   B. C. CODES
              1           0           0           1

   X - COORDINATES
    0.0000E+00   7.5000E-01   1.1667E+00   1.7917E+00

   B. C. VALUES
   FOR D.O.F. NUMBER 1
    1.5000E+03   0.0000E+00   0.0000E+00   1.5000E+02

               * ECHO OF ELEMENTS *
   ELEM  MAT  NODAL LIST
     1    1    1    2
     2    2    2    3
     3    3    3    4

               * ECHO OF PROPERTY DATA *
   MAT  PROPERTY LISTS
     1  7.2000E-01   1.0000E+00
     2  8.0000E-02   1.0000E+00
     3  5.0000E-01   1.0000E+00

   ** COMPUTED RESULTS **
   NODE, 1COORDINATES, 1 DEGREES OF FREEDOM
     1  0.00000E+00   1.50000E+03
     2  7.50000E-01   1.31250E+03
     3  1.16667E+00   3.75000E+02
     4  1.79167E+00   1.50000E+02

    NORMAL ENDING OF BEGIN.FEA
```

INDEX

A

ABACUS, 119
ACSL, 179, 193, 196
analysis function, 2, 6, 169, 170, 171
analysis interface, 4
analysis variables, 3, 6
angular velocity, 21, 182
anisotropic material, 125
ANSYS, 119, 169, 170
antisymmetry, 136, 138, 139, 140, 141, 142, 171, 173
approximate optimization, 169
arc length, 102
assembly, 133, 136, 157
attributes, 209, 210, 211, 212, 213, 214, 215, 217, 218, 219, 220
automobile, 217, 221, 222
axisymmetric solids, 126, 128, 129, 167

B

backward chaining, 208, 222
bandwidth, 132, 134
bar, 161, 163
beam, 172, 201
behavior constraint, 2
bending, 172, 187

Bezier interpolation, 67, 70, 82, 83
bilinear interpolation, 84
bill of materials, 225
bintree, 112
blackboard, 207, 208
blending functions, 62, 63, 64, 131, 132
block diagrams, 180, 193, 194, 195
body force, 162
Boolean operation, 105, 106, 107, 108, 109, 110, 111, 113, 116, 154
boundary representation, 105, 106, 111, 113
buckling, 5, 6, 7, 119, 124

C

cantilever, 172, 188
case selector, 205
cell models, 110
centrifugal loads, 144
centroid, 9, 11, 75, 77, 88, 95, 111, 115, 117
chaining, 225
chain rule, 90
CLIPS, 209
column, 5, 6, 29, 30, 132, 156, 206, 214
complete polynomial, 80
computational fluid dynamics, 124
conduction, 167
connectivity, 205